Not in our name:
Democracy and foreign policy in the UK

Not in our name:
Democracy and foreign policy in the UK

Edited by
Simon Burall
Brendan Donnelly
Stuart Weir

POLITICO'S

First published in Great Britain 2006 by
Politico's Publishing Ltd, an imprint of
Methuen Publishing Ltd
11–12 Buckingham Gate
London
SW1E 6LB

10 9 8 7 6 5 4 3 2 1

A CIP catalogue record for this book is available from the British Library.

ISBN 1 84275 150 6

Printed and bound in Great Britain by St. Edmundsbury Press, Bury St. Edmunds, Suffolk

Contents

Acknowledgements

This work would not have been possible without the help of many people. The authors would like to thank: Graham Allen, Donald (now Lord) Anderson, Martyn Atkins, Tony Baldry, Anthony Barker, Roger Beaton, David Beetham, Roger Beetham, Monica Blagescu, Thomas Blanton, Jay Branegan, Judith Bueno De Mesquita, Simon Burton, Iain Byrne, David (now Lord) Chidgey, Christine Chinkin, Niamh Collier, D. Clark, Richard Corbett, George Cubie, Wayne David, Randi Davis, Sam Daws, Lucy de Las Casas, Andrew Duff, Katherine Ferrey, Bruce George, Dorian Gerhold, Harris Gleckman, Lord Grenfell, Steven Haines, Mark Hendrick, Peter Hennessy, Lord Holme of Cheltenham, Paul Hunt, Mark Hutton, Bo Manderup Jensen, Nick Jones, Tony Kingham, Leticia Labre, Rob Lloyd, Chris Lord, Noam Lubell, Joseph Macmanus, Alice Mann, Richard Norton-Taylor, Chris Parsons, Stephen Pittam, Greg Pope, Greg Power, Steve Priestly, Andrew Puddephatt, Lord Radice, Tim Rieser, Jonathan Rose, Nilmini Rubin, Jonathan Sanford, Tom Scholar, Donald Shell, Lord Shutt of Greetland, Gavin Strang, Gisela Stuart, Lord Tomlinson, Paul (now Lord) Tyler, Andrew Tyrie, Lord Wallace of Saltaire, Justin Williams.

Foreword

Imagine what might have happened if British MPs had voted against the war in Iraq. It probably would not have prevented the war; the Bush administration was determined to go to war with or without the British fig leaf of multilateralism. Tony Blair would have had to resign unless he changed his mind before the vote.

But a British 'no' vote would have created a consensus within the European Union and would have strengthened countervailing power in the United Nations, thus enhancing the legitimacy of both organisations. Above all, a British 'no' vote would have boosted the culture of democracy in Britain, allowing those two million of us who marched against the war on 15 February 2003 to feel that participation counts.

The government deny that the 7 July bombings had anything to do with the war in Iraq. Of course, the bombings cannot be justified by the war in Iraq. But what cannot be denied is the sense of alienation and frustration that resulted from the failure of what was, in effect, a widespread and sustained popular protest. It is a well-known pattern of behaviour that when social movements fail or when people feel that their voices are not being heard or taken seriously, some elements become more extreme and turn to violence.

This is why the subject of this book is so important. Historically, democratic participation has always been circumscribed by war. This is the nature of the social contract citizens make with governments in nationally bound societies. In the western world, democracy evolved through a series of bargains often made in wartime. Governments agreed to protect citizens from external threats and, in return, civil, political and later economic and social rights were granted in peacetime. War always represented an interruption in democracy, a moment when citizens gave up their individual rights and became part of the collective nation.

In today's world, that clear separation between internal and external, domestic and foreign, peace and war is breaking down, if it ever really existed. Everyone is touched by events taking place far away, whether because they are part of a Diaspora, because of our dependence on trade, foreign investment and imported food and energy, or because, with the spread of television and the Internet, they are horrified by poverty, AIDS/HIV or human rights violations or they are worried about global warming.

We cannot any longer confine democratic debate to domestic issues because foreign policy, as the authors emphasise, has a profound impact on everyday life – we cannot, as 7 July vividly illustrated, insulate ourselves from the outside world. And we cannot claim to live in a democracy if we cannot influence the decisions that affect everyday lives.

We need, as this book proposes, to introduce new mechanisms to democratise the 'external' decision-making that affects everyday life in Britain and around the world. And we also need to find ways to strengthen multilateral institutions that take some responsibility for global decision-making, and to increase the participation of citizens and not just states in their deliberations. In the 1990s we seemed to be moving in the direction of more democratic global decision-making but 11 September and, above all, the war in Iraq have represented a tragic reversal. Despite our supposed internationalist commitments, Britain's failure to oppose the war was a significant factor in that reversal. And, in turn, that failure has to be understood as a failure of democracy. The power of the Prime Minister to steam-roller the Cabinet, Parliament and the civil service, the ease with which our system was hijacked in the service of a unilateralist American foreign policy, was a shocking indictment of British democracy.

I hope that policy makers and the public take the proposals in this book seriously and so allow us to claim back some of our democratic rights.

Professor Mary Kaldor
Director, Centre for the Study of Global Governance, London School of Economics

Introduction

The decision to invade Iraq without the approval of the United Nations – and the manner in which it was taken – threw into dramatic relief the weaknesses of the traditional means by which Parliament holds the executive to account. It is almost universally recognised that the executive in the United Kingdom exercises undue power over Parliament.[1] But this is especially the case in 'foreign policy', one of several areas where the executive has, by tradition and through the use of the royal prerogative, the ability to wage war, make treaties and engage in external negotiations outside parliamentary control. Judicial deference to the executive, especially on international and national security affairs, ensures for the most part that ministers' prerogative decisions on 'foreign policy' are in practice immune from judicial review.

However, the executive's supremacy is not a cause for concern solely in the case of military action; it matters across the whole range of Britain's 'foreign policy'. In addition to the prerogative, there are other areas of democratic shortfall. The government can deny elected representatives the ability to make it accountable and to scrutinise policy, through restrictions on the release of official information, control over parliamentary business and rigid parliamentary discipline.

Our title, *Not in Our Name*, reflects the placards that protesters carried against the Iraq war. However, this is not a protest tract: our intention is to analyse the quality and effectiveness of parliamentary oversight of the executive's external policies, not to analyse the substance of those policies. We chose this title because it expresses a wider truth. The executive is constantly engaged in making 'foreign policy' without ever being required to seek parliamentary or popular approval. The royal prerogative for the most part gives the Prime

Minister and government untouchable powers of action over the whole of 'foreign policy'. 'Foreign policy' in modern times is a wider-ranging complex set of processes, far removed from the exercise of autonomous bilateral diplomacy to which the prerogative traditionally applied. For the most part, 'foreign policy' has for many years been pursued through multilateral organisations, including the European Union, and multilateral agreements, and it affects the everyday lives of the British people in manifold ways. There is a complex interaction between international and domestic affairs – we live in a global marketplace, we feel the growing effects of global warming, we experience global migration, we combat international crime and drug-trading, we fear international terrorism and the proliferation of weapons of mass destruction, we share liability to HIV/AIDS and other diseases. Each of these challenges has its own character that prevents it from being dealt with by the national actions of an individual country. They all call for wide international understanding and responses if the interests of the British people are to be protected.

The 'foreign policy' the government pursues is therefore an amalgam of multilateral and bilateral negotiations, the policies of the European Union, or of NATO, or of the UN Security Council, or of the World Bank, or even of, say, the Universal Postal Union, rather than the independent policy of the UK. This is particularly true in the case of the European Union. The EU's dense legal structure means that a significant proportion of 'domestic' legislation derives from legislation originating in Brussels or Strasbourg (see Chapter 6).

'Foreign policy' thus touches the everyday lives of the population and can no longer be left almost out of the reach of Parliament, the judiciary and public opinion. But we need also to reconfigure the very idea and talk as much of Britain's *external policies* – aid, trade, treaty-making, bilateral and multilateral activities, relations with the European Union and the United States, the conduct of the UK in international bodies such as the World Bank, the IMF and NATO. This adjustment will in turn assist more systematic, meaningful parliamentary oversight of the policies in question. This does not, however, mean that we should not examine whether and how far bilateral policies, that is, the traditional 'foreign policy' of the past, live up to the humanitarian and objective goals that British governments proclaim and public opinion supports.

This book considers current parliamentary procedures for holding government to account for all its activities and the state of parliamentary and public access to official information. There is a particular focus on the scrutiny role of various parliamentary select committees that deal with external policies. We also examine the powers at the disposal of the executive, the roles of the relevant government departments, and the conduct of British representatives in a sample of significant international organisations and forums, including the institutions of the European Union; and we ask what is the most appropriate way for the British Parliament to secure the accountability of the UK's European policy. The focus of our studies is not necessarily to question substantive policy outcomes, but rather to question the process of oversight to which they ought to be subject. We make a series of recommendations designed to make policies more accountable and transparent.

1

Keeping watch on the executive

This study concentrates largely on parliamentary oversight of the external policies of the executive. The discussion of parliamentary oversight of external policy that follows is, therefore, both descriptive and prescriptive. As already noted, this oversight – and certainly any idea of parliamentary control of the regular process of external policy-making – is severely limited by the continuing dominance of ministers' use of the royal prerogative powers in the name of the Crown rather than of statutory powers under Acts of Parliament.[1]

The Foreign and Commonwealth Office (FCO) only rarely needs to bring Bills or statutory orders before Parliament on matters of policy, and the Ministry of Defence (MoD) not much more often. Once their annual expenditures, or budgets, are established with the Treasury, their policy work experiences little formal parliamentary constraint. The FCO does not even publish its external affairs equivalent of the annual MoD White Paper, describing current policies, which is by convention debated in both Houses of Parliament. Both Houses do hold annual debates on foreign affairs in general, from which FCO ministers can choose the issues on which they prefer to offer some response. The contrast with domestic policy is striking. The conduct of internal affairs, such as local government, housing, crime and punishment, are all dominated by the need for detailed Bills and statutory orders, as well as for public expenditure approval from the Treasury.

Of course, FCO and Defence ministers must in principle obtain the political confidence of the House of Commons in what they are saying and doing on policy issues, just as those in charge of domestic affairs must. But the absence of formal constraint and the sense of distance, even deference, in Parliament's approach to external and military policies are two sides of the same coin. These high affairs of state have passed from the hands of ruling monarchs into ruling ministers' hands today, using the Crown powers they have inherited to minimise parliamentary scrutiny; and thus the gradual introduction of select committees to monitor government departments came last to the FCO and MoD. MPs on the Foreign Affairs Committee have made (or attempted) little impact and were brushed off by the FCO on the Iraq intelligence issue. Intelligence itself remains the preserve of the executive and no select committee on security and the intelligence services yet exists (though a government advisory committee of invited senior MPs and peers accepts briefings on condition of secrecy).

We measure parliamentary 'oversight' and its fitness for its democratic purposes using the framework for assessing democracy first developed by the Democratic Audit for its audits of British democracy and now employed widely around the world.[2] In the Westminster model, executive and legislature are combined – we are ruled by the Queen in Parliament – and Parliament is the highest court in the land. (An American sees Congress and the Supreme Court as two of the three 'branches of government'.) The elected government takes on the executive role that was once the monarchy's and exercises primacy in making law and policy over Parliament. The UK Parliament does not govern; its task is to hold the government to account and exercise oversight over its legislative proposals, policies and actions (a task which is complicated in the UK by the fact that the government can usually rely on the majority party in the Commons to consent to its policies and draft laws and to sustain it in power). The audit framework for assessing democracy provides a measure by which citizens of any country can assess the performance of their parliaments or assemblies. The framework also recognises that parliamentary oversight is only half the story; the judiciary and the courts have a democratic duty to maintain the rule of law and to ensure that it applies to the executive's actions and policies as well as to legislation framed in Parliament.[3]

In assessing Parliament's oversight of the executive's external policies, we recognise the force of the argument that such policies are often very different from domestic policy, and that there are differences also between different forms of external policy. We also recognise that there are limits to parliamentary control of the executive. However, the near-limitless freedom from parliamentary oversight that the royal prerogative bestows upon ministers across the whole range of external policies cannot be justified in a modern representative democracy. Moreover, we are investigating a series of quite distinctive delegations of power to the government of the day – delegations that involve government ministers and officials negotiating policy outcomes with other governments in a heterogeneous range of international bodies, each of which has its own power parameters, decision rules and norms of appropriate behaviour. There can be no 'one size fits all' answer to the complex question of how to frame appropriate forms of oversight for the various areas of policy that concern us.

Making parliamentary oversight a reality

Parliamentary 'oversight', as we use the term, is a synthesis of the powers and processes that bring about accountable government. It is important that government should be both effective and accountable, and accountable between elections as well as at them. So while the primary means of securing accountability is through elections, there is a need to ensure that between elections the government, ministers and officials are required to 'render an account' to citizens and their representatives in Parliament. The electorate is then in a position to form a comprehensive judgment on how government has performed. Thus Parliament itself is, or should be, the main instrument of political accountability on behalf of citizens. Other institutions, agencies and processes play a part in securing parliamentary accountability – such as the National Audit Office, the ombudsman services, the Information Commissioner and freedom of information laws, various bodies and officials concerned with standards, rules of conduct for ministers and parliamentarians, party political manifestos, etc.

Accountability ought not to be merely retrospective, though in principle and practice it is in the UK Parliament. However, in a mature democracy, it is important that MPs and peers should play a public role in examining and shaping government policies as they evolve; that MPs are able to represent their constituents' views on these policies to government; and that Parliament provides a public forum in which the policies are debated and decided. It is vital for this more continuous element of accountability that policy-making within the executive is as open as possible and that both Parliament and the public have established rights to be consulted and are given access to relevant official information (with limited exemptions, subject to regulation that is independent of the executive, to protect individual privacy, commercial confidentiality, national security, etc.).

Scrutiny is a significant aspect of Parliament's role in securing accountability, executive responsiveness and a degree of public participation. Thus select committees should possess powers to investigate all aspects of government policies; the ability to summon ministers and officials to give evidence and to secure policy papers; and the resources and specialist skills and advice necessary to come to judgement. MPs and peers should be able to question ministers and obtain honest and full replies.

Finally, both Houses ought to be in control of their business. Parliament must have wider powers to initiate legislation; by which we do not mean only more opportunities for private members' Bills, but also for select committees to put Bills forward. Parliamentarians should have full and genuine opportunities to amend as well as approve the government's primary and secondary legislation, both in draft and final form. (At the moment, the time for considering government Bills is frequently restricted in the Commons and MPs rarely amend Bills while suppressing most of the Lords' decisions to do so. Statutory orders cannot be amended.) Opposition parties, MPs and peers must have sufficient time to raise issues with ministers and to initiate debates.

Seeking oversight of external policies

Parliament has long since lost its power to control public expenditure. However, it is important that the executive operates within known constitutional and statutory rules of conduct and observes established rules of convention; and that, within the UK system of government, the impartiality of the Civil Service should be preserved. The authority under which the host of modern agencies and regulatory bodies that perform executive functions operates should be clear and transparent. They are in theory answerable to Parliament through select committees, but are not in practice accountable to Parliament for their policy-making nor is that policy-making open to parliamentary and public scrutiny.

External policies raise specific issues. The executive requires a freedom of manoeuvre and response and a degree of confidentiality and discretion in conducting external policies. However, there are significant decisions with far-reaching consequences which should require for their legitimacy parliamentary consultation, scrutiny and/or approval – notably armed action overseas; the ratification of treaties; the UK stance in international trade, aid, environmental and other negotiations; the UK's input into the policies of the United Nations and its Security Council, as well as other international bodies, such as the IMF and the World Bank; and the UK position in and contributions to NATO. Decisions to intervene with military force raise particular problems, since they clearly cannot always be discussed or cleared in advance; but where parliamentary approval cannot be obtained in advance, there should be provision for subsequent approval or disavowal and agreed conditions for further engagement.

British membership of the European Union is a special case. First, two representative institutions – the European and Westminster Parliaments – are formally responsible for securing the accountability of the EU executive bodies and of the Union's decision-making procedures. There are other representative bodies within the UK, namely the Scottish Parliament and National Assembly of Wales, which have legitimate claims to exercise at least some oversight of EU business. Views differ as to how these bodies might best share their responsibilities. As a further complicating factor, a significant proportion of UK external policy-making and negotiating is now part of a common EU policy. Secondly, the EU performs a significant legislative function in Britain's domestic and economic affairs.

On all fronts, there is a danger that the UK's contribution to joint policy-making in the EU, NATO and other international bodies is concealed from public and parliamentary view and approval. Formal arrangements for ministerial consultation with Parliament over the positions to be taken in the most important international negotiations should be an altogether more central element of our democratic culture than they are today.

The rule of law in world affairs

As stated above, the actions and policies of the executive should be subject to the rule of law. The development of judicial review in the UK since the 1970s has required most executive and administrative actions to meet judicial standards. Since this process is concerned with the courts' standards for the decision-making process and not the substance or correctness of the actual decisions, judicial review is on the way to establishing a valuable place for law within UK governance (though in the absence of a written constitution, the UK prefers (elected) legislative supremacy to (appointed) judicial supremacy, as in some other democracies, such as Germany, where the constitutional court can strike down executive decisions on a broad range of grounds). The reluctance of the courts to intervene in executive decisions, especially those touching international affairs, defence and security that are covered by the royal prerogative, is a weakness so far as oversight of external policies is concerned.

British governments are also, in principle at least, committed to the rule of law internationally. The FCO has long maintained traditional notions of state sovereignty and the inviolability of international borders. The *Ministerial Code*, the rule-book for government, commits ministers to uphold the international rule of law (see page 76); and the Labour Party's 2005 election manifesto, while unapologetic about taking part in what is generally agreed to have been an illegal invasion of Iraq, committed the Labour government squarely to 'always uphold the rule of international law'. But issues around the use of force in particular have become increasingly confused in modern times; and the UK has certainly not kept to the strict letter of international law on several occasions in the recent past: for example, the UK took the lead in inspiring NATO's armed intervention in the former Yugoslavia in 1999 and shared in establishing and maintaining the no-fly zones over Iraq between the two Gulf wars (though here, at least initially, the UK, the United States and France could call in aid previous Security Council resolutions). We consider the circumstances in which the government (and Parliament) justified the invasion of Iraq in 2003 in Chapter 4.

Here we describe the general principles of international law governing the use of force, as set out in the Charter of the United Nations in 1945. Basically the Charter, coming as it did in the wake of world war and the invasions that preceded war in the 1930s, sought to re-establish international traditions against the use of force by introducing a new framework of general security limiting the grounds for military action. Article 2(4) of the Charter declares:

> All Members shall refrain in their international relations from the threat or use of force against the territorial integrity or political independence of any state, or in any other manner inconsistent with the Purposes of the United Nations.

The Charter allows nations to use force either in self-defence, individual or collective, against 'an armed attack' (under Article 51); or on the authority of the Security Council. Both these exceptions raise difficulties. Can a state or states lawfully defend themselves by taking 'anticipatory' or 'pre-emptive' military action to avert an armed attack? There is provision for 'anticipatory' self-defence in customary international law, but does the fact that a potentially hostile state possesses, or is acquiring, weapons of mass destruction constitute grounds for pre-emptive action? What moral authority does the Security Council possess? Rivalries between the five permanent members (each of whom has a veto power on UN resolutions) colour nearly all its decisions on armed or any other intervention in other states; and currently, Russia and China are hostile to any armed interventions, even when they may be 'humanitarian' interventions to prevent genocide or mass violations of human rights.

Those who argue that human rights should have priority over state rights often call in aid the 1948 Genocide Convention that specifically requires nations to 'prevent and punish' the crime of genocide. But the convention does not provide for armed intervention by states acting collectively or on their own; instead it is left to the UN organs to take what actions they consider appropriate. Thus the convention creates a collective duty, but does not resolve the difficulties of fulfilling it through the UN and the Security Council.

It is sometimes argued that customary international law, or convention, can be invoked to justify armed intervention to prevent a humanitarian crisis. Customary international law is a dynamic process that is created by the acts, intentions and attitudes of individual states and the 'international community'. There have certainly been occasions of interventions for arguably humanitarian purposes that have escaped substantial international censure, for example India's incursion into East Pakistan following the massacres in 1971, Tanzania's intervention in Idi Amin's Uganda, Vietnam's invasion of Pol Pot's Cambodia in the 1970s, the interventions of west African states in Liberia and Sierra Leone in the 1990s, and the enforcement of the no-fly zone in northern Iraq in 1991. The Security Council appears to be increasingly willing to regard humanitarian crises within states as a threat to international peace and security; and in the cases both of Kosovo and the no-fly zones over Iraq, NATO allies and the UK initially claimed that they were acting on the 'implied' authority of the Council.

However, the weight of legal opinion seems to be that no such customary principle justifying armed intervention for humanitarian goals has yet developed, though some jurists have argued that such interventions for the exclusive purpose of putting an end to large-scale atrocities may yet crystallise into a general rule of customary international law. The recent report from the United Nations High-level Panel on Threats, Challenges and Change[4] advocated the establishment of clear criteria for humanitarian intervention in a country; however, it failed to suggest that such an intervention could occur without Security Council approval. The High-level Panel report is probably the best indicator of a clear recognition by the international community that there is a need for international intervention and it talks (though only that) of trying to find a solution.

Other international reports, such as the report of the International Commission on Intervention and State Sovereignty, do go as far as advocating the need for a right to intervene that supersedes the Security Council's remit.[5] Robin Cook set out 'rules of the road' for humanitarian intervention while he was Foreign Secretary, namely that the use of armed force should be collective, proportionate, likely to achieve its objectives and carried out in accordance with international law.[6] In his Chicago speech on 'international community', Tony Blair set out five similar considerations for determining whether or not intervention was justifiable (while acknowledging that they were not 'absolute tests'): Are we sure of our case? Have we exhausted all diplomatic options? Is intervention a prudent undertaking? Are we prepared for the long term? Are our national interests involved?[7]

All this leaves the UK Parliament and its committees in a dilemma. It is important that the UK should continue to acknowledge the importance of clear and agreed objective rules governing the international use of force to an ordered world system and the protection of human life, freedom and prosperity. The doctrine of 'non-intervention' is central to the international rule-book. And yet the case for humanitarian intervention in countries like the former Yugoslavia, Iraq in the 1990s, Rwanda and Darfur is compelling, even if such intervention is likely to be selective. Thus, in monitoring any future intervention by UK governments in another country's affairs for humanitarian purposes, Parliament should at least seek to ensure that they should do so purely and exclusively for those purposes; that any intervention must be proportionate; that all diplomatic options should be exhausted; and that, so far as is possible, any military intervention should be 'collective'.

The place of the international courts

The establishment of the International Criminal Court (ICC) in The Hague has made the issue of the legality of the use of force more pressing. The ICC has jurisdiction over the three most serious categories of international crime that individuals can commit: geno-cide, war crimes and crimes against humanity. It has also struggled for some time to develop the concept of 'crimes of aggression', but has so far failed. Britain is a party to the ICC Statute and, as such, its armed forces are subject to its jurisdiction. Admiral Sir Michael Boyce, the Chief of Defence Staff, and his legal advisers sought an unequivocal assurance of the legality of the invasion of Iraq in 2003 so that he could be sure that the military chiefs and soldiers 'would not be put through the mill' at the ICC; 'I required something in writing . . . saying our proposed actions were lawful under national and international law.'[8] (In fact, regardless of the legality of the war, UK forces that committed war crimes would be liable to prosecution in any event.)

The rules on the use of force, genocide, war crimes and crimes against humanity are at the sharp end of the 'silent' development of a system of international laws that grew rapidly in the second half of the last century. This still growing system not only seeks to govern the use of force, but also promotes free trade and global economic liberalisation, sets in place rules to protect the environment and curb global warming, and enshrines fundamental human rights – not just civil and political, but economic, social and cultural too. Britain plays a leading role in the international organisations, such as the UN and the World Trade Organization, that exist to develop and enforce these complex rules; and is of course a member state of the EU. The European Court of Justice enforces the rule of law for all EU affairs and its supremacy is recognised by the British courts. The WTO also has a mechanism for resolving disputes over alleged violations of its member states' agreements, with a seven-member appellate body which adjudicates upon disputes and may authorise retaliation.

The International Court of Justice (ICJ) is the UN judicial authority responsible for the adjudication of international legal disputes. All UN member states are automatically signatories to the ICJ Statute. But though the International Court provides the institutional mechanism for the judgment of cases under international law it is an inherently weak institution. Only states may be party to full cases before the court, therefore limiting the possibility of other parties seeking redress (though non-state parties may seek an advisory judgment). Furthermore, there are two major weaknesses in the court's structure and powers. First, there is nothing to stop a state from withdrawing from a case before the court at any time, as when the United States withdrew in 1986 when it became apparent that the ICJ was going to rule against its illegal operations in Nicaragua. Secondly, the ICJ has no powers to enforce compliance with its judgments, there being no Leviathan-type enforcement authority nor a developed body of international rule of law. Thus the ICJ is a fatally weak body that powerful countries can ignore. Given this lacuna in the international mechanism, it is all the more important that the UK should be a 'law-abiding' state and that Parliament should act as the 'body of last resort' for ensuring that it is.

Such oversight is not a responsibility of the UK courts as they have no general competence to enforce international law. This does not affect only the UK's relations with the ICJ, but also its adherence to a number of UN and other legally binding treaties which in principle should govern the UK's external policies but do not. For example, the UK is obliged to contribute to securing the economic and social rights of poor people under the UN International Covenant on Economic, Social and Cultural Rights, but this is not a legal duty. Ideally the government should comply with the whole body of international law in pursuing its external policies. However, unlike in some other countries, such treaty obligations are not automatically incorporated into British law. Under Britain's 'dualist' legal system, international laws have to be separately incorporated into British law following ratification if they are to have full legal force in domestic law. Thus the European Convention on Human Rights had to be incorporated through the Human Rights Act to become directly applicable in the UK.

Government will always require a high degree of discretion in much external policy-making, but there is also a case for a statutory framework in some areas, such as aid, arms sales and environmental protection. It is also important that policies reflect the concerns and wishes of the general public, in whose name they are pursued. There is a shift away in the popular mood from the traditional pursuit of 'selfish' national self-interest towards the view that external policies should be conducted with regard for moral and humanitarian values.

The public support for action to protect the Kurds of northern Iraq and Shias in the south from Saddam Hussein's vengeance after the first Gulf war and the recent generous response to the tsunami tragedy in southern Asia are but two examples of this new attitude. There should be parliamentary oversight to ensure that the executive is open and honest in holding the balance between the national interest and humanitarian and human rights goals abroad.

2

The overweening executive

The executive in the UK is made 'strong' because the electoral system usually delivers large government majorities in the popular chamber – the House of Commons. This majority power in the popular chamber and the constitutional weakness of the House of Lords makes Parliament and its law-making powers subordinate to the will of the executive; and since Parliament's constitutional sovereignty is thereby at the disposal of the executive, the judiciary too is subordinate to the executive (though not without profound influence, as the Law Lords' decision on the detention of foreign terror suspects in 2004 made clear). The executive is not bound by a written constitution, a position the Labour government of the time was careful to protect when passing the Human Rights Act in 1998. The Act ensures that Parliament, not the courts, should retain the last word within the UK in determining civil and political rights.[1]

The position of the executive is further strengthened by the flexible and uncertain nature of constitutional arrangements: by the fusion, rather than the separation, of powers; and by the effects of rigid discipline, party loyalty and patronage upon its majority in the Commons. The principle of ministerial responsibility to Parliament ensures that the sole duty of the Civil Service is to the government of the day. It is ministers, not officials, who report to Parliament and ministers determine which officials may give evidence and normally prescribe the terms on which they do so. The new freedom-of-information regime preserves official secrecy in most sensitive areas (especially those that concern policy-making, security, defence, trade and other external matters). The Freedom of Information Act 2000 also gave Cabinet ministers a power of veto over the release of information ordered by the Information Commissioner.

The executive comprises a complex mesh of actors and institutions that, with the Prime Minister, Cabinet ministers and senior civil servants at the centre, governs the United Kingdom. It is this 'core executive' that determines Britain's external and security policies. No one political figure, not even the 'presidential' Prime Minister, has absolute power within the executive; it is the site of an interactive and shifting process of decision-making. Four Cabinet ministers – the Foreign, Defence, Trade & Industry and International Development Secretaries of State – head the departments which are largely responsible for external policies (though there is now an external element to every department's responsibilities, especially in relation to the European Union). The Foreign and Commonwealth Office usually takes the lead in making and liaising external policies; its power within Whitehall has grown because it is the 'lead' department on European affairs. There are tensions between the departments since their interests in foreign affairs differ and often clash.

Executive powers under the royal prerogative

The executive jealously preserves 'a necessary freedom of action' in its external relations and is less constrained in the pursuit of its external policies than in any other area of government. As we have noted above, the royal prerogative is the main instrument at the disposal of ministers and officials for making and pursuing these policies, for it gives them flexible decision-making powers which are unconstrained by statute, are not subject to parliamentary approval, and are usually a no-go area for judicial review. These powers, once the prerogative of the ruling monarch, are a pre-democratic residue of the 'non-statutory powers' of the Crown, or 'common law powers and immunities which are peculiar to the Crown and go beyond the powers of a private individual'.[2] While the royal prerogative applies, for example, to the summoning, prorogation and dissolution of Parliament and granting honours, the government itself recognises that 'the conduct of foreign affairs remains very reliant on the exercise of prerogative powers.'[3] They are used for:

- making treaties
- declaring and waging war
- deploying the armed forces overseas
- recognising foreign states
- accrediting diplomats.

The prerogative is widely recognised as a pre-democratic anachronism. For example, Lord Wakeham's Royal Commission on the Reform of the House of Lords stated:

> A consequence of the continuity in British political and legal structures is that the Crown still retains significant powers under common law, which are not subject to direct Parliamentary control . . . The executive action authorised by the royal prerogative at common law includes some of the most basic and important tasks of Government, including the power to declare war [and] conduct international relations . . . The controversial feature of these powers is that the Government may use them to adopt major policies and decisions without the need for any formal approval by either House of Parliament.[4]

The report of the Public Administration Select Committee (PASC) on prerogative powers recommended that they should be put on a statutory footing and singled out 'three specific areas – the decisions on military conflict, treaties and passports' where early legislative action needed to be taken.[5] The committee reported that its witnesses had 'produced a range of persuasive arguments for more systematic Parliamentary scrutiny of the Ministerial prerogative on a range of fronts. If we want to take Ministerial accountability to Parliament seriously, the case for reform is unanswerable'. The committee also published a draft Bill for reform, part of which was used as a model by Neil Gerrard MP for his Private Member's War Powers Bill which fell when Parliament was dissolved in April 2005. (At the time of writing, Clare Short, the former minister, is to introduce a similar measure.)

Treaty-making in a parliamentary vacuum

Very few people, even those interested in politics and government, know that British governments enter into around 50 treaties a year through use of prerogative powers. The treaties are integral to the UK's bilateral, European and multilateral engagements; and they are often of great significance, such as the Mutual Defence Agreement with the United States and agreements with the World Trade Organization, the International Monetary Fund and other international organisations. Yet such is the opaque nature of government policy in this area that there is no publicly available single list of all the treaties to which the UK is a party. (When we asked for a list, the FCO's Treaty Section said that not even an internal list exists. It estimates that the UK is party to 14,712 treaties, but does not know for certain how many of these are still in force.) Treaty-making largely takes place in a parliamentary vacuum. The government generally 'lays' treaties before Parliament and avoids any debate on them, unless it is in its political interests, or if the opposition or a select committee requests a debate. The FCO explained the respective roles of the executive and of Parliament in treaty-making in evidence to the Royal Commission on the future of the Lords:

> The constitutional principle is two-fold; the power to make treaties is vested in the Crown as part of the Prerogative, but treaties so made are not self-executing, in other words they do not take effect as part of the law of the land unless enacted by Statute. This two-fold principle thus preserves both the Government's necessary freedom of action in foreign relations and the legislative supremacy of Parliament: the Crown is disabled from using its treaty-making powers as a device for legislating on its own, without the consent of Parliament . . . to the extent that a treaty sounds entirely within the sphere of foreign policy, and can be implemented without legislation, its conclusion and entry into force for the United Kingdom are regarded as being under the sole responsibility of the Executive; but they are subject to ministerial accountability to Parliament in exactly the same way as any other area of activity.[6]

It is striking that the executive regards the necessity for executive 'freedom of action' in foreign relations as *axiomatic*; and that it sees no necessity for parliamentary approval or ratification if a treaty can be implemented without legislation. As we have already argued, the FCO's assumption of an absolute separation between external and domestic affairs is utterly anachronistic. As the PASC has also observed,

> treaties are no longer restricted just to high diplomacy and security. They can involve, for example, vital economic matters with profound effects on Britain and the world, including agreements between the United Kingdom and organisations such as the World Trade Organisation and the IMF.[7]

The FCO argues that treaty-making is subject to 'practices of long standing which have hardened into conventions of the constitution [see pages 35–7 below], or of rules laid down by Parliament itself.' A few treaties require parliamentary approval (e.g. those that entail ceding territory or impose charges on the public purse). Parliament does not mandate ministers in advance in treaty negotiations, as other EU member states do for European negotiations. It may legislate in advance, requiring its approval in statute for certain types of agreement – for example, increases in the powers of the European Parliament – but again this is rare. A constitutional convention, known as the 'Ponsonby rule', applies to treaties entered into subject to ratification or its equivalent (see pages 35–7 on conventions generally).[8] Meanwhile, treaties are rarely debated in Parliament, even after their signature. Most are not scrutinised. There is no parliamentary committee that oversees Britain's treaty negotiations, or a decision whether or not to ratify a particular treaty. As Philippe Sands, the international lawyer, comments, 'this is a startling gap, especially as the European Community increasingly signs up to treaties on behalf of its members.'[9]

There is clearly a need for flexibility in international negotiations. Mandating government negotiating positions in advance or requiring parliamentary approval with a high threshold for treaties (as in the US Senate, where a two-thirds majority is necessary to ratify a treaty) may hinder satisfactory negotiations. However, other nations function effectively while requiring parliamentary ratification of treaties, as a Defence Committee report on NATO enlargement found:

> Of the current sixteen NATO member states, only Canada shares with the UK a ratification process which requires no formal involvement from the legislature. In other member countries treaties are ratified by the head of state upon authorisation of the legislature, usually by a simple majority . . . In many member states parliamentary committees make recommendations to the legislature before the consideration of ratification.[10]

Meanwhile, major treaties may be ratified in the UK almost unnoticed. For example, in 2004 the government renewed the Mutual Defence Agreement (MDA) with the United States without consulting Parliament, even though, as one specialist correspondent observed, it is 'regarded in Whitehall as a cornerstone of the special relationship' and may well contravene the 1968 Treaty on the Non-Proliferation of Nuclear Weapons.[11] To give the MDA its full title, the Agreement between the UK and the USA for Cooperation in the Uses of Atomic Energy for Mutual Defence Purposes 1958 enables the UK and the US to share nuclear technology and information. A time-limited article of the MDA allowing for the transfer of nuclear materials and equipment (though not actual atomic weapons) required renewal in 2004. The government ratified the amended treaty without debate in Parliament (see further page 72).

Government's freedom to make war

British governments have not declared war against another nation since 1942, but they regularly engage in military action, as for example in (among other places) Korea, Malaya, Kenya, the Suez Canal, the Falkland Islands, Kuwait, Kosovo, Afghanistan and Iraq. The executive is concerned to preserve the 'freedom of action' that the prerogative provides in deploying armed forces abroad. In response to the PASC report on prerogative powers, the Department for Constitutional Affairs (DCA) argued that extending 'parliamentary authority in this area' would meet with difficulties. What sort of action would trigger the need for approval? What if govern-ment had to act in an emergency? The DCA argued that the existing pragmatic, flexible and retrospective approach to parliamentary scrutiny worked well:

> The Government is accountable to Parliament for any armed conflict it engages in, as for anything else, and the Government have given repeated assurances that Parliament would be given an opportunity to debate and scrutinise decisions about the deployment of British forces in armed conflicts overseas. Furthermore, the Government is also mindful of the need to keep Parliament closely informed of develop-ments during the course of a conflict through statements and adjournment debates, as necessary . . . arrangements which allow for our involvement in armed conflict to be debated and scrutinised by Parliament after the event are by no means unique to the UK.[12]

Yet the absence of formal constitutional rules for parliamentary involvement in war-making is another example of British 'exceptionalism'. For example, the French constitution demands that a declaration of war must be authorised by Parliament. More stringent rules apply in other countries. Sweden's 'Instrument of Government', part of its constitution, is more broadly drawn. It requires not only the approval of the Riksdag but also compliance with international agreements for all troop deployments, other than government's use of armed force to repel an armed attack on Sweden itself. The United States Constitution states that 'the Congress shall have Power . . . To declare War'; and – mindful of the fact that it is rare nowadays actually to declare war – Congress passed the War Powers Act in 1973 in an attempt to secure the need for its approval for military action in general (see also page 88).

Britain's part in global organisations

British ministers play a prominent role in a host of multilateral organisations using their prerogative powers. The UK is a member of all the major international organisations, including the UN and its Security Council, the World Bank, the IMF, the WTO, the G8 (the group of eight leading industrial powers), the Organisation for Economic Co-operation and Development, as well as many lesser-known bodies. Britain is also a member state of the EU and a key player in NATO, the western defence alliance. Again, UK ministers and often officials – diplomats and senior civil servants – participate in their decision-making under the prerogative. In some cases, authority is ceded to these organisations, including NATO and the EU. Most decision-making in such organisations is opaque and even further removed from parliamentary oversight. The most that MPs or peers can expect is a statement in the chamber. As Baroness Williams complained in the Lords,

> we do not discuss the World Trade Organization; we do not have the pleasure of looking at the agenda for the G8; and we do not have an opportunity to talk at great length about the global environment convention. However, we all recognise that those treaties are now shaping our world and producing decisions that affect our citizens while we are virtually voiceless in them.[13]

Executive agencies and quangos

The UK operates several agencies with an international reach. These bodies are mostly a legacy of the country's imperial past but remain active today, often in a semi-privatised form that removes them from parliamentary and public scrutiny, even though they are publicly funded. Of these, the Crown Agents, the Commonwealth Development Corporation (now known by its initials, CDC) and the Export Credits Guarantee Department (ECGD) are the most significant. The ECGD is actually a government department that reports to the trade and industry secretary. The Crown Agents work in 130 countries, managing logistics and supply for multinational and bilateral donors on projects with an estimated annual value of £7 billion – a considerable sum. The CDC and the ECGD both disburse development finance and export credits larger than the sums managed by the Department for International Development – formally the lead department for development aid. Of these organisations, the ECGD has been repeatedly controversial: in

2003/4, it provided insurance and guarantees to British manu-facturing firms worth nearly £3 billion (see pages 98–101).

A handful of non-departmental public bodies (quangos) are also active in external affairs, including UK Trade & Investment (a frequently renamed creature of the FCO and the Department of Trade and Industry), the British Council, the Westminster Foundation and the Wilton Park conference centre (responsible to the FCO). UKTI is a high-powered body of senior officials and captains of the construction and other export-oriented industries. It is tasked with developing support for the promotion of British exports and though it is formally an advisory body, it occupies a particularly informal and unaccountable position and is clearly influential.

3

Checks and balances

The main channel for oversight of the executive in the United Kingdom has traditionally been political, not legal. Ministers are formally responsible to Parliament for their policies and actions; and it falls to Parliament to make ministers accountable, both individually and collectively. The government justifies the extensive use of the royal prerogative (see page 14) in external policy-making by pointing out that ministers remain accountable to Parliament through the doctrine of collective and individual responsibility for all their actions, even if they are taken under the prerogative.[1] In fact, this doctrine was born in the Victorian era not to secure accountability to Parliament, but to unify government and protect it and the Civil Service from parliamentary and political pressure – or, in Walter Bagehot's words, to protect them from 'the incessant tyranny of Parliament' and 'the busybodies and crotchet-makers of the House and the country'.[2] In practice, the 'doctrine' is more rhetoric than substance; it is used to justify secrecy over the government's collective decision-making and to restrict parliamentary demands for information from civil servants (see below); and it is by its nature at best a post hoc remedy, whereas accountability should apply throughout the policy process, not just at its end.[3]

Further, the doctrine's pre-democratic origins mean that, with respect to external policies, it belongs to the era of bilateral 'foreign' policy, rather than multilateral or European dealings, and so is not appropriate for modern developments. As George Cubie, the Clerk of Committees, put it to us, 'Parliament holds ministers to account, not multinational organisations.'[4] Obviously, it is only through ministers (in the short term at least) that Parliament can hope to get a grasp on the performance of the EU and these global players. But

MPs and peers require a new doctrine of ministerial accountability and new ways of engaging with ministers, for the post hoc accountability of the past will always be too late.

The emphasis upon the political has also meant that, until the 1970s, the judiciary generally refrained from subjecting the executive to judicial oversight. Judges are still reluctant to trespass upon executive territory. The executive is not bound by a written constitution and is largely free from statutory rules of conduct. Non-legal – and non-binding – political 'conventions' have traditionally governed the conduct of ministers, especially in their dealings with Parliament. The *Ministerial Code*, drawn up by the Prime Minister (with advice from the Cabinet Secretary) for each parliamentary term, is a package of conventions. Its most important provision, for our purposes, is to lay an obligation upon ministers to be open and honest in their dealings with Parliament (see page 93). It also requires ministers to comply with international law and their treaty obligations.

Judicial 'deference' makes Parliament's oversight role all the more important, as do changes within the executive itself. The idea that the non-political Civil Service might act as a restraint on ministers was exploded by the advent of 'can-do' ministers in Margaret Thatcher's governments. The influence of the senior Civil Service has diminished still further under New Labour. Ministers are encouraged to seek a wider range of advisers and now employ special advisers – who are generally party political – to strengthen their power in their dealings with officials as well as with the media. Ministers also turn increasingly to outside consultants. The Prime Minister and Chancellor also exert more political power over governance from the centre, through their own special advisers and bilateral meetings. Up to three politically appointed special advisers at 10 Downing Street may be given the power by the Prime Minister to issue instructions to permanent staff.

Moreover, Tony Blair's has been a commanding premiership; 'Tony wants' were said to be the most powerful words in Whitehall, and even after gaining a third term in power on a mere 36 per cent of those voting (or 22 per cent of the electorate), he has made it clear that he will treat his electoral victory as a mandate for his policies.[5]

Various witnesses have described the existence of a de facto prime ministerial department, run by a small inner circle at No. 10, with decisions taken in bilateral and often informal meetings rather than in full Cabinet or the Cabinet sub-committee structures that have directed post-war government policy.[6] Lord Butler's *Review of Intelligence on Weapons of Mass Destruction* is the most authoritative and critical account of Blair's informal 'sofa' government and its defects.[7] The former Cabinet Secretary's report touches on two long-term concerns about trends in governance at the centre, both of which pre-date 1997: the decline in Cabinet government and the principle of a neutral Civil Service giving impartial advice to ministers. Thus the two supposed safeguards against the misuse of executive power – the collegiate nature of Cabinet decision-making and the impartial advice of senior civil servants – are compromised. Ministers are supposed to give 'due weight' to advice from civil servants and to protect the Civil Service's integrity under the *Ministerial Code*, but there are fears that the growth in special advisers and expanding use of outside consultants compromises that integrity, and especially compromises government communications. Overall, it is hard to reconcile the conduct of government under Blair, as described in Butler's inquiry report, with a reading of the *Ministerial Code* rules on the integrity of the Civil Service, the conduct of business in Cabinet and its committees, the circulation of papers and the care for accurate note-taking. It is, however, the Prime Minister who is also by convention responsible for interpreting and enforcing the code. It is therefore all the more important that Parliament should conduct effective oversight.

Weaknesses in Parliament's powers and culture

The reality of executive dominance over Parliament, formally the sovereign ruling body, and the corresponding weakness of the House of Commons was starkly put to us by Bruce George, a former chairman of the Defence Committee. Recalling the emergency debate after the invasion of the Falklands in 1982, he said how struck he was by MPs' low level of knowledge of the subject. 'I would not rely on 659 MPs having the superhuman capacity to make a collective judgement on the use of armed force,' he said. 'We should be wary of their collective ignorance . . . the executive has most of the information, most of the expertise, access to intelligence, views of allies. What does Parliament have? . . . 659 times zero still adds up to zero.'[8]

Be that as it may, we shall catalogue serious structural weaknesses in Parliament's ability to oversee the executive and make it accountable. There are also two underlying cultural weaknesses in the capacity of the House of Commons to make a government accountable. First, the House is very rarely an entity of 659 MPs exercising a collective cross-party judgement. The House of Commons is a party-political cockpit, characterised by the dominance of the government over its activities and the power of the parties over their MPs. The House as such (and Parliament the more so) has no separate identity and rarely achieves a consensual approach to any issue. While opposition MPs are more likely to take seriously the need to keep a government under scrutiny, government MPs are generally bound to put the government's (and their own) interests first.

Parliament last asserted itself to any effect on a major issue of governance in March 1997, with a resolution passed in both the Lords and the Commons. This resolution arose from the Scott report's evidence of the deliberately misleading information about arms sales to Iraq given to Parliament and the public by ministers and officials. The then Public Service Select Committee published a draft resolution which required ministers and civil servants, among other things, to 'give accurate and truthful information to Parliament'. The Major government revised the original draft in order to preserve ministerial control over the information officials gave in Parliament while complying with its demands. The revised resolution was duly passed. Thus it was the executive that framed the resolution asserting Parliament's rights over it.

For the most part there is rarely any 'parliamentary leadership' in the House of Commons as a whole (though in the Lords there are sometimes informal alliances across parties). The Speaker in the Commons is not the powerful figure found in many other legislatures and his or her counterpart in the Lords is actually a senior minister, at least for the time being. The Speaker rarely assumes any other than a symbolic public role (though on occasion the Speaker will complain about ministers' disrespect, when they announce policies in the media rather than in the House). The House of Commons Commission busies itself largely with housekeeping matters.

The House acquiesces in the executive's control of its business. The governing party determines the timing of all debates and legislation on the principle that 'government business' has precedence at every sitting. The Leader of the House, a Cabinet minister, takes charge of the business of the chamber, though through 'the usual channels' – that is, negotiation with the opposition whips. In 2000 MPs were asked by the Hansard Society Commission on Parliamentary Scrutiny (HSCPS) to rank their roles in order. They put scrutiny of government first (with 33 per cent). Voting with the party scored only 2 per cent.[9] Yet the reality is that party comes first for most MPs most of the time and the time and resources allocated by most MPs to scrutiny lag far behind the demands of MPs' constituencies and of their caseloads of individual constituents' problems and grievances. The Hansard Society noted:

> The very high level of support for the constituency role, almost 90% [of 179 MPs who returned its questionnaire] regarded the solution of constituents' grievances as very important or quite important and over 80% thought similarly about protecting the interests of the constituency.[10]

This attention to the constituency acts as a valuable buckle between elected representatives and the general public, between Parliament and people. Often it can inform concern and action in the House, as it did for example over the failures of the Child Support Agency and inadequately published changes to earnings-related state pensions. But for many MPs constituency work is instrumental. Their very survival may depend on building up a reputation as a 'good' constituency member. The more a member 'digs in', the more he or she strengthens the value of incumbency at election time. The greatly enhanced system of members' allowances contributes to very sophisticated means of trawling for support among constituents. For months before the May election in 2005 many MPs' researchers and office staff were working almost full-time on drumming up the vote. Some newly elected MPs with small majorities in the election were at once contemplating employing all their staffs on constituency work and none on political research. Thus too few MPs feel that they have time or resources to spare on effective oversight of external policies.

Meanwhile it is clear to ambitious MPs how they can best climb the greasy pole to preferment – and it is not through sustained scrutiny work on select committees. It is the parties which organise collective activity within the Commons and which determine the careers for most MPs. As the Hansard Society report acknowledges, 'promotion is more likely to be the result of partisan activity . . . than pursuing the accountability functions of Parliament.'

Parliament's slow progress on committee scrutiny

There is at the same time growing recognition of the importance of the scrutiny work of select committees at Westminster. The Liaison Committee (consisting of select and other committee chairs) has developed from an administrative role into the proactive represent-ation of the interests of select committees; it now questions the Prime Minister every six months and challenges the executive on issues such as committee access to civil servants and documents. But it is too large and unwieldy to be as effective as it might be; and the HSCPS recommended that it should be reduced in size and should then elect an even smaller executive body. Parliament First, an informal cross-party group of MPs, has achieved some media impact and facilitated cross-party collaboration on issues such as the royal prerogative. But its members are too few to have an impact in a House divided and limited by partisan politics. The committees of the House of Lords have built up a reputation for excellence, but their work is inevitably marginal while the House is unreformed. Yet as Tony Wright, who himself chairs the PASC effectively, noted wryly to us, committees in the upper chamber were probably the best bet for non-partisan and influential scrutiny – and it might be worth recommending that they took on more.[11]

Parliament is making slow progress towards becoming a modern 'committee legislature'. But it is still the chamber in the Commons which dominates its activities and seizes media attention. The big debates generate far more heat and publicity than the less partisan hearings of select committees. We should not lose sight of the significance of the chamber within Parliament. As Wright wrote recently,

> it provides an arena in which the party battle is conducted on a continuous basis, and where brute accountabilities are demanded and identified. It makes, and destroys, reputations. It is a forum in which every issue under the sun makes its appearance.[12]

But it is not an arena in which a more considered scrutiny takes place. When ministers are obliged to account for their policies and actions in the chamber, the party-political battle lines are drawn up; the opposition is rarely seeking information, explanation and constructive remedies, but rather a ministerial scalp. These set pieces make good copy but not necessarily good government.

Reinforcing executive dominance

What, then, of Parliament's ability to maintain scrutiny of government's external policies and to make the executive accountable for them? Here we draw out some general themes. Executive dominance over Parliament is reinforced, paradoxically, by the doctrine of ministerial responsibility to Parliament and by the executive's firm control of the parliamentary agenda. Under the doctrine of 'collective responsibility', once the Cabinet or (more likely) a sub-committee has come to a decision, all ministers are jointly committed to that decision. Thus ministers are able to maintain, in the words of the *Ministerial Code*, 'a united front when decisions have been reached'.[13] The code goes on: 'Decisions reached by the Cabinet or Ministerial Committees are binding on all members of the Government.' (The code is silent on decisions taken unilaterally by the Prime Minister or bilaterally with others, but it may be assumed that the same rules apply.) In order to sustain this united front, it is held that details of particular positions advanced during discussions must be confidential, and even the process through which decisions are made should not be disclosed.

Thus ministerial responsibility keeps the policy-making process largely beyond the reach of Parliament. In the absence of constitutional or statutory regulation of ministerial conduct, the oversight of external policies depends to a large extent upon making ministers politically accountable. But the doctrine of ministerial responsibility harms that means of securing accountability disproportionately, and also reinforces the tendency to official secrecy and restricts, for example, what officials may say in evidence to select committees. There is an obvious need for ministers to be able to determine their position in private, so long as they and their officials account for it, if requested, later. The doctrine, as it is practised, also reinforces the retrospective nature of parliamentary scrutiny and inhibits the development of any process of shared policy-making between the executive and Parliament.

Secondly, executive command over the parliamentary agenda, debates and even the recall of Parliament reduces the opportunities for parliamentarians to maintain oversight. The most telling recent illustration of this weakness became apparent during the autumn of 2002, when it was clear that the Prime Minister was close to engaging with the United States in the invasion of Iraq. Yet Parliament was in recess at the time and unable to discuss the matter. The government had recalled Parliament earlier in the year on the death of the Queen Mother and at first refused to recall it again. The Archbishop of Canterbury and other church leaders presented a petition to Downing Street. MPs and peers joined in the public debates, but MPs had no power to recall Parliament for a debate. Graham Allen MP then forced the Prime Minister's hand. He organised an informal recall, to which hundreds of MPs of all parties were signed up, and booked a venue for debate at Church House, Westminster (he was told the chamber itself was unavailable, despite the fact that it was clearly not in use at the time). The government backed down and reconvened Parliament officially. A number of MPs have since signed a motion demanding that Parliament be able to recall itself, which has languished on the Order Paper ever since.

There are in any case limits both to how far MPs want to exercise oversight of executive policies and actions and to how far they have the capacity to do so. The government of the day usually has a majority in the House of Commons, and very often this is a commanding majority. All members of the government and ministers' parliamentary private secretaries are bound to back its legislation, policies and actions. This 'payroll vote' provides a strong spine of support, especially when the going gets rough. Moreover, there is a strong, usually cross-party consensus where 'foreign policy' is concerned, and MPs are generally unwilling to challenge it. Certain policies are often taken for granted (for example, the Special Relationship with the US; see pages 209–12).

It is true that many MPs chafe against executive dominance. Research by Philip Cowley of the University of Nottingham shows that, after 1997, there were more than 300 rebellions against the government whip.[14] But such rebellions do not add up to the kind of systematic oversight of policies, domestic and external, that is required. Few rebellions occur over external policies, thanks in part to their bipartisan nature, though the drive to war in Iraq produced the two largest rebellions in a governing party in modern parliamentary history (February and March 2003). This bipartisan approach also means that the main opposition parties rarely press a government hard on a 'foreign policy' issue. Thus the Conservatives voted with the Labour government on the invasion of Iraq (though with rebels in their ranks), thereby securing the Commons vote for the policy decision. (The Iraq war was remarkable in that the third main party, the Liberal Democrats, did not give their support. Had Paddy Ashdown still been the Liberal Democrat leader, they might also have swung behind the Prime Minister, thus ensuring that, as with previous wars, there would have been no major parliamentary vehicle for opposition.)

Rebels are sometimes able to secure certain concessions, but overall rebellions have little influence on policies as they occur after the policies have been fully developed. Rebelling may be regarded by some backbenchers as a safe way of registering discontent; and certainly when the prospect of a government defeat looms large, as it did several times in Tony Blair's second term, the size of rebellions adjusts accordingly. Faced with the possibility of defeating their government and damaging their party, MPs are reluctant to defy the whip. Rebellions thus have an indirect influence, especially where the opposition is poised to vote against a government, but they are no substitute for the practice of systematic parliamentary oversight. Their impact on the media is generally far more substantial than the concessions they achieve on public policy.

The parliamentary reforms initiated since 1997, welcome as they are, have had very little impact upon the oversight of external policies. Scrutiny of draft Bills, for example, hardly touches upon such policies as they are by nature not legislative. For instance, 29 draft Bills (or parts of draft Bills) received pre-legislative scrutiny by

Table 1: Westminster Hall debates, December 2004*	
2 December	*The Caribbean*
7 December	Incapacity Benefit (Coalfield Communities); Royal Regiment of Fusiliers; Parents (Family Policy); School Closures; *Democratic Republic of Congo*
8 December	Electoral Registration (Service Personnel); *Christian Community (Iraq)*; *Procurement of Army Uniforms* [debate had an external trade policy element]; Withdrawal of Pension Books
9 December	Long-term Savings
14 December	Health Services (Norfolk); Road Safety (West Derbyshire); Regional Television; Small Businesses (Swindon); Rural Diversification
15 December	Anti-Semitic Incitement; British Transport Police; Health and Safety (Railways); Travellers' Sites; Coastal Defences (Newbiggin-by-the-Sea)
16 December	House of Commons Commission (Annual Report)
* Policy issues with clear or borderline external relevance are in italics. They make up four of twenty-two debates.	

parliamentary committees from 1997/8 to 2003/4. But of the 29, only three Bills were clearly related to external policy: the Export Control and Non-Proliferation, the Extradition and the International Development Bills. The International Criminal Court Bill, though published in draft form in 1999/2000, went unexamined in its pre-legislative phase. The practice of using Westminster Hall for additional debates gives MPs the opportunity to raise subjects with ministers. Analysis of the topics covered in Westminster Hall in December 2004 (see Table 1) suggests that external policy matters do receive some coverage, but not a great deal. Indeed, we found a strong tendency towards the parochial, another sign of MPs' emphasis on the constituency link, and even matters at the level of national policy were not often raised.

Tools of accountability

In the remainder of this chapter we examine the various means by which the executive may be made accountable in Parliament. First, we discuss the extent of statutory regulation of external policies, which is confined largely to the rules for dispensing development aid and governing trade and exports. We then describe the role of conventions, the non-binding 'rules of the game', which exist to govern relations between the executive and Parliament. The *Ministerial Code*, the rule-book for ministers, is the single most important collection of conventions. We then go on to describe the means at Parliament's disposal to exercise oversight over government policies, principally through select committees in both Houses and parliamentary questions. Finally, we analyse the freedom-of-information regime that came into force in January 2005.

The statutory framework for governance

We have emphasised that the executive conducts most external policy, through the prerogative, outside parliamentary oversight. Very little is carried out under, or regulated by, statute, whether Acts or statutory orders. As part of Labour's manifesto commitment in

1997 to a more ethical foreign policy the government introduced two important Acts governing international development and trade policy.

The rules for international development
Broadly just over half of the UK's international development aid is dispensed bilaterally (53 per cent in 1999/2000) and the remainder through the EU and other multinational bodies. The provision of bilateral aid by the international development secretary is governed by the International Development Act 2002 (which replaced the Overseas Development and Co-operation Act 1980). The then international development secretary, Clare Short, told Parliament that the 2002 Act was intended to entrench the concept of poverty reduction, to prevent the use of aid for political or commercial purposes, and eliminate 'tied aid' (which is not specifically banned under the Act, allegedly because of drafting difficulties). The Act is loosely framed and the only prerequisite for making most decisions on aid is that the secretary of state is 'satisfied' that it will contribute to a reduction in poverty (except in British overseas territories, where even that goal is not necessary). The Act does not define 'poverty'. There is also scope for humanitarian responses to disasters and emergencies, the commissioning of research and other activities, and support for organisations and programmes promoting awareness of global poverty.

The Act is also narrowly drawn. It only governs 30 per cent of the UK aid budget that is dispensed by the EU – the rest can legally be spent by the EU on other political or administrative considerations. Nor does it set rules for the policies with a bearing upon aid and development that British ministers and officials pursue in organisations such as the International Monetary Fund, the World Bank or the World Trade Organization. Thus multilateral organisations, dispensing UK aid, of which the EU receives the largest share and spends much of the aid money on administration, escape parliamentary oversight almost entirely. During the committee stage of the Bill, an amendment was tabled – then withdrawn – calling for all multilateral humanitarian assistance to meet the same standards as bilateral aid. A similar amendment was debated at report stage. MPs were also concerned that the EU may pursue objectives that differed from the Act's emphasis upon poverty reduction, such as political stabilisation at its borders. Chris Mullin, then the junior minister responsible, responded that the international development secretary supported the EU Development Fund, the UN and other organisations and provided funds 'if he is satisfied that to do so is likely to contribute to a reduction in poverty'. In other words, this was a matter for ministerial discretion.

There is minimal parliamentary oversight of the secretary of state's power (with Treasury approval) to lay orders for contributions to be made to multilateral development banks, such as the World Bank and the regional development banks. The drafts of such orders must be laid before the House of Commons for approval. Provision can also be made by Order in Council to introduce privileges and immunities for various international financial institutions, subject to approval by resolution in each House. All other orders relating to payments made under the 2002 Act come into effect automatically unless a 'negative resolution' is passed within the 40 days during which it is laid before Parliament. Negative resolutions are very rare. In theory an MP can put down a motion to that effect, as an early day motion, but no time will be available to discuss it unless, perhaps, there are an extremely large number of signatories. If the official opposition puts down a motion, a debate may be organised, but even then not necessarily.

Statutory control of exports

The Export Control Act 2002 came into being to end the illegitimate postwar use of a 1939 emergency wartime measure which gave governments general and undefined powers to impose import and export controls with no parliamentary scrutiny. The 2002 Act sets out the purposes of export controls and provides for parliamentary scrutiny. Controls of any kind may be imposed 'for the purpose of giving effect to any Community provision or other international obligation of the United Kingdom'. The government may also impose controls over the export of arms, military equipment and technology, actual or potential, and goods likely to have an adverse effect on the security of the UK, EU member states and other 'friendly' states or on peace, security or stability anywhere in the world. Among such goods are those which facilitate the production or use of weapons of mass destruction (WMD), acts of terrorism or serious crime, or 'breaches of international law and human rights'. Controls may also be imposed 'in relation to objects of cultural interest'. Orders under the Act have immediate effect but must be approved by affirmative resolution in both Houses of Parliament and the government is required to report annually to Parliament on the workings of the Act.

Conventions – the 'rules of the game'

In Britain, conventions often stand in for binding constitutional and statutory rules. Conventions do not have the force of law. They are 'rules of the game' that belong to an earlier ethic of the gentleman's club; they remain, however, important political rules that serve to facilitate parliamentary oversight and ministerial responsibility to Parliament. They are especially important to the conduct of external policies, given the prominent role of the royal prerogative.

Conventions are created and altered by political actions as they set precedents and thus shift and adapt over time. There is no doubt that they, being thus flexible, make a significant contribution to good governance and parliamentary oversight in the UK. They are also by their very nature uncertain devices that may be interpreted in different ways; and at any time the executive can ignore or unmake a convention. Margaret Thatcher, for example, was renowned as Prime Minister for having made a 'bonfire of conventions'. In foreign policy, it was once held that the Foreign Secretary should always sit in the House of Commons to ensure that he (in those days) would be answerable to elected members for his conduct of affairs under the royal prerogative. However, Harold Macmillan and then Thatcher breached this convention and made it redundant. Differences of interpretation arose when the government refused to publish the Attorney General's advice on the legality of the invasion of Iraq (until finally it was leaked). Ministers argued that it was convention that such advice was never published, citing precedents in their favour; those who demanded that the advice should be published also furnished precedents. The unsurprising conclusion seems to be that governments do as they see fit at the time (see pages 89–95); and this rule of thumb probably holds good for most conventions. Thus while it is now widely said that the two votes the government conceded over the invasion of Iraq in 2003 have established a new convention obliging a future government to seek parliamentary approval for military action abroad, much would depend on the circumstances of any situation that may require military intervention. Only time will tell.

The 'Ponsonby rule' is perhaps the most notable convention that gives Parliament a potential voice in external policy-making. This rule came into being in 1924 when Arthur Ponsonby, Under-Secretary of State for Foreign Affairs in the first Labour administration, undertook to lay any treaty subject to ratification before the House of Commons for 21 sitting days and to inform the House of all other 'agreements, commitments and understandings which may in any way bind the nation to specific action in certain circumstances'. At that time treaties binding upon the UK were presented to Parliament only after they had entered into force. Ponsonby was responding to anger over secret treaties, and secret clauses in treaties, which had supposedly helped bring about the First World War. He stated that 'if there is a formal demand for discussion forwarded through the usual channels from the opposition or any other party, time will be found for the discussion of the treaty in question.' The convention is now that the rule, except in times of emergency, applies both to ratification and accession to treaties.

The government has since January 1997 published explanatory memoranda with all treaties laid before the House under the Ponsonby rule. Yet not only is Parliament still denied the right to approve (or disapprove) treaties, it rarely even discusses them. The Defence Committee complained in 1999:

> Hardly any treaties laid under the 'Ponsonby Rule' are debated on the floor of the House; whether or not a treaty is debated is a matter for the Government and its business managers, although it is conceivable that the Opposition or a backbencher could secure a debate.

In 2000, the government then extended the Ponsonby rule again, declaring that it was 'happy to undertake normally to provide the opportunity for the debate of any treaty involving major political, military and diplomatic issues, if the relevant select committee and the Liaison Committee so request'.[15]

Parliamentary committee scrutiny of external affairs

The most significant means at the disposal of Parliament to check and scrutinise executive policies and actions are the eighteen departmental select committees in the House of Commons. For external policies, the relevant committees in the Commons are the Defence Committee, the Foreign Affairs Committee, the International Development Committee and the Trade and Industry Committee; and in the Lords, the Economic Affairs Committee. The European Scrutiny Committee in the Commons and the Lords' European Committee (and its sub-committees) share the responsibility for scrutiny of EU business, but most EU legislative activity is also relevant to the work of the 'home' committees (see Chapter 5). Further, the Commons Liaison Committee, comprising the chairs of the House's committees, interrogates the Prime Minister at six-monthly intervals; and the Intelligence and Security Committee, comprising of parliamentarians but responsible to the Prime Minister and not the House, attempts to oversee the policies and actions of the secret intelligence services. The Joint Committee on Human Rights, comprising members of both Houses, has taken on a significant initiative in scrutinising the UK's compliance with the international human rights instruments to which this country is a signatory.

Select committees do not of course escape executive influence. The party whips decide their composition, which reflects the balance of power within the chamber. Thus, though they may have a chairperson from an opposition party, the government party has a majority on them all. There is usually a real effort to achieve a non-partisan ethos on committees. While MPs from the governing party are generally willing to be critical as scrutineers of government policies and actions, they are inhibited by their party loyalty and usually will not press an issue which might seriously embarrass their government.

The committees discharge their responsibilities largely through reports on issues within the domain of the department they shadow. They largely proceed by hearing witnesses on the issue they are investigating. Members take it in turns to ask their own questions. Some chairmen do try and organise the questioning, but MPs will often chase their own preoccupations and valuable lines of inquiry come to an abrupt end when one MP succeeds another. There are other limitations on their capacity to uncover the truth, as the inquiries into the Iraq war demonstrated (see pages 83–4). Ministers can simply refuse information and cooperation.

Anthony Sampson, in the last of his *Anatomy of Britain* series, was struck by the contrast between the rather cumbersome procedures employed by the UK select committees and the working practice of committees in the US Congress, which employ 'teams of lawyers and researchers to amass volumes of evidence and who can conduct hearings like major trials, attracting both publicity and respect'.[16] Select committees are certainly more humdrum: their hearings and reports rarely attract publicity in the media (indeed, some of their officials seem to regard media interest with dismay); the reports are conservatively produced and usually blandly written. However, they provide the only real opportunities within Parliament to question ministers and officials closely about their policies and actions. They also act as forums for pressure groups, organised interests and academic and other specialists to contribute to policy thinking and critiques of government policy. There is undoubtedly a growing interest in Parliament in subjecting the executive to effective scrutiny, stimulated by the uncertain progress of select committees since they were introduced in 1979. Compare for example the executive's ability to suppress any parliamentary or public inquiry into the disastrous Suez invasion in 1956; and seven specific inquiry reports within the parliamentary and public sphere (including the Butler and Hutton inquiries) into the decision to join the invasion of Iraq in 2003, as well as other select committee reports that touch on it.

However, the Iraq war demonstrated once again the weaknesses that drain Parliament's ability to make the executive accountable. Select committees have the formal power to send for 'persons and papers', but in practice they cannot make full use of this power. They are able to require ministers (except for the Prime Minister) to attend, but they cannot require him or her to answer their questions. Ministers can obstruct their requests for civil servants and ministers' special advisers to give evidence to committes. (Politically appointed special advisers have proved particularly shy. For example, Jonathan Powell, the Prime Minister's Chief of Staff since 1997, has never appeared before the Public Administration or any other select committee, though he has been asked.[17]) Even when civil servants do attend, ministers can dictate what they may or may not say (see page 41).[18] These constraints derive from the doctrine of ministerial responsibility to Parliament, which holds that civil servants, when giving evidence to select committees, do so on behalf of ministers, not themselves (since ministers are answerable to Parliament for their departments and their officials are answerable only to them). The constraints prohibit officials from going 'beyond explaining the reasoning which, in the Government's judgement, supports its policy'. They cannot discuss 'alternative policies where this is politically contentious' or 'the advice which they have given to Departments, or would give if asked'.

Moreover, while committees may formally demand 'papers', the government severely restricts what they get. Ministers will supply 'memoranda, written replies to Committee's questions and oral evidence from Ministers and officials', but the rules insist that they will not give 'access to internal files, private correspondence, including advice given on a confidential basis or working papers'.[19]

By contrast, the Butler and Hutton inquiries received (in Lord Butler's words) full cooperation from departments, 'a huge volume of documents' and impressive lists of witnesses. The disparity between the cooperation that these inquiries received from the executive, and that which select committees are used to, dramatically illustrates the weaknesses which undermine the latter (see also Chapter 4). The Prime Minister, the chairman of the Joint Intelligence Committee (JIC) and the chief of the SIS were among those who gave evidence on the record to the non-statutory Hutton inquiry. In January 2004, the Commons Liaison Committee noted the disparity between this turnout and the list of recent occasions on which committees of the House had been refused requests to question ministers and officials.[20]

Further, the Liaison Committee pointed out that no select committee would 'be given the form of documentary evidence supplied to Hutton . . . [such as] the correspondence or loose minutes between senior officials and the mass of e-mails'; it 'would not be given the nature of documentary evidence supplied to Hutton, much of which would fall into the categories of advice to Ministers or paper [sic] whose release would adversely affect the candour of internal discussions'; 'a select committee would not be given (and might not ask for) documentary evidence as opposed to information.' The committee listed the sorts of papers that might be helpful to select committees: 'full records of past events and decisions, including those of the Cabinet and its sub-committees; internal reports, detailed options papers, documents passed between departments (including HM Treasury); and departmental work programmes and agendas such as are available at divisional or central level to management of a department and to Ministers'. Finally, it was noted that the inquiry received documents far faster than select committees could expect.

The weakness of Parliament in this respect is underlined by the fact that it has no effective means of even registering its discontent at the government's refusal to give documentary evidence or send witnesses. In March, the Foreign Affairs Committee (FAC) noted that, when meeting with a lack of executive cooperation with its Iraq inquiry,

> the only way in which the Committee could have sought to insist on the attendance of official witnesses or the production of official papers would have been to make a Special Report to the House, or to table an appropriate Motion. Either course of action would have required the Government's agreement for a debate to be held in government time.[21]

In other words, the government would have to approve a challenge to its own authority. The FAC also complained that the non-parliamentary Intelligence and Security Committee received greater cooperation for its inquiry than the FAC experienced.

Tony Wright drew the attention of MPs in a Commons debate to the 'paradox' that Hutton, with no formal powers, was able to demand cooperation from government that select committees, formally equipped with all the powers to send for persons and papers, fail to achieve. 'I have come to the conclusion that we have a choice, and it is a very important one,' he said: 'we must either equip ourselves to hold the sort of inquiries that need to be held, or abandon the field altogether and leave it to the Lord Huttons of the world. That is the decision before the House of Commons.'[22]

In the 'wrong box'

In February 2004, the Prime Minister accepted a request from the Liaison Committee to see what lessons could be learned from the experience of the Hutton inquiry. After further pressure from the committee, Peter Hain, then the Leader of the House of Commons, produced a consultation paper on revisions to the 'Osmotherly rules', which govern the evidence of officials to select committees. They may prove to represent limited progress, although they are yet to be tested. The paper proposed to introduce a presumption that ministers will comply when a select committee asks to take evidence from a 'particular named official, including special advisers', or made a request for information. The idea of 'presumption' and the reference to special advisers are both new; whether 'information' means actual documents, rather than specially prepared memoranda, is unclear. However, the final say will remain with ministers, not Parliament.

Ministers will retain their wide discretion over just how far they wish to cooperate with committee inquiries and they therefore can, if they wish, obstruct legitimate investigations which could prove politically embarrassing. We were told in interviews with chairmen and members of select committees that they depend heavily upon the goodwill of individual ministers and the relationships they develop with them. They may be offered confidential briefings, but these are an unsatisfactory alternative to the open supply of information since committees cannot refer to them in their reports. In the words of Bruce George, then chairman of the Defence Committee, 'if they give you classified information, you're screwed.' Moreover, securing the attendance of a minister at a session in itself achieves little. George told us: 'If the Secretary of State doesn't want to give us information, we can't force him – we can force them to come but we can't force them to answer our questions.'[23]

Moreover, parliamentary inquiries will not, it seems, be given the kind of access that led to the tantalising glimpses of the internal workings of government associated with the executive-convened Iraq inquiries. In discussing the proposals with the committee, Hain explained that the Butler and Hutton inquiries 'were in a different box from Select Committee activity'. The committee chairman noted that the obvious conclusion was 'that if you want a comprehensive inquiry you have to go outside Parliament because you are not going to get one within Parliament.'[24]

So what distinguishes the two boxes from each other? Butler told the PASC:

> I think there is a difficulty for select committees in this respect and that is – I notice Lord Hutton made this point to you – that select committees inevitably bring in the party political aspect and governments are less confident about revealing very sensitive papers to select committees that contain members of other political parties. Select committees, I believe, go out of their way to behave very responsibly and honourably about this but it is a factor one just cannot ignore and I think that is what makes it more difficult for select committees to get access to the most sensitive papers.[25]

No doubt Butler has accurately identified the obstacle to the executive's openness to Parliament. However, the executive's position does seem to be constitutionally – and certainly democratically – improper since members of Parliament and of select committees are present as the elected representatives of the people; and information should not be withheld from them for party political reasons, however responsibly or irresponsibly they may behave.

The executive often shows committees scant respect in other ways. For example, as the Liaison Committee's 2003 annual report noted, ministers and their departments may not bother to meet the two-month deadline for responding to committee reports, or may, on the other hand, simply return poor-quality, 'rapid rebuttal' responses.

Ministerial influence over 'independent' inquiries

For the purposes of oversight, non-parliamentary inquiries such as Hutton and Butler are not satisfactory alternatives to select committee investigation. As the PASC noted,

> although known as 'independent public inquiries' this description is subject to some qualification. Invariably it is Ministers who set up inquiries in response to political or public pressure or, more cynically, as a means of deferring a potential problem. It is Ministers who therefore are responsible for an inquiry's composition, its terms of reference, and the powers and resources at its disposal. They may also influence its form; not all independent inquiries are necessarily conducted in public.[26]

They may also serve as a convenient means at the executive's disposal to take the heat out of public concerns.

MPs as 'welfare officers'

We deal with the resourcing of select committees in the next section. Here we deal with a less obvious dimension of the resources question. Fewer than half of MPs serve on select committees.[27] Committee chairmen and clerks pointed out to us that the greatest constraint on the work of committees is the time that their thirteen members can devote to their participation. MPs are obliged to juggle with a variety of demands upon their time, both at Westminster and in their constituencies. (We advocate one solution to this constraint which may also assist in foregrounding scrutiny – that all backbench MPs should serve on larger select committees – in Chapter 7.) In particular, as we have noted above, the emphasis MPs give to constituency casework greatly restricts the time and attention that they can devote to scrutiny work on committees. In the words of Donald Anderson MP, chairman of the Foreign Affairs Committee, 'We [MPs] don't survive if we're not a welfare officer.' He recounted how the constituency emphasis even affects MPs' conduct on inquiries. When his committee members visit an army barracks, their first interest is in whether there is a constituent there, so they can have their photo taken with them for local press purposes.[28] He also referred warmly to the German *Landesliste*, the list of top-up members elected to the German Parliament under the alternative-member electoral system (variants of which are in use in Scotland and Wales), saying that as the German top-up members have no constituency duties, they can devote more time to scrutiny.[29] (Directly elected German MPs are not 'welfare officers' either, so the difference runs deeper. The welfare role seems to be an Anglo-American phenomenon.)

Constraints of this kind mean that select committees must pick and choose the issues into which they inquire. The scale and size of departmental activity makes it impossible to determine a systematic set of priorities for scrutiny. Select committees also show signs of 'going native', accommodating to the direction of departmental assumptions, being sympathetic about the difficulties that confront ministers and officials, taking the part of particular interest groups, either public employees or within particular policy communities. The former Defence Committee chairman has gone on the record as describing his committee as 'champions of the regimental system'. Dominant chairpersons can impose their own priorities on the work of their committees. Further, committees take great care to avoid trespassing on areas where the responsibility for scrutiny may overlap or is confused, thus leaving significant issues unexamined. In our interviews, the Defence and Foreign Affairs Committee chairs assured us that they are able to sort out demarcation uncertainties.

Overall, executive dominance and resource, combined with political and cultural weaknesses in the Commons mean that select committees do not succeed in subjecting government policies and actions to systematic scrutiny. It is questionable whether they ever could. Mark Hutton, Clerk of the Defence Committee, expressed the view that rather than achieving systematic and comprehensive coverage, select committees achieve accountability by creating the feeling within government that they could potentially investigate any particular area, rather than the certainty that they would.[30] In other words, their role is akin to a 'police officer on the beat'.

Setting priorities for scrutiny
In June 2002, the Liaison Committee attempted to tackle the

unsystematic nature of select committee activities by promulgating a set of 'core tasks' for committees. Our research indicates that committee members and staff do not regard their work as being driven by the 'core tasks'. Annual reports by select committees may refer to fulfilment of the tasks, but often in a very unsystematic way. Indeed, some at least regard the core tasks an unwanted and unnecessary restriction on their freedom of action. The core tasks may come to be adopted over time, but how this might come about is not entirely clear, given the much-prized autonomy of MPs. Of the tasks set out under Objective A, which deals with policy oversight, Task 2 encourages committees to 'identify and examine areas of emerging policy, or where existing policy is deficient, and make proposals'. The Liaison Committee noted: 'This calls for Committees to identify areas where, based on judgement of Members, views of others, etc, a Committee inquiry would be worthwhile.' This is a particularly important task with respect to external policies that literally involve a whole world of developing or overlooked issues. However, a seasoned committee chair with a clear external policy remit told us that he did not see it as his job to identify problems or issues – even major humanitarian crises – that the government was failing to address. Rather his committee was supposed merely to respond to actual policy.

Task 4 enjoins committees to 'examine specific output from the department expressed in documents or other decisions', with a formal framework to ensure that they are informed of 'secondary legislation, circulars and guidance, treaties and previously identified casework decisions, so that they can if needed be drawn to a Committee's attention'. The interviews we have conducted have not revealed anything as distinct as a 'formal framework' of the sort referred to here. The International Development Committee, for example, does not receive advance sight of orders to be made under the International Development Act 2002.[31] An open process, whereby the texts of the Liaison Committee's list of documents should be officially deposited with the relevant committees (and published on their websites) seems the most appropriate way of ensuring effective oversight in this respect.

Objective B is 'to examine the expenditure of the department'. Here is an example of an area which, if it was to be thoroughly covered by select committees, could absorb a number of extra staff to assist members without reducing the accountability of committees to the MPs who sit on them. The same could be said of the next objective,[32] Objective C, 'to examine the administration of the department', including scrutinising 'major appointments made by the department'. The Foreign Affairs Committee is committed to carrying out valuable work examining ambassadorial appointments from outside the Diplomatic Service (see also page 62).

The 'awkward squad'

The fact that the party whips determine the composition of the select committees is widely seen as another aspect of their weakness. There is anecdotal evidence of party whips keeping members of the 'awkward squad' off committees and some degree of selection of more appropriate MPs to others such as Defence (but here a strong element of self-selection must also be allowed for). Preselection of members of some committees in conjunction with chairs does occur in order to prevent MPs with non-consensual views on external policy matters being placed on sensitive committees. Bruce George said that he believed in 'socialising' committee members into consensual decision-making, and that had someone with particularly difficult views been placed on his committee, he would have resigned.[33] Chairs and even committee places are also treated by party managers as spoils, usually as rewards to the loyal. The most spectacular example of this was the whips' attempt to substitute former minister Chris Smith for the greatly respected Donald Anderson as chair of the Foreign Affairs Committee in 2001, as Tony Blair wanted to soften the blow to Smith of losing his seat in the Cabinet. At the same time, the whips tried to evict Gwyneth Dunwoody from the chair of Transport, because she was seen as a thorn in the government's side. For once the House rose up in rebellion and the two chairpersons were reinstated. Robin Cook, the then Leader of the House, gave MPs the opportunity of freeing the committees from the dominion of the whips, but MPs voted to retain their chains. It is argued that there are practical grounds for having done so, as the whips are likely to be more consistent in the way they allocate MPs to committees than members in general will be; and they do enable committees to be set up quickly after general elections (though this has not been the case after the 2005 election). However, there is not much sign of the whips seeking to match MPs with known expertise or knowledge to appropriate committees. MPs do themselves sometimes at least try to match their enthusiasms with service on a particular committee – for example, Tony Baldry, the International Development chair, describes his committee as 'a conspiracy in Parliament of those concerned with development'. The danger is that enthusiasts tend to go native (but International Development seems to do so intelligently: see Chapter 6).

Resourcing committee scrutiny

It would be unrealistic to expect committees in the UK to match their equivalents in the US; there in 1999 the House Foreign Affairs Committee had 68 staff, and the Armed Services Committee 57; the two equivalent Senate committees had 50 and 48 staffers. The US takes the idea of the separation of powers seriously and recognises that Congress requires substantial support to maintain oversight of the enormous and complex external engagements of the US. However, given the tendency for the UK to 'punch above its weight' in external affairs, the relevant parliamentary committees do need more substantial resources. But here they are part of a general tendency that expects to get Parliament on the cheap.

The salaries of MPs have increased greatly since 1997, they receive staffing allowances, now worth £77,534 annually, and other expense allowances. Many MPs are now able to employ up to three full-time employees. Opposition parties in both Houses also receive funds for assistance in their 'parliamentary business', research, travel and 'associated expenses'. In 2003/4, the allocations for 'Short money' (as it is known) in the Commons came to over £5.2 million, and 'Cranborne money' in the Lords for the Conservatives, Liberal Democrats and cross-bench convenor totalled £639,792. In addition, the leader of the opposition, his chief and assistant chief whip received salaries of £66,782, £37,796 and £24,324 respectively over and above their salaries as MPs. Very little information is available about the parties' use of these funds. There have been accusations that some of the money has been funnelled off into party political campaign work. Our concern is with research for the purposes of oversight; and our view is that most of the funds go into facilitating the work of the party whips and offices and thus benefit the executive by ensuring that the conduct of parliamentary business – its business – runs smoothly.

The resources at the command of select committees have not kept pace with those devoted to individual MPs. They are in the midst of a modest boost to their staffing – a three-year programme, beginning in 2003/4, is designed to provide each of them with an additional 1.5 staff members 'to assist them with inquiry management and administrative functions'. By 2006, each committee should broadly have some 6.5 staff. In Germany, parliamentary scrutiny committees have about 14 full-time staff each.

Our researches indicate that they are considerably under-resourced for the tasks of keeping government under scrutiny, if it is to be fully performed, and fulfilling the 'core tasks' which are supposed to guide their work. They are likely to remain under-resourced for the foreseeable future. In 2002/3, the last year for which we have figures, select committees in the House of Commons received a total of £10.6 million, to shadow a government leviathan that spent £430 *billion*. In 2005, the select committees that oversee external policies are not generously staffed (see Table 2).

The research staff are typically young people at the outset of their careers, which is why chairs such as Bruce George say they also need access to experienced heavyweights in their fields. Committees rely heavily upon information from the departments they are shadowing and make up for the shortfall in independent research by engaging specialist advisers, who are commonly academics, for the inquiries they undertake. Defence can employ up to four extra specialists for a particular inquiry and draws upon an informal network of advisers when it needs advice. This is particularly useful, George says, if the committee wants 'to take on the Ministry'. The advantage to the Exchequer of these arrangements is that committees get their advice on the cheap. The rewards for advisers are counted in terms of contributing to public debate, having a marginal influence on policy, gaining in prestige. The fees are low and at least one committee

Table 2: Staffing levels of committees that oversee external policies					
Committee	Senior officials	Researchers & specialists	Secretarial assistance	Others	Total
Foreign Affairs	2 clerks	2 specialists	1 assistant; 1 secretary; 1 office clerk	0	7
Defence	2 clerks	1 specialist; 1 audit adviser	1 assistant; 1 secretary; 1 office clerk	1 inquiry manager	8
International Development	2 clerks	2 specialists	1 assistant; 1 secretary; 1 office clerk	0	7
Trade & Industry	2 clerks	1 specialist	1 assistant; 1 secretary	1 inquiry manager	6

chairman has publicly apologised to a consultant about the low level of remuneration.

There is, however, considerable resistance among members to expanding their research staffs. MPs are quite reasonably jealous of their representational role and they fear that expanded staffs would take a more dominant role in amassing evidence and coming to conclusions at the expense of their control. This, both MPs and the senior officials argue, would reduce the level of accountability to the MPs on whom the legitimacy of committee activity rests. (The ministers, whom the committees are tracking, often rely on thousands of officials apparently without worrying about the dilution of their legitimacy. No more do the well-resourced legislative committee members in Washington or Berlin.)

Select committees in the Commons are also able to draw upon the expertise of a new Scrutiny Unit and the House of Commons Library. The Scrutiny Unit was set up in November 2002 to provide (in the words of the Liaison Committee's 2003 annual report) 'specialist support for committees on expenditure matters and draft Bills together with an element of "surge" capacity at times of

unexpected demand or temporary staffing shortages'. The unit
employs ten specialists, six of whom are seconded (three from the
National Audit Office, a public expenditure expert from a Whitehall
department, a House of Commons Library statistician and a
performance audit adviser from the Audit Commission), two lawyers
and two economic/social policy experts on short-term contracts; and
seven core staff. By March 2004, they had carried out more than 100
tasks for select committees, varying in size. At first they concentrated
on expenditure matters, but from mid-2003 onwards they spent most
time on scrutiny of draft Bills for joint committees. The unit's most
notable contribution to scrutiny of external policy was the assistance
given to the largest of the joint committees, the Quadripartite
Committee, for its examination of secondary legislation on export
controls (see page 97 for more on this committee's work). Figures
from the Liaison Committee indicate that while the International
Development, and to a lesser degree Trade and Industry, committees
made considerable use of the Scrutiny Unit, the Foreign Affairs and
Defence committees could make only scant use of this new resource.

The House of Commons Library provides a central research service
employing, in total, 233 staff. There are fewer than 50 research
specialists, of whom only six concentrate on international affairs. The
library's services are there for the 659 MPs in general. Its researchers
provide skilled briefings for MPs on current legislation and important
issues as well as taking on limited research tasks. The library is
therefore only secondarily at the disposal of select committees.

Scrutiny in the Lords
Members of the House of Lords are chronically under-resourced for
their responsibilities as scrutineers of government policies and
legislation. Peers often refer to the Lords as 'a voluntary chamber'.
Even the so-called 'working peers' typically share offices, and have
just a desk, a computer and a telephone. Even though they may have
considerable committee duties, they receive no secretarial or research
facilities, except in the case of those opposition peers paid for their
part in facilitating 'parliamentary business'. These weaknesses are
significant largely for the House's revising work, especially as the
executive now tends to use the chamber for its own second thoughts

on legislation going through Parliament. Yet its committees have traditionally carried out valuable oversight of policies, and in recent years there has been a considerable expansion in their number. We discuss the Committee on the European Union, with its six sub-committees labelled A to F, in Chapter 5. There are also committees on science and technology, with two sub-committees and one ad hoc committee, on constitutional affairs, on economic affairs (with a sub-committee on the Finance Bill) and an extra sub-committee for the EU Committee. Peers also serve with MPs on the Joint Committee on Human Rights. The Committee Office staff has risen from 29 six years ago to 46 now.

Tony Wright MP, an authority on parliamentary affairs, has suggested that committees in the House of Lords could carry out scrutiny of the executive more effectively than Commons select committees can (see page 27). Some peers have proposed establishing more committees. For example, Lord Lester has advocated setting up a treaties committee in the Lords. Recently, the Earl of Sandwich and Lord Blaker called for an international affairs committee. They identified a need for 'a forum other than the EU committees in which all aspects of foreign affairs – including development aid – can be debated'. Additionally, they argued:

> There are longer-term, less obvious topical issues not all of which are being taken up by the Commons or the Lords EU committees. Current examples might be: China, Nepal, security in Afghanistan, islands and smaller states, intervention in failed states/humanitarian catastrophes, conflict resolution in Africa, the UN Security Council and so on.

They also drew attention to the need to address 'non EU-related developing countries which often receive less attention'. However, the House of Lords Liaison Committee noted that it had

> considered the question of whether or not to establish such a committee on two previous occasions, in 1999 and 2000. We then recommended that the committee should not be appointed on the grounds that its remit would overlap with the House of Commons

Foreign Affairs Committee. We remain of that view. The work of such a committee would also overlap into the work of the European Union Committee.[34]

For resource reasons, the Lords' Liaison Committee has resisted establishing new committees. The fear of overlap with the FAC in the Commons is mostly a question of protocol, as that committee is overburdened and does not take on the kind of inquiries that Sandwich and Blaker had suggested. Discussion of a reformed second chamber should take such ideas into consideration.

The Prime Minister's security committee

There is no select committee for the intelligence agencies despite their importance to external policy-making. Instead the Prime Minister of the day appoints nine parliamentarians from both Houses to the Intelligence and Security Committee (ISC) in consultation with the leader of the opposition. The ISC, a statutory body, is tasked with oversight of the UK's three main intelligence and security agencies: the Secret Intelligence Service (SIS, commonly known as MI6), Government Communications Headquarters (GCHQ) and the Security Service (MI5), as well as the Defence Intelligence Staff and the JIC. The committee reports to the Prime Minister, not to Parliament, and the Cabinet Office supplies its Clerk and staff. Its members act within the so-called 'ring of secrecy' and issue annual and ad hoc reports which are published, with some deletions for security reasons.

The ISC is in a privileged position under the Intelligence Services Act 1994. The committee can request information from the heads of agencies which they are bound to supply, provided it is not (crucially, in their judgement) 'sensitive' and unsafe to disclose. The secretary of state can veto disclosure on the grounds that 'the information appears to him to be of such a nature that, if he were requested to produce it before a Departmental Select Committee of the House of Commons, he would think it proper not to do so.' The ISC benefits from this special relationship, but on the other hand it has no formal powers to obtain information from anyone else and is plainly dependent on the agencies.[35] The FAC has complained that the ISC has better access both to witnesses (including senior ministers and officials) and papers.

When Douglas Hurd, the then Foreign Secretary, created the ISC, he assured the House that it would not 'truncate in any way the existing responsibilities of existing committees'. Yet his successors have on several occasions refused to give the FAC access to the agencies on the grounds that the ISC is responsible for their parliamentary scrutiny. The argument is that select committees had no such access prior to 1994 and so their remit has not 'been truncated'. Yet the ISC's scrutiny is not *parliamentary*, and both the Home Affairs Committee (in 1999) and the FAC (in 2003) have recommended that the ISC become a committee of the House. For all its limitations, informed observers have found that its reports are often valuable.

The role of parliamentary questions

There is 'no more valuable safeguard against maladministration', a former Clerk of the Commons observed, than the 'searchlight' that parliamentary questions (PQs) bring to bear upon the activities of the executive. PQs, both written and oral, are still supposed to be integral to the concept of ministerial accountability, and MPs use written questions in particular to seek basic information. But as Civil Service evidence to the Scott inquiry revealed, the adversarial dynamics of parliamentary politics has always meant that the 'reactive purpose' of government replies to PQs is 'to avoid having a hard time'; and answers to PQs on defence exports to Iraq were (in Scott's words) 'inadequate and misleading'.[36] Still today, as Steven Haines, formerly an MoD official, told us, within Whitehall PQs are regarded as an irritation rather than being part of a meaningful oversight process. A recent Public Administration Select Committee report noted:

since the inception of Questions in broadly the current form following the Balfour reforms at the beginning of the last century, the Government's approach to answering Questions has, at times, been characterised as minimising the opportunity for scrutiny of its actions through careful and skilful crafting of answers.[37]

The PASC report shows that some departments with clear external policy remits are among the most likely to refuse to answer a written question. The Ministry of Defence is the most likely to refuse answers, having turned down 193 PQs in 2001/2 (over 4 per cent of the total its ministers were asked). The PASC also criticised late and 'poor quality' responses to written questions. Oral questions generally belong to the arena of point-scoring partisan politics and only rarely contribute to Parliament's oversight work.

However, it is a mistake entirely to write off PQs as an instrument of oversight. Persistent and skilful questioning can pay off. As we show in Chapter 4, two separate series of PQs from the Liberal Democrat MP Menzies Campbell and Labour's Alan Simpson uncovered details about aggression to Iraq prior to the invasion and the renewal of a defence agreement with the US (though ministers withheld some information from Simpson).

Access to official information

Sir Richard Scott's 1996 report into arms to Iraq observed that 'in circumstances where disclosure might be politically or administratively inconvenient, the balance struck by government comes down, time and time again, against full disclosure'. The latest-known example of such reticence came in 2000, when the International Development Committee was investigating the role of the Export Credits Guarantee Department (ECGD) in financing the Ilisu dam project in Turkey. There were fears that the dam would harm the human rights of residents in the region. The FCO said that it had given the ECGD advice on the human rights implications of the project, but refused to release the advice to the committee. The chairman complained to the Parliamentary Commissioner for Administration – that is, the Parliamentary Ombudsman – who upheld the complaint. Thus the committee obtained the information it needed, not from the FCO but from the Ombudsman's report which showed that its advice had been inadequate.

The Scott report recommended that there should be statutory access to official information. The new Freedom of Information (FOI) Act that came into force on 1 January 2005 provides statutory access and will therefore be of great significance to parliamentary accountability. Access to official information is a key aspect of parliamentary scrutiny and oversight as well as of public understanding and participation in governance. Quite how far the new FOI regime will reform Britain's ancient tradition of executive secrecy, especially with regard to external policies, remains to be seen. On the eve of its introduction, the *Guardian* noted that 'about 75% of the disclosures in the Hutton and Butler inquiries . . . would not be permitted under the new law.'[38]

The new regime could well prove to be less liberal than that which existed under the preceding voluntary code for disclosure. The FOI Act contains 23 clauses specifying 36 distinct exemptions to disclosure. (Many other pieces of legislation, primary and secondary, can also provide reasons for keeping information secret). The exemptions may apply to an entire class of information, or be subject to a 'prejudice test'. The latter entails official bodies assessing whether disclosure would prejudice the interest or activities to which the particular exemption applies. As Table 3 shows, where an exemption is 'absolute', it means that authorities do not have to consider releasing the information. If an exemption is class based or prejudice based, a 'public interest test' must be applied, determining whether disclosure would be in the wider public interest. Since the Act contains no clear statement of an intention to be as open as possible, it is unclear how the public interest should be determined.

The weight of exemptions falls heavily on external policies. Just over half – 19 – of the 36 exemptions relate to external policies, such as the framing of these policies, intelligence, legal advice, trade and commercial confidentiality, certain EU matters, defence and international relations (see Appendix A). It is also in these areas that executive freedom from parliamentary scrutiny is most pronounced.

Ministers' power of veto

It is ministers and officials who classify the information that is asked for, apply the tests if necessary and decide whether to release or withhold the information. The Information Commissioner, Richard Thomas, can review these decisions; and either the applicant or the public authority can appeal against his decision to the Information

Table 3: Categories of information that may be kept secret			
Categories of exempt official information	**Process for refusal or disclosure**	**Main types of official information covered**	**Role of the Information Commissioner**
Absolute class	No prejudice test or public interest test applies: the whole class of information is exempt	a) *Security services and organisations*	The Information Commissioner (IC) can review the public authority's decision to check that the information requested is actually covered by the exemption.
Qualified class	No prejudice test; the whole class of information is exempt. The public interest test applies: information is not disclosed unless the public interest in disclosure outweighs the public interest in withholding the information	a) *Policy making* b) *Legal professional privilege* c) *Trade secrets*	The IC can review the public authority's decision to check that the information requested is actually covered by the exemption; and can then investigate the authority's assessment of the public interest, and reverse or uphold a refusal to disclose information. But the relevant Cabinet minister

			can subsequently veto the IC's decision to disclose inform-ation on public interest grounds.
Prejudice based	Prejudice test applies: decisions on information release depend on whether disclosure would prejudice the activity or interest concerned Public interest test applies: information is not disclosed unless the public interest in disclosure outweighs the public interest in withholding the information	a) *Defence* b) *International relations* c) *Commercial interests*	The IC can check that the information requested is actually covered by the exemption; and can then investigate the authority's application of the prejudice test and its assessment of the public interest, and reverse or uphold a refusal to disclose information. But the relevant Cabinet minister can subsequently veto the IC's decision to disclose information on public interest grounds.

Note Types of information affected that relate to external policy are in italics (see col. 2)
Source Analysis in FOI section, www.democraticaudit.com

Tribunal (and then the courts). Cabinet ministers can, however, veto any decision by the Information Commissioner (the veto may be subject to judicial review).

The FOI regime is less liberal than a number of international equivalents. For example, in the Irish Republic, exemptions are far more limited. In the US, exemptions are subject to a justiciable harm test on a case-by-case basis. Much will depend on the spirit in which civil servants and ministers interpret the Act's provisions. There are hopes that the Act will contribute to a cultural shift towards greater openness in government. However, there are already some indications of Whitehall resistance. The MoD has reportedly lobbied on behalf of arms firms in order to allow confidentiality agreements in government contracts that would block disclosure. Officials wrote to some arms firms in December 2004, 'promising them a virtual veto and "the opportunity to seek a legal remedy" before files are disclosed'.[39]

The Information Commissioner has recently said that permanent secretaries are concerned about the effect the Act (that is, openness) might have on 'effective government', but that they are committed to making it work. He added that he believes it is not a 'damp squib Act' and he intends to develop and make use of the 'public interest' test – something the Parliamentary Ombudsman was slow to do.

Much will depend upon ministers' willingness to use the veto. The Prime Minister was strongly against the release of the Attorney General's advice on the legality of the Iraq war, and held out until leaks forced his hand. There was nothing in the advice to justify such obduracy and it would arguably have been in the government's interests to publish it sooner. Any veto must be laid before Parliament and the Commissioner will report vetoes to the Constitutional Affairs Committee. In more than a decade, ministers have not used the equivalent veto in New Zealand. However, ministers in the UK have refused to comply with the Ombudsman (to whom appeals were previously made) in the past, even over relatively trivial matters.

4

Pursuing British interests abroad

This chapter is about Britain's 'bilateral' policy – that is, Britain's one-to-one relations with other states. In the past such dealings would have been the major component of external policy: 'foreign policy' in the traditional sense of the term. As we have seen, the advent of globalisation, the rise of supranational organisations and the continuing development of international law mean that bilateral policy is no longer the kingpin of Britain's external policies. But that is not to say that bilateral policy has ceased or become irrelevant. Indeed, it can be extremely important, both on a long-term basis (notably the 'Special Relationship' with the United States) and in particular circumstances (for example, the dispute with Iceland over fishing rights.)

The UK's colonial past has left a legacy of bilateral difficulties, with Spain (over Gibraltar), Argentina (over the Falkland Islands) and with China (over Hong Kong). Some would argue that the UK has a special responsibility to former inhabitants of its empire, requiring it to oppose regimes such as those of apartheid-era South Africa, and Zimbabwe under Robert Mugabe. This has involved both bilateral and multilateral (through the Commonwealth) activity.

There is finally another hangover of traditional foreign policy – which we may call 'unilateral' policy. Unilateral policy initiatives are increasingly rare. One crucial example was the Attlee government's decision to build a British atomic bomb following the withdrawal of US cooperation after the Second World War. This decision has had immense external policy implications to this day. Another example, arguably, was Margaret Thatcher's decision in 1982 (in which the US finally acquiesced) to retake the Falkland Islands by force after bilateral and multilateral negotiations had proved fruitless. (The Falklands action, though unilateral, was not the subject of great controversy in international law.)

We present three studies of bilateral policy in action in this chapter. Their parliamentary oversight of course takes place within a multilateral and European context. Britain is a member of the United Nations and other global organisations and has pooled parts of its sovereignty with other European Union member states and in bodies such as NATO (see further Chapters 5 and 6). Britain is also committed to and is subject to international law (in principle at least). Consequently, all Britain's dealings with other countries are subject to multifarious external considerations in a way they would not have been a century ago. Moreover, the UK's ability to act bilaterally is formally limited in crucial areas. As a customs union, for example, the EU conducts trade negotiations on behalf of its members. While Britain may use armed force under international law if acting in self-defence, any other military action ought to be authorised by – and conducted under the auspices of – the United Nations (the development of the principle of humanitarian intervention notwith-standing).

Thus bilateral policy often merges into multilateral activity and back again. Britain's policy towards Iraq provides the most striking recent example of this. At one level, intense personal negotiations between Tony Blair and President Bush resulted in the formation of an agreed bilateral strategy which resulted in both nations participating in multilateral initiatives at the UN Security Council, as well as further bilateral negotiations within western Europe. The Azores summit of March 2003, attended by the heads of state or government of the US, the UK, Spain and Portugal in advance of the invasion of Iraq, was a multinational event set in place by bilateral negotiations. Within the EU, bilateral relations between the UK and individual member states – especially France and Germany – are part and parcel of the union's policy-making processes.

There is, however, a key distinction between multilateral and European policy on the one hand, and bilateral policy on the other. Multilateral and European negotiations and policy-making occur, by definition, within formal organisations with set procedures, in known locations and on specific occasions, and almost always demand inter-departmental coordination within government. These wider dealings are conducted under the royal prerogative and transparency and accountability are often lacking, but the outcomes are at least publicly announced on the record. For example, the EU Council of Ministers publishes skeleton summaries of agreements and records that a vote has been taken (but not which way countries voted). Whether or not it was adhered to, we know when the Kyoto protocol on climate change was signed, who signed it, and what its contents were.

By contrast, bilateral policy-making can be more nebulous and has been so at critical moments in recent history, from the aborted taking of Suez to the invasion of Iraq. There is no official record or announcement of any agreement between the Prime Minister and President Bush about the goals of the agreed policy on Iraq. It has never been officially divulged, nor even reported to the full Cabinet, whether Blair committed the UK to the President's objective of 'regime change' in Iraq; whether he made a specific agreement to join the US in an invasion of Iraq; and – if he did – when it was entered into, and what its contents were. (Circumstantial evidence suggests that he did, as we discuss below.)

Many of the means by which parliamentary oversight of external policy might be conducted are inherited from the period of old-fashioned foreign policy and bilateral and unilateral action. The very notion of ministerial responsibility to Parliament is founded upon the idea that retrospective accountability is sufficient for the oversight of government policies. However, it was never an effective means of holding ministers accountable, and it is less so in the infinitely more complex and extensive world of the modern state. External policies are formed and developed over the long term in a variety of international forums, involving changing webs of actors, pressures and events. They necessarily involve compromises and may take unforeseen directions. For British ministers to come to Parliament or appear before a committee to give a post hoc statement is gesture politics. They can often plausibly claim that events were outside their control and therefore also out of Parliament's reach.

It may seem that it would be easier to maintain oversight of simpler one-to-one dealings. But the doctrine of ministerial responsibility works no better even in the case of bilateral policy. The royal prerogative still holds sway, reinforced by the strong tradition of secrecy that surrounds bilateral negotiations. The Blair–Bush talks are a case in point. But informal agreements between nations are constantly being made and need never be formally revealed. Bruce George MP drew our attention to a session the Defence Committee had with the defence secretary, Geoff Hoon, in the last parliament. Hoon simply would not reveal details about the decision taken with the US for the redeployment of troops within Iraq.

An example of the way in which the executive can exert control over bilateral policy without formal reference to the legislature is through the appointment of ambassadors. There is a temptation for ministers to politicise such appointments, as took place recently when Paul Boateng, a Labour minister, was made high commissioner to South Africa. Since the regulation of the Home Civil Service and the Diplomatic Service is carried out under the royal prerogative, Parliament is not officially consulted on such decisions. The Foreign Affairs Committee served notice in 2003 that it would examine any future political appointments to such posts, and it can be expected to do so shortly.

It is also possible for political allies of the government to be given informal diplomatic roles – most notably, Lord Levy, who was described by Dod's as 'Personal Envoy to the Prime Minister and Adviser on the Middle East'. Levy was a personal friend of the Prime Minister and a high-level fund-raiser for the Labour Party. Such unpaid appointments are subject to less accountability even than special advisers, who are theoretically subject to a code of conduct. Responding to pressure from the Committee on Standards in Public Life, in September 2003, the government agreed to introduce greater clarity to the roles of unpaid advisers, such as Levy, agreeing they would be subject to the code of conduct, but some ambiguity remains. For instance, the government rejected the committee's proposal that it should present Parliament annually with a comprehensive list of all its paid and unpaid advisers and a description of their functions. (This proposal does not appear to have been followed up by MPs.)

The 'Special Relationship' with the United States

The Special Relationship has been the keystone of UK external policy since the end of the Second World War. Within it, the UK is a junior partner. Peter Riddell, the *Times*'s political writer, said in a recent study: 'The most significant feature of transatlantic relations . . . has been the desire of . . . prime ministers to be insiders in the Washington policy debate.' For its part, he argues, the US values the Special Relationship because 'despite recurrent unilateralist rhetoric, the US has seldom liked operating alone . . . On several occasions this has involved a desire for British military involvement, not just because of admiration for the quality of British forces but as a symbol that America is not on its own.'[1]

The Special Relationship was forged at a time of British economic and military dependence upon the US while that nation was remaking the international order and the world was dividing into the two blocs of the cold war. It remains the product of two inter-linking imperatives. The first is often unspoken. Beneath the need for the protection that American military power offered Britain and the west, formalised in the North Atlantic Treaty Organisation (NATO), the United Kingdom came over time to feed off the developed US nuclear war-making capacity, especially after 1962.

More openly, it has always been argued that in return for acting as junior partner to the US in world affairs, the UK achieves influence over the policy of the dominant world power that it would not otherwise have. All of this rests in part on the view that through its past experience as a great power and cultural links, the UK has something to offer which the US needs. As Prime Minister during the late 1950s and early 1960s Harold Macmillan believed that the UK could fulfil the role of Greece to the US's Rome. Others doubt this. Roger Beetham, formerly the UK Permanent Representative to the Council of Europe, told us that successive politicians in the UK have tended to 'confuse access with influence'.[2] Sir Percy Cradock, the senior figure in the diplomatic and intelligence world who became Margaret Thatcher's foreign policy adviser, also took the view that 'the American connection was too readily overvalued'; the 'hard-headed' Americans valued the UK for what they could get, especially in Europe.[3]

The choice between Europe and America

In the immediate postwar era, it was natural for Britain to turn to the ally with which it had the closest historical and cultural links and which offered the means of economic recovery. However, the UK was also seeking a new role to compensate for its diminishing imperial power. One possible response was to utilise the empire in a different way, perhaps turning it into an autarchic trading bloc. Another was to establish continental ties, an initiative contemplated long before UK membership of the European Economic Community. There was also the prospect of closer association with the US. Winston Churchill hoped that the UK could maintain a balance between imperial, continental and US approaches – what he called the 'three circles'. But over time hopes of building upon the Commonwealth crumbled with the loss of imperial power; in 1968, the Commonwealth Office was merged into the Foreign Office. Only two of Churchill's three circles remained viable options: Europe and America.

To what extent has Parliament debated either the choice between these two options or the possibility of riding both horses? Did Parliament oversee the triumph of the Special Relationship over a commitment to the EU? How far have Parliament and the public been involved in endorsing either course? More immediately, with the advent of a neo-conservative US President, has Parliament reappraised the value of the Special Relationship in the light of changes in US policies and a changing world situation? In the immediate aftermath of the 2005 general election, Sir Menzies Campbell, the Liberal Democrat foreign affairs spokesperson, said that such a reappraisal was an urgent priority.

The potential choice between ties with the US or western Europe has never as such been presented to Parliament or the people. It is the case that sentiment has long been on the side of the US; and the bonds and constraints of the Special Relationship, real though they are, are less evidently binding than those demanded by the legal structures of the developing EU. Edward Heath, after 1970, was the first and only British premier not to give primacy to the relationship with the US. Heath was a convinced European who wanted a united Europe and was prepared to develop a common foreign policy with other member states. His brief premiership constituted a 'revolution' in Britain's postwar foreign policy, as Henry Kissinger, the White House national security adviser then Secretary of State during this period, recognised. But entry into the then EEC, with the legal and political obligations that it entailed, could not be managed as an issue of bilateral policy, as relations with the US have been. Instead, the negotiations had to be carried out in public and accession to the Treaty of Rome required the passing of the European Communities Act in 1972.

Moreover, the two main parties and the public were divided over the desirability of entry. Hostility centred then as now on the idea of loss of sovereignty. In response, Parliament was given three votes on the principle of joining the EEC. The first two, in 1961 and 1967, were free votes; for the third in 1971, Harold Wilson, then leader of the opposition, whipped against. Three years after the 1972 Act, Wilson as Prime Minister was obliged by divisions in his own party to resolve the issue again by putting Britain's continued EEC membership to a referendum, partially suspending collective Cabinet responsibility for the duration of the campaign.

Europe remains a divisive issue, however, and the Labour government has committed itself to holding a referendum both on signing up to the new EU constitution and before joining the single currency. (A Bill for the referendum on the European constitution was prepared, but put on hold after the 'no' votes in France and the Netherlands in 2005.) Presently, there are specific arrangements, including committees in both Houses, for parliamentary oversight in the UK of European matters (see Chapter 5), as well as at Strasbourg and Brussels, where elected UK members take part.

In other words, Parliament and electorate have been consulted on whether or not they want the UK to participate in European integration. There was wide public debate, not entirely driven by partisan considerations. The Treaty of Rome was available to anyone who wished to consult it. By the time the UK joined the EEC in 1973, it had been functioning for fifteen years and was in that sense a known quantity. This is not to claim that the British political discussion of European issues has always been straightforward and open, nor that parliamentary oversight of the process or continuing participation has been perfect or without flaws. Rather it does throw into relief the absence of participation and oversight of the Special Relationship with the US.

Unlike entry into the then EEC, which entailed joining a specific body on a particular date, subsequent Acts of Parliament and ratification of treaties, the Special Relationship with the US has developed more gradually and unobtrusively, with different aspects of it emerging over time. Indeed, relations with the US have throughout been a classic example of bilateral policy-making, generally under the direction of the Prime Minister of the day. Only parts of the evolving Special Relationship were subject to parliamentary scrutiny – for example, there were debates over the financial negotiations conducted by the two countries during the Second World War, an early phase in the Special Relationship. Parliament was generally only permitted to endorse decisions after they were taken. On 28 June 1950, the Labour Prime Minister, Clement Attlee, made a statement to the House announcing the decision to participate in the US-led multinational force supporting South Korea. While Parliament was granted a debate on a substantive motion (more than it received over, for instance, the Falklands war or Kosovo conflict), it was only held after the fact on 5 July 1950.

The unspoken and unquestioned 'treaty' with the US

The ties with the US are considerably closer than is generally realised; to a great extent, Britain is irreversibly committed to an implicit treaty with the US that has never been put to Parliament or the public. In 2001, the FCO submitted evidence to the FAC that attempted to spell out the full extent of the Special Relationship:

> The British–US relationship goes far wider than the traditional co-operation over foreign policy and in the political, military and intelligence fields. There are almost no areas of public policy with which UK posts in the US do not deal. They embrace all aspects of the relationship from public health to trade policy, from transport to immigration and civil liberties, from aid policy to financial services and banking, from welfare to education, from drugs control to policing.[4]

Parliament has never specifically examined the question of whether the UK should be party to the Special Relationship and if so, what form it should take. There has been no Act to put the relationship on a statutory footing; no treaty has been placed before Parliament for ratification; no referendum has been held to gain public approval. The profound shock of the Suez crisis of 1956, when America forced Britain to end the military adventure, inspired some attempts to reappraise British policy and to consider switching to a European alliance. But Harold Macmillan, the new Prime Minister, set about at once to repair the Special Relationship and deepened the UK's dependence on the US with the deal at Nassau to rely on the Polaris submarine for the country's nuclear defence. (In doing so, he set back his other aim of joining the then EEC.) However, apart from a short-lived burst of fury among Conservative MPs, Parliament was not involved in any reappraisal and there was no parliamentary inquiry into the debacle.

Yet the impact of the affair on policy-makers was deep and long-lasting. They concluded that never again should the UK seek to act against the wishes of the US and an elite consensus formed around maintaining the Special Relationship. By the time Tony Blair had become Prime Minister, this doctrine had evolved still further: for Blair, it was axiomatic that the 'US should not be left to act alone'.

Thus the Special Relationship has become more strongly still the centrepiece of the UK's external policies. Generally, the main parties have been unquestioningly committed to its maintenance and so therefore has Parliament. (From the 1950s to the early 1980s, Labour in opposition flirted with unilateral nuclear disarmament and it once briefly became party policy.) There are no specific arrangements for oversight of the Special Relationship, unlike those in place for European policy (however imperfect they may be); select committees do not hold inquiries into its value to Britain. Indeed, it is part of the natural order of life.

Donald Anderson (now Lord Anderson) was until May 2005 the chair of the FAC, the body most responsible for oversight of the Special Relationship. He told us that he found dealing with the CIA easier than UK intelligence agencies because 'they accept that, broadly speaking, we are on the same side as them.'[5] When we asked him in 2004 whether he would feel able to conduct an inquiry into the Special Relationship, Anderson replied that the FAC had inquired into it as part of its rolling inquiry since 2001 into the war on terror.[6] These reports do indeed refer to UK/US bilateral relations – indeed, it is hard to envisage an investigation of that particular subject which did not. However, they do not explicitly assess the underlying nature, form or value of the Special Relationship to which the UK is party. Anderson agrees that an investigation of the Special Relationship would be an appropriate area of activity for a future FAC.

In general, where there is possible divergence between the UK and the US over policy related to the war on terror – notably over Israel – the committee normally recommends that the UK use its good offices to 'influence' the US – in other words, that the UK should work within the existing framework. As the FAC put it in *Foreign Policy Aspects of the War against Terrorism* in July 2004, 'We *once again* [our emphasis] recommend that the Government work to encourage the US to send a high-level emissary to the Middle East with dedicated aim of resolving this long-standing conflict.'[7] In 2001, the FAC actually conducted an investigation entitled *British–US Relations* – to which the FCO submitted the evidence we quote above (see page 209), making it clear that for the government the Special Relationship was of immense importance. This surely merited critical analysis. The FAC did not attempt this, stating in its final conclusion, without supporting evidence, that

> the response of the British Government to September 11 has demonstrated once again that the relationship between the United Kingdom and the United States remains special. It is the firm view of the Foreign Affairs Committee that it is in the interests of both countries that it remains so.[8]

This report was of course undertaken at a time when pro-American sentiment was running high in the UK in the aftermath of the attacks of 11 September 2001. It would be fair, however, to suggest that even then the new directions of American policy in the world were becoming increasingly clear. Since George Bush had become the US

President, concerns had accumulated over the strongly unilateral reshaping of US policies – for example, over the US renunciation of the Kyoto agreement, its plans for ballistic missile defence and the damage to the test ban treaty, the US hostility to trade agreements on small arms, its refusal to accept the International Criminal Court – quite apart from major differences over policy in the Middle East. As Philippe Sands has commented, 'with the election of Bush in November 2000, a US Administration took office that was outspoken in its determination to challenge global rules. Soon it turned into a full-scale assault, a war on law. This began even before 9/11 . . .'[9]

Bush's State of the Nation address in January 2002, with its reference to the 'axis of evil' (Iraq, Iran and North Korea), made the unilateralist shift in US external policy more evident still. America was clearly considering the option of 'regime change' and looking to work through 'coalitions of the willing' (which it could lead) rather than through established alliances. Chris Patten, the EU's External Policy Commissioner and a convinced Atlanticist, warned on several occasions that the US was in danger of going into 'unilateralist overdrive' and urged the US to cooperate with Europe. Individual MPs raised their voices too, but the FAC remained a bystander while the government 'was often silent or, in certain respects, a willing handmaiden to some of the worst violations of international law'.[10] Blair explained his rationale to British diplomats in January 2003:

> We should remain the closest ally of the United States, and as allies influence them to continue broadening their agenda. The price of influence is that we do not leave the United States to face the tricky issues alone. By tricky, I mean the ones which people wish weren't there.[11]

Blair's commitment to the Special Relationship is so intense and, indeed, personal that it raises the issue of how it has largely become the preserve of the Prime Minister over the past quarter of a century. Margaret Thatcher and now Blair have both taken personal charge of dealings with the US President of the day and made their own personal relationships with Presidents Reagan, Clinton and Bush a particular feature of the Special Relationship. (There is a negative aspect to this development: both Neil Kinnock and Michael Howard, as leaders of the main opposition party, have been snubbed by a US President in a calculated political manner.) It may well be that this is an inevitable result of the way that modern politics is personalised in general, but it also illustrates how the royal pre-rogative can in effect make foreign policy a personal fiefdom.

Defence drivers of the Special Relationship

The UK's military and intelligence links with the US are also deeply embedded and effectively irreversible, and are kept highly secret. The UK surveillance system is an integral part of the US's world-wide system; the intelligence forces share information; the US maintains air bases in the UK; and British military plans assume that its forces will conduct operations in tandem with US forces.

Defence procurement and intelligence are in fact two of the drivers of the Special Relationship, but the Defence Committee does not examine the benefits that accrue to the UK in these two fields, nor does it explore the underlying nature of the Special Relationship. This is particularly important since, as Lord Garden (the former Air Marshal Commandant and Director of the Royal Institute of International Affairs, now Liberal Democrat defence spokesman) told us, military equipment programmes serve to lock the UK into carrying out future operations in conjunction with the US. Decisions over capabilities are taken on the assumption that UK forces will be working in tandem with the US military. Yet, as has been noted already, the priority of the Defence Committee, as indicated by its chairman, is to obtain the best armed forces for the money available, not to investigate overarching strategic considerations nor potential alternatives to the current interlocking arrangements.

Central to the Special Relationship is cooperation between intelligence agencies. As has already been noted, ministers are not accountable to Parliament for the UK intelligence and security agencies. The Intelligence and Security Committee (ISC), which undertakes oversight of the agencies, is not a parliamentary committee and serves the executive (through the Prime Minister). Moreover, though the agencies are now established on a statutory footing, their operations are kept strictly private. The ISC has not specifically investigated the Special Relationship. These arrangements detract from parliamentary oversight of the Special Relationship.

Britain's participation in the US ballistic missile defence programme has been a significant recent manifestation of the military and intelligence content of the Special Relationship. In 1999, President Clinton's administration revived the 'star wars' idea for the nuclear defence of the US from attacks by so-called rogue states and Bush took on the policy after 2000, pulling out of the 1972 Anti-Ballistic Missile Treaty in order to do so. The Blair government twice informed Parliament, in 1998 and 2001, that it did not regard the threat of ballistic missile proliferation as urgent. However, early in Bush's presidency he asked Blair for UK cooperation and the use of early warning facilities at Fylingdales. This request, as Peter Riddell recounts, 'could never have been refused without causing immense damage to the alliance'; and Blair's response 'was to play the issue long, avoiding an early request to use the facilities at Fylingdales which, he knew, would ignite substantial opposition within the Labour Party'.

Geoff Hoon, the defence secretary, indicated in the Commons in 2000 that the government would consider any request by the US to cooperate with the US anti-missile programme and in October 2002, he informed the House that he was launching a public discussion paper on missile defence. The US made a formal request for the upgrade of the early warning radar at RAF Fylingdales for missile defence purposes on 17 December 2002. Some Labour MPs did express concern, but the mainstream parliamentary consensus over the Special Relationship held with strong Conservative backing. There was not even a formal vote in Parliament over what was a significant decision. The Defence Committee argued in January 2003 that

> the UK should agree to the [Fylingdales] upgrade. The factors in favour of that agreement – the importance of the UK–US relationship, the improvement to the early warning capability, the opportunity to keep open the prospect of future missile defence for the UK and the potential for UK industrial participation in the programme's further development – outweigh the arguments against.[12]

Hoon announced in a written statement to the House on 5 February 2003 that he was agreeing to the US request and in October 2004, the government placed a memorandum of understanding between the US and UK over missile defence in the House of Commons Library, but with parts left out, apparently at the request of the US government. It now seems likely that actual interceptor missiles will be deployed in the UK. Meanwhile not all defence experts agree with the Defence Committee, warning that the decision could make the UK more likely to be attacked and questioning the prospects for 'UK industrial participation' in the US programme.

Another international agreement of great import to the Special Relationship, but never approved by Parliament, is the Mutual Defence Agreement (MDA, full title Agreement between the UK and the USA for Cooperation in the Uses of Atomic Energy for Mutual Defence Purposes 1958). It enables the UK and US to share nuclear technology and information. In the words of one writer, the MDA is 'regarded in Whitehall as a cornerstone of the Special Relationship.'[13] It could be seen as in contravention of the UN Treaty on the Non-Proliferation of Nuclear Weapons 1968. Article III bis of the MDA, added in 1959, permits the transfer of nuclear materials and equipment (though the transfer of actual atomic weapons is forbidden under the agreement), but given the important issues such transfers raise, both of policy and international law, it is time limited and requires regular renewal.

This crucial article, which binds the UK for ten years at a time, was renewed in 2004. In the US, the renewal had to be laid before Congress for 60 days and was theoretically subject to negative veto (through a simple majority in both houses). In the UK, the Ponsonby rule on treaties applied to its renewal, meaning that the order formally renewing it had to be tabled before Parliament for 21 sitting days. However, Parliament does not have the power to veto (or approve) treaties. The Ponsonby rule, a convention only (see page 36), dictates that the government need make time to debate a treaty within the 21-day period only if it decides to hold a debate, or it is asked to do so by an opposition party or the relevant select committee.

The renewal of Article III bis surely merited debate, given the significant issues involved. But none was held although a lone MP, Alan Simpson, did ask for one. Peter Hain, then Leader of the House of Commons, wrote to Simpson on 2 March 2004, stating: 'I agree with you that the issues related to our nuclear cooperation with the US are of great importance and that they fully merit the scrutiny to which you refer [a parliamentary debate]. But I cannot undertake to find Government time for a debate.' The opposition did not request one and the Defence Committee decided that no debate was required because it did not involve 'major political, military and diplomatic issues'. Even the committee's decision itself was not immediately published. (Under the Freedom of Information Act, such minutes are now published promptly.)

Simpson's attempts to probe the government over the MDA and its renewal revealed some of the potential value and limitations of (written) parliamentary questions (PQs). Written questions on such subjects as the discussions taking place between the UK and US met with minimal responses but at least confirmed they were taking place. In April 2004, Simpson received a detailed response on the numbers of UK personnel visiting various plants, laboratories and test sites in the US. In the same month, he asked: 'How many personnel are employed in the renegotiation of the 1958 US/UK Mutual Defence Agreement?' The answer provided was: 'A number of personnel are involved.' In responding to other questions, the government withheld technical information and details of cooperation with France under the exemption for defence, security, and international relations matters (the refusal was then under the former voluntary code of practice on access to government information, now incorporated in FOI legislation).

The value to Britain of the Special Relationship
The whole of Europe, indeed the west, has found security under the umbrella of American power. We examine Britain's membership of the principal western alliance, the North Atlantic Treaty Organisation, and its role in NATO policy-making in Chapter 6. Clearly NATO is a significant aspect of the Special Relationship, but the UK could be part of the alliance without being locked into a

Special Relationship. So what tangible benefits accrue to the UK from this additional and less formal alliance? Tony Blair's appearances in front of the Liaison Committee have provided some opportunity for examination of the Special Relationship and a small measure of parliamentary oversight. In July 2002, Donald Anderson said to Blair:

> The Special Relationship with the US is clearly the key part of our security policy and the closeness, the unwillingness to criticise is justified by the fact that we have special influence on the US administration. Can you give to the Committee any example of ways in which that influence has changed or modified US policy?

Blair's response was:

> I never like to approach it in that way because it suggests almost as if you go along as a supplicant to the US and you make a case and if you are lucky you win a verdict on points. It is just not like that. The truth is we are very interlocked in our strategic relationship and we discuss and deal with issues the whole time together . . . we worked then very, very closely with them on all the strategic details of that Afghan campaign. To give you another example where we have worked closely, the new NATO–Russia relationship, which is very, very important, is a huge breakthrough because it allows Russia to move closer to the West, puts the whole of that relationship and the tensions within it on a new and better footing . . . Now whether you describe that as having influence, I prefer to look at it as a partnership.[14]

Blair's statement, especially his description of an 'interlocked . . . strategic relationship' and assertion that the relationship was a 'partnership' arguably merited further investigation of a sort which Parliament has so far not supplied.

Since Parliament has failed to try and measure the military and intelligence value of the Special Relationship, it is hard to discern what the UK gets out of it. Peter Riddell records that before the US formally came out in support of the retaking of the Falkland Islands in 1982, the Pentagon followed a 'Special Relationship' of its own with the UK, supplying 'vital equipment and intelligence without which the Falklands could probably not have been retaken'.[15] In 2000, Vice-Admiral Sir Alan West, then Chief of Defence Intelligence, remarked to the Defence Committee after Kosovo: 'America's intelligence capability is amazing. We are lucky that we have got such a good ally.'[16] Yet Sir Rodric Braithwaite, former chairman of the Joint Intelligence Committee (JIC), has dismissed the Special Relationship as 'an emotional comfort blanket for a declining power'. He asserted in an article in *Prospect* that the traffic was one-way, for while the Americans rarely accommodated UK needs, the close links in nuclear defence and intelligence reinforced UK dependence on the US.[17] Riddell, a thoughtful and sympathetic observer, suggests that the 'bargain is lopsided'. The US President takes the decisions; American interests come first; a British Prime Minister has a say, but his or her 'influence is seldom crucial'.[18]

The Prime Minister's broader argument for the Special Relationship centres on the view that America's allies have a duty and responsibility to act alongside the US. In part this argument implicitly at least incorporates the idea that in doing so, these allies can restrain the US. Thus when the UK and others back the US on the 'tricky issues', 'we should, in return, expect these issues to be confronted with the international community, proportionately, sensibly, and in a way that delivers a better prospect of long-term peace, security and justice'.[19] The ultimate test of this wider goal is first, in today's world, an American response on peace in the Middle East, and specifically, a more balanced approach to the Israel–Palestine conflict; global poverty, especially in Africa; global warming; and respect for international law and treaties. Britain's presidency of the G8 is putting that test squarely to the US on two of these issues. As for justice, the US continues to violate human rights norms at Guantanamo Bay and other places, and Britain's only response has been to argue for the release of a few British-born victims.

With the collapse of the Soviet bloc in 1989–91, there has been an apparent tendency for the interests of Europe and the US to diverge. In the absence of another superpower, at least for the time being, the US has become increasingly impatient about the restraints of international laws that challenge its sovereignty and its perception of its interests. This impatience has increased notably, as we have noted above, under George W. Bush's presidency. According to the American neo-conservative Robert Kagan, a former US State Department official turned academic,

> it is time to stop pretending that Europeans and Americans share a common view of the world, or even that they occupy the same world. On the all-important question of power – the efficacy of power, the morality of power, the desirability of power – American and European perspectives are diverging. Europe is turning away from power, or to put it a little differently, it is moving beyond power into a self-contained world of laws and rules and transnational negotiation and cooperation . . . Meanwhile, the United States remains mired in history, exercising power in an anarchic Hobbesian world where international laws and rules are unreliable, and where true security and the defense and promotion of a liberal order still depend on the possession and use of military might.[20]

Blair has striven hard to justify Britain's role in the Special Relationship as a 'bridge' between Europe and the US. There is of course an element of special pleading in this view – it serves to justify the UK's closeness to the US in Europe. It also creates resentment in the rest of Europe, as events since 9/11 have put relations between the US/UK and much of Europe under strain. Gerhard Schroeder, the former German Chancellor, is said to have commented that the traffic across Blair's bridge always seemed to be in one direction.[21] The effect of Blair's interpretation of the Special Relationship on the UK's position in Europe and the EU is another aspect of this alliance that requires parliamentary attention which it has not received.

The critical shift in defence and security thinking in the US is also significant for the UK because Britain is a close military ally of the US and its military and intelligence capacity is integrated with that of the US. The US doctrine of anticipatory self-defence, or pre-emption, provoked by 9/11 and its lead and actions in the 'war on terror' puts this country's commitment to international law and human rights under strain. The UK is formally committed to the maintenance of the international rule of law and the *Ministerial Code* requires ministers to conform to international law and treaty obligations. But the position of its most powerful ally has presented the government with dilemmas. Bush was bent on 'regime change' in Iraq from the very beginning and the US has violated human rights norms in his pursuit of the war on terror.

As we shall see, the Prime Minister tried desperately to reconcile his commitment to Bush and the US with the wider British commitment to the UN and international law (see below).Yet a number of eminent experts on international law strongly disputed the legality of the US stance in advance of the invasion of Iraq. For example, Professor Christopher Greenwood QC wrote: 'So far as talk of a doctrine of "pre-emption" is intended to refer to a broader right to respond to threats which might materialise some time in the future, I believe that such a doctrine has no basis in law.'[22]

The US detention of terrorist suspects at Guantanamo Bay and other prisons has aroused considerable criticism, and the UK's position has been limited to securing the release of some British-born suspects. British complicity in the torture of other suspects has, however, received less attention. Article 15 of the UN Convention against Torture, ratified by the UK, unequivocally states that this country should 'ensure that any statement . . . made as a result of torture shall not be invoked as evidence in any proceedings, except against a person accused of torture as evidence that the statement was made'. Yet both the government and some senior members of the judiciary accept only that this principle should apply to evidence obtained by the British authorities, and have proved more willing to accept information obtained by torture overseas. For example, the Foreign and Commonwealth Office brushed aside protests in July 2004 by the British ambassador to Uzbekistan about the supply of information to the US and UK obtained under torture by the Uzbek authorities, saying: 'Where there was reliable intelligence with a direct bearing on terrorist threats it would be irresponsible to ignore it out of hand.' It seems also that US aircraft taking 'suspects' to third countries where they are likely to be tortured touch down in the UK on their way to those destinations without any intervention from the UK authorities.[23] Further, in August 2004, the Court of Appeal decided (by a two-to-one majority) to reject the appeals of ten men held under indefinite detention on the grounds that evidence used against them may have been extracted under torture from detainees in Guantanamo Bay.[24] The distinction for the court rested on the fact that the alleged torture was committed by foreign as opposed to British officials.

Parliament has played a part in probing the contradictions of the doctrine of pre-emptive strike. On 21 April 2004, a PQ from Lord Thomas of Gresford prompted a detailed response from the Attorney General, Lord Goldsmith, outlining the government's position on the right of pre-emptive armed attack. Philippe Sands describes Goldsmith's answer as 'clear, reasonable and balanced, and [it] accurately summarises the current state of international law'.[25] The FAC took much evidence from senior witnesses on the subject of international law, as part of its ongoing investigations of the war against terrorism. In July 2004 it recommended changes to the doctrine of anticipatory self-defence taking into account terrorist threats, but warned that 'the Government should be very cautious to limit the application of the doctrine of anticipatory self-defence so as to prevent its abuse by states pursuing their national interest.' It argued that Britain should explain how 'it will persuade its allies to limit the use of the doctrine [of anticipatory self-defence] to a "threat of catastrophic attack".'[26]

Making war against Iraq

The decision to go to war against Iraq and the manner in which it was taken became a major election issue in May 2005. Unresolved public anger about the war undermined public trust in the Prime Minister and his party and contributed to Labour's losses in votes and seats. Academics on the British Election Study at the University of Essex have since released figures which suggest that the war has cost the Prime Minister 'the authority to persuade voters' on the crucial issue of the then prospective referendum on the European constitution.[27]

The long-term background to the Iraq war indicates how the policies of British governments towards Iraq have shifted from support for Saddam Hussein to limited war to regime change, without respect to ethical concerns, giving full and honest account to Parliament, or being subject to public scrutiny. In the 1980s Iraq was a 'de facto ally – standing up to the Islamic threat represented by Iran on behalf of the West'.[28] During that period, for geopolitical and commercial reasons, the UK government deliberately breached its own published guidelines on exports to Iraq and Iran in order to facilitate the export of arms-manufacturing equipment to Iraq and connived at the delivery of arms to Iraq via third countries. In 1988 the Foreign Secretary, Geoffrey Howe, in full knowledge of the brutality of Saddam's regime, secretly relaxed export controls to Iraq to enhance Britain's commercial interests. But, as he explained to Sir Richard Scott in the course of the Scott inquiry into arms sales to Iraq and Iran, the change in policy could not be explained to MPs and the public because of the 'emotional way in which such debates are conducted in public'.[29]

The Scott inquiry into arms to Iraq took evidence showing that intelligence information was interpreted to suit political requirements. Evidence that Iraq might pose a military threat was underplayed. The ability of executive leaders to distort intelligence in order to support pre-existing policy objectives was re-emphasised when Tony Blair's administration did the same in the run-up to the invasion of 2003, this time to *over-play* the threat posed by Iraq. Amongst many witnesses, Rear Admiral Nick Wilkinson, secretary to the D-Notice Committee between 1999 and 2004, told John Ware for a *Panorama* documentary broadcast on 20 March 2005: 'The government perhaps allowed the public to be misled as to the degree of certainty about weapons of mass destruction.'

One of the most controversial actions by the government was to publish intelligence information from the JIC, the expert Cabinet Office body that analyses and assesses all UK intelligence material for government, as a public document, entitled *Iraq's Weapons of Mass Destruction*, in the run-up to war in September 2002 – the first time JIC work has been issued in such a way. This dossier had a foreword by the Prime Minister and was clearly designed to have a major impact on parliamentary and public opinion. Officially, 'ownership' of the dossier lay with the JIC and its chairman, John Scarlett, but evidence to the Hutton inquiry revealed the extensive influence that Alastair Campbell, the Prime Minister's Director of Communications and Strategy, a political appointment, and Downing Street advisers and publicity officials had over the contents and phrasing. In large part, Campbell or Downing Street 'owned' the dossier, but Scarlett asserted his ownership in his evidence to Hutton (who accepted his claim). The dossier exaggerated the threat that Saddam posed to UK national interests, claimed on dubious authority that he could deploy chemical and biological weapons within 45 minutes and contained false information on his uranium procurement activities. The misleading 45-minute claim was given the prominence in media reports that some observers suspected it was designed to attract. Both Lord Butler and the ISC were critical of the way in which intelligence information was presented without the caveats that usually accompany such material.[30] Lord Hutton concluded that No. 10 may have exercised subconscious influence over the document. Other observers felt that Downing Street's influence was very conscious indeed.[31]

In February 2003, Campbell oversaw the publication of another dossier that was designed to feed the media with further material supporting the case for action against Saddam (the dossier was merely given to some journalists and deposited in the Commons Library). There was no consultation in advance with the JIC or the intelligence services, even though it contained some intelligence information, nor with any minister other than the Prime Minister. He presented it as 'further intelligence', apparently being unaware that most of its contents did not derive from UK intelligence sources. Campbell – this time indisputably – 'owned' the process. The document soon became known as the 'dodgy dossier', partly because some sections consisted of unattributed and altered quotations from published material written by Dr Al-Marashi, an international expert on weapons in Iraq. Jack Straw, the Foreign Secretary, disowned the document and Robin Cook, his predecessor, told the FAC that it was 'a glorious, spectacular, own goal'. The FAC condemned the process by which the dossier was compiled and concluded that 'the effect of the February dossier was almost wholly counterproductive.'[32]

Parliamentary oversight of the war against Iraq
There is no doubt that the House of Commons as a whole, and a number of individual MPs, were greatly concerned about the

prospect of an invasion of Iraq as it became clear that the Prime Minister was being increasingly drawn into a policy of 'regime change' in Iraq alongside President Bush. By the spring of 2002 it was widely known that the invasion of Iraq would follow that of Afghanistan, even though there was no evidence of any link between Saddam and Al-Qaeda and both Iran and North Korea had more advanced nuclear programmes.

Parliament exercised its oversight role with respect to the Iraq war in the following ways:

Activity in the chamber

The meeting between Bush and Blair at Crawford, Texas in April 2002 provoked exchanges with Labour MPs on Blair's next appearance in the House of Commons, who expressed concern about the possibility of military action and were not impressed, as Peter Riddell notes, 'by his assurances that nothing precipitate would be done'. The President's 'axis of evil' speech a few months earlier had fed this concern and MPs stressed the need to work within the UN on any measures that would be taken to deal with Iraq. When Blair indicated that action against Saddam was a high priority in a speech at Sedgefield in September 2002, parliamentarians forced a recall of the House, against the initial wishes of the executive, and a vote was held on a mere procedural motion – a standard means of avoiding debate on a tangible commitment. The House was not allowed a debate on a substantive resolution until 25 November, and then in support of UN Resolution 1441, which rode on MPs' backing for action through the UN and may well have been a means of making war appear legal.

Votes on substantive motions

As we point out above (page 29), Parliament cannot recall itself: this power rests exclusively with the executive. Thus the Prime Minister was able to 'play it long' with regard to Parliament, seeking to delay full debate on the options until he had assembled the strongest possible response to parliamentary concerns, especially on the vexed issue of Security Council backing for the use of force; and until a refusal to approve invasion would have precipitated his resignation and a major political crisis. Blair's hand was finally forced by Graham Allen, the de facto whip for the opposition to war, who made plans for an unofficial parliamentary debate at Church House, Westminster (see page 29). Cook's memoir records that, as Leader of the House of Commons, he insisted that MPs should be given the chance to vote on a substantive motion supporting the invasion. He notes that Straw supported him. Many MPs (from both the Labour and Conservative parties) broke with the whip in the votes of 26 February and 18 March 2003, which marked the two largest rebellions of modern political times. In February, thirteen Conservative (plus one teller) and 121 Labour MPs (plus one teller) voted for an amendment to the government motion. In March, the respective number of rebels was fifteen (plus one) and 138 (plus one). John Dickie argues in *The New Mandarins* that

> the decision to go to war with Iraq brought Parliament right into the centre of the policy-making process for the first time since the Suez crisis in 1956. Substantive debates resulting in a rebellion of 139 Labour MPs on 18 March 2003 brought home to the government the need to take Parliament more into account.[33]

Parliamentary questions

But there is compelling evidence that the die was already cast by February 2003. Certainly, joint US and UK military hostilities against Iraq had already begun. Answers to PQs tabled by Menzies Campbell MP, the Liberal Democrat foreign affairs spokesman, in November 2002 suggest that the Prime Minister ordered air strikes possibly as part of joint plans for regime change as early as May 2002 – that is, long before Parliament had discussed the question and before UN Resolution 1441, the claimed legal basis for the war, was passed. The leaked minutes of the July 2002 Downing Street meeting on Iraq record that the defence secretary informed those present that 'the US had already begun "spikes of activity" to put pressure on the regime.' A written answer to Campbell reveals 'spikes of activity' on Britain's part. The release of ordnance in the southern Iraq no-fly zones by UK aircraft rose from zero in March and April 2002 to 4.9 tons in May and as high as 21.1 for September 2002.[34]

This bombing campaign was justified as being necessary to enforce the no-fly zones, which were in place to deter attacks on Iraq's Kurdish and Shia populations. FCO legal advice, attached to the briefing paper for the July meeting, warned that the intensified strikes would have been illegal even if undertaken as part of a 'muscular' strategy to show Saddam that he would incur military action if he continued to evade UN resolutions and wriggle out of openly declaring his possession of WMD. But the context of the July 2002 meeting (see page 93) and *American Soldier*, the autobiography of Tommy Franks, the American allied commander, indicate that the 'spikes of activity' were designed to weaken Iraq's defences and possibly to goad Saddam into retaliation – that is, they were part of an early undeclared stage of the invasion of Iraq. So while Parliament obtained information about the release of ordnance in late 2002, it seems that MPs were kept in the dark about government plans for participation in a US-led invasion, as was the full Cabinet.

There were other PQs on the substantive policy, and on the role of Parliament during this period.

Select committee scrutiny
The Prime Minister has been asked about Iraq at every session with the Liaison Committee since these exchanges were instigated in July 2002 until the most recent in February 2005. The Defence Committee published no Iraq-specific inquiry in 2002/3 and published *Lessons of Iraq* in March 2004. The FAC published *The Decision to Go to War in Iraq* in July 2003 but, unlike its report on Kosovo, this report was not a thorough investigation of every aspect of the war, concentrating mainly on the veracity of dossiers published by the government to justify its policy, the issue of political controversy at the time. In March 2004, the FAC published a special report, *Implications for the Work of the House and its Committees of the Government's Lack of Co-operation with the Foreign Affairs Committee's Inquiry into the Decision to Go to War in Iraq*. Its ongoing work on the war on terror has frequently taken in Iraq, including a discussion of the legality of a possible invasion in late 2002, described below.

The International Development Committee published *Preparing for the Humanitarian Consequences of Possible Military Action Against Iraq* in

March 2003. In April 2005 the committee published *Development Assistance in Iraq: Interim Report.*

In September 2004, the Public Accounts Committee published *Ministry of Defence: Operation TELIC – United Kingdom Military Operations in Iraq.*

There was, then, substantial parliamentary engagement in the issue of the war against Iraq, both before and after the invasion. The two debates in the Chamber were generally very thoughtful and MPs raised the significant issue of the legality of the war. But the continuing public anger over the war, made manifest during the 2005 general election campaign and by Labour's losses, suggests that the public was not satisfied that the Prime Minister in particular had been made properly accountable for his conduct. Weaknesses in the scrutiny process also raise serious concerns about the oversight that Parliament and its select committees can bring to bear and about other aspects of governance in the UK that diminish Parliament's role. We address these concerns in turn.

Non-parliamentary inquiries

The very fact that the government responded to public disquiet about the war, the death of the government's WMD specialist, Dr David Kelly, and the use of intelligence information in the September 2002 dossier by establishing two non-parliamentary inquiries illustrates Parliament's essential weakness in its relationship with the executive. British governments have long used special inquiries, set up under the executive's terms of reference, as a means of evading immediate political scrutiny in Parliament (see pages 39–43).[35]

But the stark disparity between the cooperation which the Hutton and Butler inquiries received in terms of witnesses and information and that which select committees receive confirmed once again the weaknesses of select committees as tools of scrutiny and accountability. We have already enumerated the complaints of the Liaison Committee in January 2004, comparing the impressive turn-out of witnesses to the inquiries with a list of recent refusals of select committee requests to question ministers and officials; comparing the nature and form of detailed documentary evidence (much of which would normally be withheld under FOI rules) to the two inquiries with lower-level information given to committees; listing the kinds of document that select committees require to perform their duties; and pointing out how slowly documents are given to committees (see Chapter 3, page 40).[36] As we have seen, Lord Butler has stated that parliamentary select committees are not trusted with politically sensitive information because of their partisan make-up (see page 42).

We have also already drawn attention to the FAC's complaints that committees have no effective means of enforcing their formal powers to call for 'persons and papers' when those persons or papers belong to the executive; and that the non-parliamentary ISC received greater cooperation for its inquiry than it, the FAC, had experienced (see also page 53).[37] Even when defence secretary Geoff Hoon agreed to allow Dr Kelly to attend the FAC, it was on the condition that he was asked only about the evidence Andrew Gilligan had given to the committee, rather than about weapons of mass destruction. In other words, a minister was imposing conditions upon the committee, not the witness – a novel and unwelcome development. (The FAC accepted the conditions Hoon demanded, but during the course of the session, some of its members broke them.)

The government managed to evade an inquiry into the central question which still dogs public debate about the war – the circumstances in which the decision was taken, the legal and political considerations that informed it, and the relationship between policy and its presentation. Neither of the two independent inquiries undertook an analysis of policy. The FAC report, entitled *The Decision to Go to War in Iraq*, did not, in fact, deal with the decision, but focused in part on the third of the questions, examining as it did the veracity of government dossiers such as *Iraq's Weapons of Mass Destruction*, published in September 2002. This was a significant issue, but ancillary to that of why and how the UK came to participate in the invasion.

Prime ministerial government

Parliamentary accountability in the UK depends on the principles of collective Cabinet government. The participation of Cabinet ministers, all of whom are members of Parliament, in collective decision-making is supposed first and foremost to be the 'buckle' between Parliament and the executive. But it is more often justified as a safeguard against arbitrary rule. There is ample evidence that Tony Blair took a highly personal lead throughout the Iraq crisis; that the critical decision-making came from No. 10; and that the Prime Minister's advisers played a more central role even than ministers who were nominally responsible for some of the decisions involved. The Cabinet in fact discussed Iraq as a specific agenda item 24 times before the war, as well as in the course of other discussions. Nevertheless the discussions on detailed papers – and the decision-making itself – were confined to a small, informal prime ministerial group. Cabinet safeguards were further undermined by the fact that two ministers who played a significant role, Lord Goldsmith, the Attorney General, and Lord Falconer, were friends of the Prime Minister whom he had made peers to summon them into his government.

Clare Short's account and the Butler review agree that the critical decision-making was informal – and minutes of meetings were often not kept. Ministers were not circulated with papers in advance of Cabinet meetings and did not even receive the Attorney General's legal advice in full. Patricia Hewitt admits that she saw it for the first time when it was finally published on the No. 10 website during the May election two years later. Parliamentary oversight is made more difficult when the actual location of authority is difficult to establish or scrutinise and the 'buckle' between government and legislature is bypassed. No. 10 aides did not appear before any parliamentary committee investigating the Iraq war (with the exception of Alastair Campbell. who determined to attend the FAC in furtherance of his own agenda).

Under Tony Blair, prime ministerial – as opposed to collective Cabinet – control of the intelligence agencies became more pronounced. The Butler report found that changes in the way intelligence was overseen after 11 September 2001 meant that the Cabinet Secretary, 'who attends Cabinet and maintains the machinery to support their decision-making, [was] less directly involved personally in advising the Prime Minister on security and intelligence issues'. Campbell evidently moved into the vacuum and provided a less dispassionate link between the supply of intelligence and the presentation of policy. The link between Campbell and John Scarlett conflated the JIC's function of providing and assessing objective intelligence assessments with servicing narrow political objectives. Butler found it 'wrong in principle that the Chairman of the [JIC] should be outranked not only by heads of the agencies, but also by the two other heavyweight Permanent Secretaries on his Committee'. The report said the post should be 'held by someone with experience of dealing with Ministers in a very senior role, and who is demonstrably beyond influence, and thus probably in his last post'.

There is a need in government to keep the production of intelligence apart from the politics of government, as a government's needs can colour the direction and interpretation of the intelligence. If Parliament and the public are presented with unreliable information, accountability is undermined. So too is public confidence in the work of the security forces – and in government generally. In BRMB polling research for the Committee on Standards in Public Life 'telling the truth' (not itself mentioned in the committee's seven founding principles) emerged above even 'not taking bribes' as an important aspect of conduct in public life with the general public.

Did people generally trust ministers or MPs actually to tell the truth? Not by a long chalk – 70 per cent of respondents did not trust ministers to tell the truth and only 24 per cent did (a credibility gap of minus 46 per cent). Nearly three-quarters do not expect ministers to 'own up' to their mistakes. The war against Iraq has undoubtedly increased public scepticism. When asked to mention events which may have influenced their answers, 74 per cent of respondents who did cite recent events (29 per cent of all respondents) mentioned events associated with the war.[38]

The royal prerogative
It is often suggested that at least one good came of the Iraq crisis – namely, that the House of Commons voted twice on the question of going to war and that these two votes have created a new

constitutional convention that any future military action overseas will require similar parliamentary approval. It is true that Blair, for political reasons, felt obliged finally to hold the two votes in the Commons. But he was able to delay the votes until long after he had taken the key decisions to go to war and to determine the timing and wording of the resolutions, which contained no detail as to long-term policy objectives or costs.

In January 2003, shortly before the invasion, Tony Wright asked Blair at the Liaison Committee: 'Will you give an undertaking that there will be a vote in the Commons in the event of military action being decided upon?' Blair replied: 'I have got absolutely no doubt at all that in the event of us having military action there will be a vote in the House of Commons.' Yet he was careful to add:

> What I am not promising is that you can necessarily do that in all sets of circumstances before the action is taken . . . Do not tie me down to an absolute, specific time, but I have got no doubt that as soon as possible it is right that Parliament expresses its view.[39]

The contrast with the position in the US Congress under the War Powers Act is striking. Of course the American Act has its strengths and weaknesses, but it does at least seek to 'tie down' the President over the timing, nature and duration of military action overseas. It is quite clear that it is not always possible for an executive to seek approval in advance for the use of force (though in this case it was clearly possible for the government to do so). The US War Powers Act sets out clear rules for obtaining the approval of Congress in advance or, where this is not possible, as soon as is practicable. But it goes further. It also requires the President to seek Congress's renewed consent at specific points while US troops are deployed in potential or actual combat.

During the occupation of Iraq, however, the British government has redeployed troops without being required to inform Parliament or seek parliamentary approval. Moreover, the Prime Minister clearly regarded the issue of parliamentary approval as being in his power to give, and not for Parliament to demand on a statutory footing. And he was quite right: the royal prerogative gives government flexible and undefined war-making powers (see page 172).

Robin Cook was of the opinion that the Iraq precedent gives Parliament the right to be consulted on military action in the future. But it is doubtful that such a clear convention now exists, even in this limited fashion. The government has certainly not acknowledged the existence of any such thing. In July 2004, in its reply to the PASC's report on the royal prerogative, the government stated its faith in 'the pragmatic [i.e. current unregulated] approach, allowing the circumstances of Parliamentary scrutiny to reflect the circumstances of the armed conflict'.[40] Blair told the Commons Liaison Committee on 8 February 2005: 'I am slightly reluctant to go and bind whatever future governments may do . . . I think you have got always to have the ability, as a government, to take immediate action if that is necessary, which is why I do not actually myself favour changing the constitutional prerogative.'[41]

The saga of the Attorney General's advice on the war

In order to assess the legality of the war, it is necessary to seek to disentangle the Prime Minister's motivations for taking that course, since there has never been a clear and distinct account on the public record. According to John Kampfner's book *Blair's Wars*, based on interviews with those closely involved, Blair took the decision that the UK should stand shoulder to shoulder with the US in the invasion of Iraq because it was inconceivable that Britain would not support its closest ally, once President Bush had decided on regime change in Iraq. It is clear that he held the view that Britain could not allow the US to become internationally isolated. Blair's decision, however, seems also to have been motivated in part by the humanitarian instincts that prompted his drive towards armed intervention in Kosovo and a genuine conviction that Saddam Hussein's ownership of WMD posed a threat to security in the world as well as his desire to prove that Britain is the US's most reliable ally.

Kampfner relates that Blair's Chicago speech in April 1999, opening the way to humanitarian interference in other countries (see page 9), caused 'consternation' in the FCO, especially the legal department.[42] Neither Sir John Kerr, the permanent secretary, nor his senior officials had been consulted in advance; and they tried and failed to incorporate the speech into the FCO's more orthodox policy on intervention. As we have explained, the case for armed intervention on humanitarian grounds without the Security Council's express authorisation is of doubtful legitimacy in international law (see Chapter 1); and the FAC's report on the intervention in Kosovo in 1999 concluded that 'at the very least, the doctrine of human-itarian intervention has a tenuous basis in current international customary law' (see page 171).[43] Yet the British public has at least proved sympathetic to armed intervention, both in Kosovo and in Sierra Leone, as well as in the case of the no-fly zone that John Major and George Bush Senior previously set in place to protect the Kurds in northern Iraq. But Blair did not base the case for regime change in Iraq on humanitarian grounds. Instead, as has been extensively documented, he sought on the advice of the Attorney General to justify the invasion on Saddam's non-compliance with UN resolu-tions and the dangers his supposed possession of WMD posed to the UK and the west.

A document leaked to the *Sunday Times* and published on 1 May 2005 shows that, contrary to his public positions, Blair was committed to participate in the removal of Saddam as early as mid-2002.[44] At a meeting of top officials held by the Prime Minister on 23 July that year, the head of the Secret Intelligence Service, Sir Richard Dearlove, stated that in the US 'military action [against Iraq] was now seen as inevitable.' The Foreign Secretary noted:

> The case was thin. Saddam was not threatening his neighbours, and his WMD capability was less than that of Libya, North Korea, or Iran. We should work up a plan for an ultimatum to Saddam to allow back in the UN weapons inspectors. This would also help with the legal justification for the use of force.[45]

He was aware that the US was resistent to the idea of using an ultimatum. The Prime Minister took the view that 'if the political context were right, people would support regime change.' The use of an ultimatum was the course of action eventually followed.

A key conclusion of the meeting was that 'we should work on the assumption that the UK would take part in any military action.' Neither the full Cabinet nor Parliament was made aware that such a decision had been taken. Debates held in the legislature were therefore held on a false premise: that the US and UK aim was to resolve the Iraq crisis peacefully, not that the ultimatum issued to Iraq was a political and legal device to justify war; and that the intensified air strikes in the no-fly zone over southern Iraq were to enforce the zone and keep up the pressure on Saddam to comply with UN resolutions, rather than to soften up Iraq for invasion..

In late 2002, following the introduction of UN Security Council (UNSC) Resolution 1441 and a troop build-up in the region, Saddam agreed to admit weapons inspectors. By March 2003, they had not yet completed their job, and there was no evidence of considerable stocks of WMD hidden in the country. The US and the UK, along with other allies, argued that Iraq was in material breach of the resolution, on the grounds that Saddam had not fully cooperated with the inspections (though others pointed out that, if not absolute, the cooperation being provided was considerable). They sought another resolution specifically authorising military action, but, when it was clear that other UNSC members including France would veto it, invaded without one. The legal justification presented by the UK government at the time was the so-called 'revival argument', based in the view that Resolution 1441 revived the authorisation to use force contained in UNSC Resolution 678, issued in 1990 following Iraq's invasion of Kuwait.

There were doubts over whether the action was legal in the absence of an additional resolution. Robin Cook, who thought it was not, quit the Cabinet over the issue. There was, as Butler puts it, 'disagreement inside the FCO on whether a further decision of the Security Council would be needed'. Elizabeth Wilmshurst, deputy legal adviser in the FCO, resigned because she thought the invasion was illegal. But there was a lack of transparency around the actual internal legal view of the invasion, making it difficult for both Parliament (which was asked to register substantive support for the operation) and the public to assess. The ability of prime ministers to finesse constitutional conventions, such as those contained in the *Ministerial Code*, became apparent, too.

The Butler review states: 'We have examined the Attorney General's advice on the legality of war in Iraq.' According to Butler,

> the Attorney General informed [three senior prime ministerial aides] of his view of the legal position at a meeting on 28 February 2003. The Prime Minister's office subsequently asked the Attorney General to put those views in writing, which he did in a formal minute to the Prime Minister on 7 March 2003.

That advice ruled that neither self-defence nor humanitarian reasons provided a legal justification for going to war in this case. It had to rest on WMD and Saddam's refusals to comply with UN resolutions. Lord Goldsmith was equivocal on the idea that Resolution 1441 sufficed on its own to justify armed attack, rehearsing the arguments for and against relying on it and the need for a second resolution. Thus Blair could not make the removal of Saddam an explicit objective of the invasion, and the government's campaign objectives were drawn up on a basis of Iraq's continuing possession of WMD.

On 12 March, the legal adviser to the Ministry of Defence wrote to the legal secretary of the Law Officers, asking for confirmation of the legal position, so that the Chief of the Defence Staff could order the armed forces to commit to military action. The following day, the Attorney General informed Lord Falconer and Baroness Morgan, close associates of the Prime Minister, of (in Butler's words) his 'clear view' that it would be lawful to proceed without another UNSC resolution. According to Short, at the time

> there were rumours across Whitehall that the Attorney thought there was no legal authority and was planning to resign. The military made it clear that, without the Attorney's approval, they would not go. Then we got a short opinion saying there was no problem and no discussion . . . Looking back it is difficult not to believe he was leant on . . . The later rumour was that he went shopping to find the one UK international lawyer who would say [UNSC Resolution] 1441 gave authority for war.[46]

Cabinet, Parliament and public were not provided with the 7 March advice, only a brief summary by way of a parliamentary answer on 17 March 2003. The full advice only came into the open when parts of it were leaked during the 2005 general election campaign, prompting the government to publish it in full. There is in general a sensible case for keeping the government's legal advice confidential; it does not do to disclose one's hand in advance in legal matters. That is why the *Ministerial Code* rules that 'the fact and content of opinions or advice given by the Law Officers . . . must not be disclosed outside Government without their authority.' But when Parliament is faced with the decision on whether or not to approve going to war, and the legality of that war is in doubt, then it is essential that the advice is made public and subject to analysis and parliamentary and public debate.

As it is, even the Cabinet had to make do with the brief summary of that advice, which was distributed around the table on 17 March. Clare Short alleges that 'no discussion was allowed' and charges that 'by failing to reveal his full legal advice and the considerations that underpinned his final advice, the Attorney misled the Cabinet and therefore helped obtain support for military action improperly.'[47]

It seems likely that the Attorney General was consulted in good time, for the leaked July 2002 document shows that he was inside the loop from early on. (That issue aside, it is difficult to judge whether the law officers have been properly consulted over any issue since, as Butler noted, 'there is no set procedure for seeking the advice of the Law Officers.') Yet the *Ministerial Code* rules (in paragraph 23) that he should make the full advice available to Cabinet. On 10 March 2005, Tony Wright questioned the Cabinet Secretary, Sir Andrew Turnbull, about 'whether the Cabinet saw the full legal advice from the Attorney General'. Turnbull replied that on 17 March the Attorney General gave the Cabinet 'his definitive view at that time. He has said that this was not a summary of something, it was his view which he had formed at the time . . . this requirement that the Attorney's views are accurately represented, they are not paraphrased, they are not chosen selectively, was covered by inviting him personally to attend the meeting.' Wright responded that 'paragraph 23 does not say, "Oh, by the way, if he wants to turn up instead, we need not have the full legal advice available."'[48]

There is evidence for the view, presented in particular by Philippe Sands, that prior to the 7 March advice the Attorney General was put under pressure from US sources to alter his initial assessment that a second UN resolution was required. A leaked section of Wilmshurst's resignation letter – which the government had withheld under the FOI Act – showed that she felt he changed his mind twice, before the 7 March opinion and when his final view was expressed. Sands raises the possibility that a meeting Goldsmith had with John Bellinger III, legal adviser to the White House's National Security Council, on 11 February 2003 might have influenced a shift in his views. According to Sands, Bellinger said later: 'We had trouble with your Attorney; we got him there eventually' (but Bellinger would not confirm this statement to Sands). Sands affirms that this was when the Attorney's views shifted and he came to the view that Resolution 1441 was sufficent on its own.[49] Goldsmith's 7 March opinion acknowledges that he accepted a reasonable case could be made that Resolution 1441 'revived' earlier authorisations to take military action partly on a basis of 'the arguments of the US Administration which I heard in Washington'.

Parliament was not shown the Attorney General's opinion, but the FAC report in December 2002, in advance of the invasion, did set out a detailed legal assessment of the position over Iraq, drawing on a range of expert opinion. The committee's conclusions were close to his original view:

> UN Security Council Resolution 1441 would not provide unambiguous authorisation for military action, were Iraq to fail to comply with its provisions. We therefore recommend that, in the case of Iraq's violation of Resolution 1441, the Government do its utmost to ensure the adoption of a further Security Council resolution authorising the use of 'all necessary means' to enforce Iraqi disarmament . . . We recommend that the Government clarify, in its response to this Report, whether it believes that a further United Nations Security Council Resolution is legally necessary before military action is taken against Iraq.[50]

In that sense, the legislature was publicly providing an expert view on the legality of the coming conflict. Yet a press search for the words

'Foreign Affairs Committee' around the time of the report's public-ation yields no hits whatsoever in the national or regional press in the UK, despite the prominence given to the Iraq crisis by the media. In its response of 25 February 2003, shortly before the invasion, the FCO stated: 'Our strong preference is for a second Resolution.'

Britain's export policy

The UK's trade policy is primarily determined in the EU (since the EU member states constitute a customs union) and by the EU in multilateral negotiations and agreements in the World Trade Organization and other international bodies. But while the EU decides policy and takes the lead, there remains a bilateral element to UK trade policy: for instance, with respect to decisions over whether certain countries should be permitted to purchase certain goods, particularly arms; and determining state assistance to UK exporters.

The government passed the Export Control Act 2002 to replace the Import, Export and Customs Powers (Defence) Act 1939, an emergency wartime measure that gave successive governments wide-ranging powers to impose import and export controls. In 1996, the Scott report condemned the continuing use of the emergency 1939 Act, which enabled ministers to control imports and exports as they pleased in the absence of parliamentary scrutiny of secondary legislation made under the Act. The 2002 Act was preceded by a White Paper in 1998 which provided for parliamentary scrutiny of future secondary legislation on new 'strategic' controls.

What are the criteria for export control? The Act allows first for controls giving effect to any EU provision or the UK's other multi-lateral obligations. Thereafter the main purpose of controls is to regulate the UK arms trade and prevent the development of WMD, to protect the security of the UK and the world against terrorism and serious crime, and to uphold international law and human rights. The secretary of state is also obliged to give guidance over 'issues relating to sustainable development' and may act to protect the UK's cultural heritage. A schedule attached to the Act gives further details of the controls which 'may be imposed in relation to' military equipment and technology, actual or potential. The emphasis is on prevention; the controls are in place

- to prevent exports that are likely to have an 'adverse effect' on 'the national security; or . . . the security of members of the armed forces, of the United Kingdom (or any dependency), any Member state or any other friendly State', or a possible adverse effect on 'peace, security or stability in any region of the world or within any country'; and
- to prevent the 'carrying out anywhere in the world of acts which facilitate the development, production or use of weapons of mass destruction', acts of terrorism or serious crime or their facilitation 'anywhere in the world' and various 'breaches of international law and human rights'.

The orders are subject to the affirmative resolution procedure of both Houses of Parliament. Any order made has immediate effect but will fall if it is not approved by both Houses within 40 days. The secretary of state is required to report annually to Parliament on the workings of the Act, but the reports are already taking longer than a year to appear (the first, for 1997, was published in March 1999).

When making decisions on issuing export licences, the government applies consolidated EU and national criteria. In that sense, the policy is a bilateral/European hybrid, with additional reference to multilateral organisations, such as the UN, which may, for example, have introduced an embargo on a particular country. (For the criteria in full, see Appendix C.) The FCO policy is that

> an export licence will not be issued if the arguments for doing so are outweighed by the need to comply with the UK's international obligations and commitments, by concern that the goods might be used for internal repression or international aggression, by the risks to regional stability or by other considerations as described in these criteria.

The wording is slightly ambiguous and the statement could be read as meaning that failure to comply with the criteria is acceptable if the arguments in favour of issuing a licence are sufficiently strong.

Parliament has recently demonstrated some ability to hold the executive to account for export policy. It was able to cause severe embarassment to the government over the arms-to-Africa scandal in 1998, when the UK company Sandline stated that its activities in Sierra Leone were undertaken with the approval of the government. The FAC forced the Foreign Secretary to retract and correct a statement he had made to the House in May 1998, and the permanent secretary at the FCO, Sir John Kerr, had to alter a statement he had made to the FAC. An MP who leaked an advance copy of the committee's report to Robin Cook resigned from the FAC.

Since 1999, the Quadripartite Committee, composed of the Defence, Foreign Affairs, International Development and Trade and Industry select committees, has investigated government regulation of the export of military equipment, meeting government obstacles and identifying flaws in oversight arrangements. It receives confidential briefings on individual licence applications, but not 'the detailed assessments available to Ministers on which they base decisions to permit or deny an export licence in cases presenting real difficulty – for example, of the integrity of an end-user, or the risk of diversion of goods for internal repression'.[51] The government has cited the Code of Practice on Access to Government Information (now superceded by the Freedom of Information Act 2000) when refusing to answer the committee's requests for information, even though the committee asked to be informed in confidence, not for purposes of publication.

The committee has, in its own words, 'consistently urged the Government to introduce a system for the prior parliamentary scrutiny of export licence applications, which would enable Members of Parliament to make recommendations to the Government on individual licence applications before a final decision had been taken on whether to allow or refuse them.' The government has repeatedly declined to introduce such a system. The committee has also complained that 'the [government] information systems used for retrieving licensing information are inadequate';[52] that 'the Government's Annual Reports fail on two counts: the information that they contain is sometimes misleading because it is incomplete; and the information is no longer topical by the time that it is published'; and that there is insufficient information available on the end use of exports.[53]

Overall the committee believes that 'the right decisions' are being taken on export licence applications. But it does have 'concerns about several specific licensing decisions'. In 2003, for example, it recorded unease at British Aerospace's negotiations for the sale of a Hawk training jet to India, and 'licences granted to Pakistan during 2001 for production equipment and components for heavy artillery'.[54]

In its final report of the 2001–2005 parliament, the Quadripartite Committee recommended that new government information systems for export controls be designed to make it easier to furnish the committee with information that had been withheld from it on grounds of practicality. The report stated that the government's record of timeliness in responding to reports and inquiries was getting worse. It complained about witnesses not being able to answer questions that fell outside their strict departmental areas – despite an understanding that they would. The committee has introduced a single website location for its work, which was previously spread across the four constituent committees. It expressed concern about the increased usage of open licences, as opposed to single ones, and about the impact of efficiency savings upon the government's Export Control Organisation.[55]

The Export Credits Guarantee Department

The Export Credits Guarantee Department (ECGD) was the first organisation of its sort in the world. Many countries now have an equivalent. It was set up in 1919 to help UK firms win back markets after the First World War. It provides insurance, finance facilities and guarantees, and project financing. A government department, responsible to the Secretary of State for Trade and Industry, it is regulated by the Export and Investment Guarantees Act 1991. Claims from insured firms are ultimately met by the taxpayer. The majority of developing world debt to the UK consists of unpaid export credits. The ECGD can only write off debt according to Paris Club regulations (see Chapter 6), with Treasury permission. If debt remission goes beyond Paris Club plans, the ECGD is reimbursed by the Department for International Development.

Table 4: markets for ECGD guarantees for 2002–3		
Country	**Amount (£m) %**	**FCO human rights assessment**
Saudi Arabia	£1,013.48, 29%	One of the highest figures for use of the death penalty in the world (including for adultery). Cruel, public executions. Maltreatment and torture of prisoners. Discrimination against women and Shiites. Infringements on freedom of expression, assembly and religion.
Oman	£348.05, 10%	Physical and sexual abuse against foreign female workers. Withholding of wages from foreign workers. Restrictions on freedom of speech and the press. Discrimination against women.
Malaysia	£225.46, 6%	–
Chile	£224.97, 6%	–
Turkey	£161.38, 5%	Torture, police violence, restrictions on freedom of assembly, religious discrimination, impunity for law officials.
Indonesia	£148.01, 4%	Human rights abuses by military and censorship in Aceh and Papua regions.
Nigeria	£127.21, 4%	'Police brutality and abuse is rife.' Use of death penalty. Sharia penal code adopted in twelve states (including stoning for Muslim adulterers). Problem with street children 'significant'.
Sweden	£118.21, 3%	–
Romania	£107.06, 3%	Despite recent improvements, 'we are concerned about police brutality; press freedom; treatment of disadvantaged children; and treatment of minorities, particularly Roma.' 11% of population in poverty. Corruption. People-trafficking.
Qatar	£99.74%, 3%	Non-payment of migrant workers. No political parties. Trafficking of child slaves as camel jockeys. Restrictions on freedom of speech and the press (excepting Al-Jazeera).
Other	£958.49, 27%	–

The ECGD mission statement is: 'To benefit the UK economy by helping exporters of UK goods and services win business and UK firms to invest overseas, by providing guarantees, insurance and reinsurance against loss, taking into account the Government's international policies.' The 'international policies' referred to include the promotion of human rights, sustainable development and good governance – there is not a specific reference to controlling arms sales. (For the ECGD mission statement in full, see Appendix D.)

The markets for ECGD guarantees for 2002–3, amounting to £3.532 billion, are set out in Table 4. In order to see how far the ECGD's activities are sensitive to human rights considerations, we include excerpts, where relevant, from the assessment of countries as contained in the FCO's Human Rights Annual Report 2004. These monies or guarantees were allocated as follows between types of project: defence, 50 per cent; Airbus, 14.5 per cent; other aerospace, 0.5 per cent; civil, 35 per cent.

From September 1997, the government has pursued a policy of a moratorium on export credits to selected developing-world countries for projects which are deemed 'unproductive', restricting the credits to activities supporting economic and social improvement. The ECGD website states that it will 'restrict cover for the poorest countries to transactions which pass a productive expenditure test'.

ECGD annual reports are not subject to scrutiny of the sort applied to annual reports on strategic export controls by the Quadripartite Committee. Since 1999 the ECGD has been investigated by the International Development Committee in 2000, and the Trade and Industry Committee in 2000 and 2004. The more general problems of parliamentary oversight associated with such agencies have been discussed earlier in this book. In both of its reports, the Trade and Industry Committee concluded that the existence of the ECGD was necessary to avoid putting UK firms at a disadvantage in the competitive international market. However, the ECGD has itself conceded that it is difficult to measure how valuable its services are, and whether they could be provided equally well, or better, by the private sector. In 2000, the International Development Committee called for the ECGD to incorporate development into its core objectives (which it did). The committee raised concerns about the concentration on arms exports possibly at the expense of civil exports. It called for research into the impact of the ECGD and export agencies generally upon development, and for an international development framework within which they could operate.[56]

During 2004 there were allegations reported in the press that the ECGD had made its new anti-bribery guidelines less stringent. They were first issued in May but in November arguably weaker revised ones were introduced following discussions with industry.

Human rights and bilateral trade policy

The *Ministerial Code* refers to 'the overarching duty on Ministers to comply with the law, including international law and treaty obligations'. Treaties to which the UK is a signatory include a number of human rights–related agreements. It is reasonable to conclude that part of Parliament's oversight role for bilateral trade policy is to assist the government in fulfilling the obligations that are entailed.

The FAC remarked in 1998:

> Bilateral relationships may pose different challenges to the Government in respect of the consistency and coherence of a foreign policy which seeks to promote universal human rights standards. Several countries in which the United Kingdom has particular and key strategic or commercial interests are recognised as having human rights records which fall significantly below the standards we hope the Government would seek to promote. We recognise that there are inherent difficulties in maintaining a consistent approach to human rights abuses in respect of countries which have relatively small markets and unfavourable geostrategic locations and of countries which are major trading partners or key allies. To put it bluntly, successive Governments have, for example, found it easier to denounce military repression of indigenous people in Central America than to condemn lack of religious freedom in the Gulf.[57]

Parliamentary assessment of the human rights aspects of government activity is not consistent. In September 2003, the Trade and Industry

Committee – which has carried out valuable work on the human rights agenda at other times, including its participation in the Quadripartite Committee – produced a report entitled *Trade and Investment Opportunities with China and Taiwan*.[58] Such an investigation surely merited a section dealing with human rights issues. Yet there was none. Indeed, the phrase 'human rights' occurs at no point in the report, which deals with how to open up markets to UK firms.

The ECGD, given its mission statement and the breakdown of its financial allocations included above, should be monitored carefully from a human rights perspective. It is not. The Trade and Industry Committee report of 2004 – the first full investigation of the ECGD since 2000 by a parliamentary committee – did not deal with human rights. The previous Trade and Industry Committee report from 2000 similarly did not. As discussed, the International Development Committee report of 2000 dealt with third-generation human rights such as development, but not other types.

The Quadripartite Committee has a strong record of raising human rights issues. For example, it recorded in 2003 that 'it is doubtful whether the Government should have granted a licence for oversized handcuffs in one particular case, given the nature of licence applications which the Government had previously received . . . We have been asked by the Government not to identify the destination of the cuffs.' In another case, the committee noted that that an 'administrative failure' had led to the export of a set of oversized handcuffs, since 'basic checks on the end-user of this equipment . . . would have revealed concerns about how the oversized cuffs might be used.' Continuing 'measures to minimise the risk that military equipment supplied to the Sri Lankan armed forces . . . will be misused' were recommended.[59]

The Duke of York's part in overseas trade

UK Trade & Investment (UKTI), previously known as British Trade International (BTI), was renamed in October 2003. It also takes in the former brand names Trade Partners UK and Invest UK. Its objective is 'to enhance the competitiveness of companies in the UK through overseas trade and investments; and attract a continuing level of quality foreign direct investment'. There is no reference to human rights objectives in this statement. BTI was established in 1999, combining previously separate DTI and FCO functions. UKTI brings together staff in British embassies, overseas FCO posts and government departments. The responsible minister is the Minister for Trade and Investment and Foreign Affairs. Ultimate ministerial responsibility is split – arguably not an ideal arrangement for accountability – between the Foreign Secretary and the trade and industry secretary. The current annual budget is £290 million, spent on such items as overseas promotion and advisory services.

After leaving the Navy in 2001, the Duke of York (Prince Andrew) took up a role for UKTI as the UK Special Representative for International Trade and Investment. His role and responsibilities, in what is an official function on behalf of the UK government, are unclear. In response to a written question about the special representative's appointment, role and responsibilities, Graham Allen MP was informed on 7 April 2005 that 'the Duke of York was appointed to the role . . . by Her Majesty the Queen, after consultation with the Cabinet Office, BTI and the Foreign and Commonwealth Office . . . The roles and responsibilities . . . are set out in the 2004 UK Trade and Investment Departmental Report.' But that report merely states that 'HRH works closely with UK Trade & Investment . . . in support of . . . overseas trade and inward investment objectives [through] an extensive programme of targeted engagements at home and overseas.'

Other information in the public domain lists the Duke's 'nearly 250 trade and investment-related engagements annually within the UK, and around five overseas trade-related visits'. Again, a list of the countries and markets he has courted is likely to prompt raised eyebrows among readers of the FCO's human rights report. The Duke's upcoming and recent engagements (as listed on the official royal website) include a Middle East Association lunch; a visit to the Gulf states, including Oman, Qatar and Bahrain; visits to China and Russia; a visit to Turkey and Jordan; a meeting of the Oman–British Friendship Society; a meeting with the Omani Young Presidents group; an Anglo-Arab dinner; a visit to south-east Asia; attending an Emerging Markets and Political Risk conference in London; and a

China Association lunch. In some of these cases, that he will be dealing with countries with poor human rights records is not absolutely certain, but in all there is at least a possibility. The Duke's role is not clearly set out and the suspicion that it is exercised without due attention to human rights concerns cannot be allayed.

Golf, however, may well receive attention. The royal website states that 'the Duke has in recent years taken up golf, with a current handicap of seven.' He is now 'working on behalf of the game to ensure that as many can participate and play as possible'. His list of engagements as UK Special Representative for International Trade and Investment includes, on 9 April 2004 in the US, 'attending a UK Trade and Investment reception during the US Masters'.

No doubt the glamour of members of the royal family can be a valuable asset in furthering British trade interests. It is unlikely that his opportunities to combine playing golf with his duties promoting British trade will make a big contribution to getting his golf handicap down below seven. However, there must be concern about the vague terms of reference for his role, particularly with regard to human rights. We have already noted that commercial interests prompted the British government to deal favourably with Saddam Hussein in the 1980s, even though the brutal conduct of his regime was well known to ministers (see page 79). It is important that Parliament can be vigilant in ensuring that Britain does not promote commercial gain with no concern for human rights in its negotiations with other nations; and it must have oversight of the conduct of royals, as with ministers and officials, in such negotiations.

The transcript of a speech the Duke gave at one of the functions he attended as special representative suggests that there is cause for concern. On 25 October he spoke in Moscow to an audience of leading businessmen, investors and others from Britain and Russia. Russia is criticised by the human rights report for 'the use of torture by law enforcement officials, rising racism and extremism, restrictions on media freedom, discrimination and violence against women, suppression of religious rights and abuse of child rights'. The conduct of the conflict in Chechnya, for which the Russian authorities (as well as the terrorists active there) have been criticised, is given an entire section of its own in the report.

The Duke did not refer to any of this in his talk – the drafting of which the FCO must surely have had a hand in. Instead, he concentrated on the idea that 'our mutual prosperity and now, even more particularly, our security, are intertwined.' The only course of action he urged upon the Russian government was to ensure that it met President Vladimir Putin's 'goals of doubling GDP by 2010, improving living standards and greater international economic integration'.

The notion that trade, growth and military security were the only concerns of the UK government in its dealings with Russia was underlined by the following statement:

> In order for you to clearly understand where we place our trading relationship, and from where the UK is looking to Russia, I need to remind you that it was four hundred and fifty years ago that Richard Chancellor sailed from Britain to Russia in order to secure the right to free trade from the Tsar. This was an insightful move by Tsar Ivan IV; he understood that greater trade would lead to greater prosperity, diplomacy and security between our two countries.

Whether support for the policies of Ivan the Terrible is official UK policy, or is regarded as compatible with respect for international human rights obligations, is not clear.

5

Britain in Europe

British membership of the European Union has a substantial impact on domestic UK legislation. As an EU member, Britain jointly decides with the other member states the rules and regulations governing not only the single market but also other areas of cooperation at the European level, such as judicial affairs or foreign and security policy. If the British Parliament is fully to carry out its responsibilities to the British electorate, it needs to exercise appropriate scrutiny and supervision not merely in the domestic context but in the European arena as well. Parliament is clearly aware of this need and has sought to set up arrangements for scrutiny in both Houses of Parliament. These arrangements are only comprehensible against the background of the specific decision-making processes of the EU. This chapter therefore begins with a brief review of the EU's institutional and decision-making structures.

Making policy and law in Europe

The **European Council** is the meeting of heads of state and government which takes place at least twice a year to agree on strategic aims. Despite its high prestige, the European Council has no powers to adopt European legislation, which is the responsibility of the Council of Ministers.

The **Council of the European Union**, usually referred to as the **Council of Ministers**, is composed of ministerial representatives of the 25 member states. It is the main legislative and policy-making body of the EU. Normally, it takes its decisions by consensus, without a formal vote. When a formal vote occurs, the Council of

Ministers decides by unanimity or by a qualified majority vote, depending on the policy area. It meets in different formations of specialised ministers, such as the Environment Council, where the national ministers responsible for the environment are represented, or the Agriculture Council, where the agricultural ministers meet. Altogether the council meets some 60 times a year in its different compositions.

The **European Parliament** is the directly elected body, with 732 members, which exercises parliamentary scrutiny of the European Commission and acts as a co-legislator with the Council of Ministers in a wide range of policy areas.

The **European Commission** is the 'guardian' of the European treaties, ensuring that the treaties and the legislation derived from them are observed. It consists of 25 commissioners, one from each member state. The Commission is obviously an influential body through its role in proposing and drafting legislative texts and the commissioners are often seen as the EU's representatives and spokespersons. Yet the commission is not generally a decision-making body and merely implements and enforces decisions taken by the Council of Ministers and the European Parliament.

Legislation decided at the European level can take two forms. A **directive** requires member states to ensure that their national legal frameworks comply with its aims. This does not necessarily lead to changes in domestic legislation. The directive's requirements may already be part of domestic legislation, or changes may be incorporated into legislation the government was planning to put forward in any case. But any future revision of domestic legislation has to take place within the framework of the existing European directives, thus limiting the room for manoeuvre of future national legislators.

A **regulation**, in contrast, is directly applicable in all member states and is more likely to have a direct impact on relevant domestic legislation. Decisions on both directives and regulations are taken by the Council of Ministers, meeting in the specific configuration of the policy area concerned, sometimes in co-decision with the European Parliament. The European Parliament can and frequently does amend legislative proposals. Once adopted, directives or regulations are binding on the member states until revised or revoked. It is not possible for an individual EU member state to 'opt out' of European legislation at its own discretion.

This legal framework of the EU has specific implications for parliamentary scrutiny in Westminster. There are admittedly similarities between the actions of the British government when it operates in the context of EU affairs and when it is conducting its bilateral foreign policy or working through international organisations. However, in contrast to other areas of classical external policy, the British government's negotiations within the EU result in a substantial body of legal texts, binding upon the British Parliament and electorate alike. Much of the British Parliament's EU business is in effect 'pre-legislative scrutiny'. In other words, committees in both Houses seek to consider all the legislative proposals emanating from the European Commission, necessarily to a greater or lesser degree. On the basis of this scrutiny, Parliament seeks to monitor and hold to account the British government in its European negotiations. Through the influence it can and should exercise over the British government, Parliament has the means indirectly to influence the legislative decisions of the Council of Ministers, of which the British government is a member.

It is important to stress that the House of Commons and the House of Lords can only act 'at arm's length' from the European Council of Ministers. The EU institutions have their own structure for democratic accountability and scrutiny, principally through the European Parliament. In the directly elected European Parliament, British MEPs play a role in scrutinising the work of the European Commission, and as a co-legislator with the Council of Ministers, it performs at the European level the traditional legislative and oversight role of the Westminster Parliament towards the UK government. It is difficult to see how national parliamentarians can or should replicate this precise role in the European arena. We assume in this chapter that the principal proper and viable role for the British Parliament in the European decision-making system is to scrutinise and hold to account the actions of its own national government when negotiating and taking decisions in the EU's Council of Ministers.[1]

Parliamentary scrutiny of EU business

The British Parliament has, since UK accession to the then European Community in 1973, introduced specific scrutiny procedures for European business, and revised those at various times, the last time being in 1998. However, there still seems to be a general perception, shared by voices from all parties, that EU scrutiny procedures are unsatisfactory and in clear need of improvement. This is why the Committee on the Modernisation of the House published at the end of the last parliament its report *Scrutiny of European Business*,[2] which suggests several proposals for reform which will be discussed later in this chapter. The government evidently also accepted the need for reform and submitted its own reform proposals to the committee.

Parliamentary scrutiny of European business faces the challenge that it needs to cover both legislative proposals emanating from the EU and the negotiating positions taken by the government when dealing with issues such as the EU's Common Foreign and Security Policy. In both instances the House of Commons and the House of Lords have their own scrutiny procedures.

Scrutiny by the House of Commons

The fact that EU legislation has a direct impact on UK domestic legislation requires special parliamentary scrutiny procedures. These procedures differ from scrutiny of other aspects of British external policy in that this is an almost entirely document-based process.

At the centre of pre-legislative scrutiny of EU documents is the European Scrutiny Committee. This select committee sifts all documents emanating from the EU institutions. It considers the political and legal importance of each document and refers important documents either to one of the three European standing committees or for debate on the floor of the House. The European Scrutiny Committee possesses the usual powers of select committees, such as calling for written evidence and examining witnesses. It also, however, has the unique power to seek an opinion from any other departmental select committee, in a specific period of time. But in practice the committee only rarely makes use of this power.

Its sixteen members, who are nominated on a government motion, have to consider and report on a vast and diverse range of EU documents[3] – over 1,000 documents annually. They get through around 40 documents at each weekly committee meeting. The committee is one of the best-staffed committees in the House of Commons. It has fourteen staff, headed by the clerk, and can also call on the Speaker's Counsel for advice. The committee has four specialist advisers, who are senior policy experts, such as former ambassadors and former senior officials from government departments. They divide the examination of documents between them by policy areas.

The Foreign and Commonwealth Office is required to deposit all documents it receives from the EU institutions to the European Scrutiny Committee within two days of having received them. Every document will at this point also be available to MPs in the Vote Office. The FCO is also expected to provide the Scrutiny Committee with an explanatory memorandum within ten days, although on some occasions other responsible departments provide these memos.

This memorandum plays a central role in the scrutiny process. It is signed by the minister and therefore constitutes the minister's evidence to Parliament.[4] In rare cases a supplementary memorandum is issued, for example when additional information, such as a regulatory impact assessment, is delivered after the original memorandum. When an already discussed document changes as a result of negotiations and new developments at the EU level, the original memorandum will usually be revised and deposited again.

The European Scrutiny Committee reports every week after its deliberations to the House of Commons. The first decision the committee has to take on each document is whether it is 'of political or legal importance'. A document that is judged not to be of political or legal importance is automatically cleared. Approximately 500 out of the over 1,000 documents considered each year by the committee are classified as 'of political or legal importance'.

The committee then decides on how to proceed with the documents it considers important. It can either:

1. clear a document, if it is satisfied with the information provided by the relevant lead department and the government's stance;
2. recommend a particularly important document for debate in one of the three European standing committees (on a government motion which will be voted on) or on the floor of the House.
3. request further information from the government, if the committee decides it has not received enough information on a specific EU document (the document will in this case not count as cleared).

The government is required under the Scrutiny Reserve Resolution (see below) not to agree in the Council of Ministers to the specific proposals contained in any document that the committee has not cleared.

Members take these decisions on the basis of the government's explanatory memorandum and a briefing note prepared by the committee's advisers which includes a recommendation on whether the document should be classified as politically and/or legally important and whether it should be cleared or debated. In practice, however, a clear distinction between the importance and the merit of a document cannot always easily be drawn.

Meetings of the European Scrutiny Committee take place in private. The chairman reads out the number of each document received and, if there are no objections, the advisers' recommendation is agreed. Otherwise there is a discussion by committee members. Some nine out of ten documents get 'waved through' this way.

The real debate on a specific document, covering the contents and the merits of specific proposals that have been marked as important, then takes place in a 'second stage', either in one of the three European standing committees or on the floor of the House. The standing committees cover different policy areas and shadow the relevant government departments.[5] Unlike select committees, they have no power to conduct inquiries or call for evidence and examine witnesses. They meet solely to question a minister on a specific document and debate and vote on a motion that he or she moves. Each committee has thirteen members (excluding the chair, chosen from the Chairman's Panel), chosen according to the standing order for their expertise. Additionally any MP may attend and speak, but not vote.

The first hour or hour-and-a-half of their meetings consist of questions to the responsible minister, followed by a 90-minute-long debate on his or her motion. Members may move amendments. The chairman then reports to the House the resolution the committee has adopted (or that there was no resolution) and generally a few days later a motion relating to the documents is moved in the House (this does not have to be the same motion as discussed and possibly amended by the committee). There is a formal vote, but no more discussion in the House. This completes the scrutiny process.

The Scrutiny Reserve Resolution

Unique to the system of scrutiny of EU documents in the UK Parliament is that this process is subject to the Scrutiny Reserve Resolution. This resolution aims to prevent the government from agreeing to proposals in EU negotiations before they have been cleared by Parliament. The Scrutiny Reserve Resolution applies to all documents deposited by the government and can only be overridden in exceptional circumstances (generally a particularly pressing timetable) in which case the government has to provide an explanation of its actions (see page 116).

Parliament's observer post in Brussels

The European Scrutiny Committee, and indeed all other committees of the House of Commons, can draw on the resource of the UK National Parliament Representative based in Brussels. This position was created in autumn 1999, arising from the recommendations of the Modernisation Committee's 1998 report on parliamentary scrutiny of European business.[6] The National Parliament Representative is a clerk of the Parliament who, with the assistance of one local employee, acts as a 'forward observer post' for Parliament. (The House of Lords has recently also created an equivalent position, which will initially be attached to the Conference on Community and European Affairs Committees of Parliaments of the European Union (COSAC, see page 132), as part of the UK Presidency troika.)

The role of the National Parliament Representative is to act as the 'eyes and ears' of Parliament in Brussels. He (currently a man) keeps the European Scrutiny Committee, as well as other select committees, updated on developments in the EU institutions and alerts them to possible future issues of importance. He does this by sending a weekly confidential briefing back to Westminster as well as by responding to specific requests from the committees on particular subject areas. As part of his role he maintains an informal exchange of information with representatives of Parliaments of other EU member states, but has no mandate to speak on behalf of the UK Parliament or the European Scrutiny Committee.

Scrutiny of ministers' actions

An important element of the role of the Commons when holding the government to account in EU affairs is to scrutinise ministers' actions when representing the UK at the EU level in the meetings of the Council of Ministers. The European Scrutiny Committee generally asks the Foreign Secretary or the Minister for Europe to come before the committee after a meeting of the European Council (which normally takes place twice a year), while the Foreign Affairs Committee regularly takes evidence from these ministers before each council.

The European Scrutiny Committee regularly receives reports from ministers of other departments on developments in the sectoral, policy-specific Council formations at ministerial level. This takes the form of a written question to the minister by the chair of the European Scrutiny Committee and is published in Hansard. However, there are no other procedures for routinely and systematically scrutinising ministers' actions in the various policy formations of the council.

Holding inquiries on major EU issues

There is a notable gap in the scrutiny of EU business in the Commons. In addition to pre-legislative scrutiny, the European Scrutiny Committee seeks sometimes to conduct longer inquiries on EU issues which it considers significant – even though there is no specific reference in its standing orders for doing so. But these inquiries are relatively rare, as they impinge on the committee's time to be spent on the weekly assessment of documents. In the last parliament for instance the committee held an inquiry into aspects of the EU's Constitutional Treaty. Earlier, in 2003, it held an inquiry into the proposals of the Convention on the Future of Europe on criminal justice. Additionally the committee often hears ad hoc evidence from ministers on a specific issue.

The FAC, under whose remit the FCO and therefore EU affairs officially fall, does not generally conduct inquiries into EU issues. Evidence suggests that this is due to a lack of time, as the FAC has a very wide range of geographic areas and policy issues to cover.

Scrutiny by the House of Lords

All European documents are also deposited by the FCO to the House of Lords EU Committee and the Scrutiny Reserve Resolution also applies. In contrast to the House of Commons, however, EU scrutiny in the House of Lords concentrates more on substantial inquiries into specific documents or broader issues than on commenting on each individual document. Unlike its Commons equivalent, the House of Lords EU Committee considers the substantive merits of documents and not just whether they should be deemed politically and/or legally important. The committee sifts all documents it receives with a view to judging their importance, and refers those deemed as important to one of its seven sub-committees. The EU Committee of the Lords regularly takes evidence from the incoming EU Presidency as well as from the minister for Europe after European Council meetings. It also conducts inquiries into cross-cutting issues.

The EU Committee's seven sub-committees specialise in different policy areas.[7] The clerks of these sub-committees report to their members on the documents that the chair of the main committee has, with assistance of staff and advisers, passed down to them as being relevant to their policy area. The sub-committees consider these documents as well as conducting inquiries into specific issues. A committee meeting generally sees the first half hour spent on considering documents, and the remaining hour to hour-and-a-half on evidence sessions for the inquiries. Issues for inquiries often relate to a specific document, with the inquiry looking at the broader context into which it fits.

About 70 peers are involved in scrutiny of European business. Some serve both on the EU Committee as well as on a sub-committee, but most serve only on one committee. They represent a very broad range of expertise, and include former ambassadors, former senior defence staff, lawyers, academics and businesspeople. As the EU committees in the House of Lords consider the contents, or merits, of proposals, this expertise is necessary to be able to make an assessment on the often highly technical documents and issues considered.

Each sub-committee has one clerk and one clerical/administrative staff, and the committees share three researchers and two legal advisers. Additionally to this they share a press and IT officer. Advisers are also drawn in on a day-to-day basis. These staffing levels are significantly less than those of a departmental select committee in the House of Commons (see page 48).

How effective is parliamentary scrutiny of EU policy?

On the face of it, the European Scrutiny Committee in the Commons performs its role of considering all documents emanating from the EU and assessing their importance in a satisfactory manner. During our study no witness suggested that potentially important documents slipped through the net of scrutiny inadvertently. The system of scrutiny has the undeniable advantage of being comprehensive, making sure that all documents are considered and not just a selected few. The corresponding disadvantage of this approach is that it puts an enormous strain on committee members, who have to deal with a large number of highly technical documents, making them heavily reliant on the recommendations by the committee's advisers. This has led to criticisms of the system as being too staff driven, a potentially embarrassing issue for both staff and members of the Scrutiny Committee alike.

The weight of documents with which the committee deals also limits the time it has available for general analysis and reflection on broader European questions. The same time constraint applies to the

FAC, which, in addition to its EU-related responsibilities, has a heavy workload of non-EU business. There is no committee in the House of Commons which regularly dedicates time to inquiries into broader or cross-cutting EU topics, such as the European budget or the EU's enlargement.

Overriding the scrutiny safeguard

The Scrutiny Reserve Resolution is a powerful (and potentially very powerful) tool in ensuring that government hears Parliament's view before agreeing to EU proposals. Evidence suggests government takes this mechanism increasingly seriously. It now provides Parliament every six months with a list of the occasions on which it has overridden scrutiny reserves. Over the eighteen months up to the end of 2004, there were 77 such overrides (out of the total of approximately 1,500 documents over the period), with significantly fewer overrides in the most recent reporting period than in the two preceding six-month periods. The committee's response to government overrides of the Scrutiny Reserve is for obvious reasons limited to post hoc review. In each case the committee receives a letter of explanation by the respective minister, which sometimes leads to further written exchange between the committee and the minister.

The committee may take the matter further by asking a minister to come before it if its members are not satisfied with an explanation. This happened in November 2004, when the committee questioned the then Minister of State for Work and Pensions on an override regarding a draft regulation on the European Agency for Health and Safety at Work, which the committee had not cleared as it believed it to be founded on the wrong legal basis.[8] Reasons for overrides usually relate to problems of timing, either because of a parliamentary recess or because a proposal supposedly needs to be rushed through the Council. Both the Commons' European Scrutiny Committee and the Lords' EU Committee highlight the fact that the Common Foreign and Security Policy is an area of particular concern regarding overrides.

Gaps in scrutiny of ministers' actions

There is no systematic mechanism in the House of Commons for pre- or post-Council scrutiny. We have already drawn attention to the fact that the thrice-yearly meetings of the European Council are looked at by both the FAC and the European Scrutiny Committee, with one committee talking to the Foreign Secretary or the Europe minister before the European Council meeting and the other one after. We found, however, no evidence of cooperation between the two committees in their interrogation of ministers. Similarly, when a new EU member state takes on the EU Presidency (every six months) both committees may want separately, and without coordination between them, to take evidence from the member state concerned. This can involve interviews with the London-based ambassador of the country involved or visits to Brussels by both committees. Recipients of these visits have commented on the lack of coordination between the committees.

Ministers taking part in meetings of the Council of Ministers are subject to systematic and regular scrutiny only in form of a written parliamentary question by the chairman of the European Scrutiny Committee. The answers to these questions often leave much to be desired in terms of detail (such as the minister's voting record). A much stronger mechanism would be to make ministers regularly and routinely appear before the committee, linking their appearances to meetings of the Council of Ministers. Given the regularity with which the Council of Ministers meets (there were 22 meetings in the last quarter of 2004 alone), such a system would be time-consuming for the committee.

Turf wars between parliamentary committees

One often-repeated observation from those we interviewed when examining EU scrutiny procedures in the Westminster Parliament was that there is no formal cooperation or coordination between the House of Commons and the House of Lords. The two Houses are of course aware of each other's work, but there is no formal mechanism to avoid overlap in their activities or to ensure that there are no gaps in scrutiny. The clerks of the committee have regular informal contact and 'make sure they get the most out of each other', but the chairmen of the committees seem to have no regular contact with each other.

Furthermore, there is no cooperation or coordination between the European Scrutiny Committee and other committees in the House of Commons. This is particularly striking in the case with the FAC, which has the remit of overseeing the FCO. Evidence suggests that the relations, or lack thereof, between the two committees can be described as a 'turf war'. (This precise phrase was mentioned unprompted virtually every time we asked an interviewee about relations between the committees.)

Although the European Scrutiny Committee regularly sends departmental select committees EU documents it considers relevant to their work, this is only a one-way procedure which does not lead to further exchange or follow-up. As we state above, the European Scrutiny Committee hardly ever uses its power to ask any select committee for its opinion on a specific EU document. The reason seems to be that select committees resist taking on this work, largely because of their already intense workload and stretched resources. The European Scrutiny Committee therefore generally refrains from using its power, on the basis that an opinion produced by an unwilling committee will not be of much value.

This lack of cooperation from departmental committees derives perhaps from an underlying view that EU affairs should be treated as an isolated policy area which has no impact on other policy areas. This bears little relationship to the reality. By treating EU business as a separate and discrete area of business, the House of Commons fails to make the best use of the technical expertise on policy available in its committees in order to oversee policy and legislation emanating from the EU.

The 'black hole' in Commons scrutiny

This failure is also reflected in the 'second stage' of the scrutiny process, after a document has been declared as important by the European Scrutiny Committee (we were informed: 'After the Scrutiny Committee the document disappears in a black hole.'). As stated above, the Scrutiny Committee refers important EU documents either to one of the three European standing committees or for debate on the floor of the House. The political balance in a standing committee reflects the overall make-up of the House of Commons. The government therefore has a majority in these committees, and they are subject to a party whip. Debates on documents in a European standing committee are often perceived as a 'rubber-stamping' exercise rather than a genuine discussion. Attendance is correspondingly low. In the standing committees on the Convention the quorum was often not met and the committee had to interrupt its work until they had found another member.

According to the standing orders, members of the standing committees are selected for their expertise. However, even the most expert members may find it difficult to debate highly specialised documents, covering a broad range of policy areas, with no committee staff for support and often at short notice. This can lead to debates in which general views on the merits or otherwise of the EU are simply rehearsed by partisans of differing viewpoints. All MPs are allowed to attend and speak at the meetings of standing committees, even if they cannot vote. Those MPs who feel particularly strongly about European questions (whether positively or negatively) can on occasion 'hijack' the work of the committees by their insistence on repeating their familiar general positions on the overall topic of European integration.

This vulnerability of the European standing committees to 'hijack' for the expression of partisan views is not merely a functional problem. It is also a symptom of a potentially more serious barrier to serious scrutiny of European policies and legislation by the House of Commons. This barrier is the widespread indifference within the House to European questions in general, and the detailed scrutiny of European legislation in particular. On the whole, European questions are not regarded by MPs as glamorous or good for their career or public profile. They would prefer to devote their anyway limited professional time to activities more calculated to help their re-election or other political advancement. Only a distinct minority within the House of Commons is sufficiently stirred by European questions to see them as crucial to a well-rounded parliamentary existence.

Whatever procedural changes might or should be adopted by the Commons for its better scrutiny of European policy, these improved procedures can only be a part of the solution. Truly effective European scrutiny will only take place within the House of Commons if the general parliamentary culture permits and encourages it much more than is currently the case.

The expertise in the House of Lords

Oversight of EU policy in the House of Lords focuses, as we have seen, mainly on in-depth inquiries into specific issues of EU affairs. In contrast to the House of Commons, scrutiny in the Lords does not consider every document received from the government, but concentrates on a select few documents, or on a broader issue arising from them.

Despite that, we heard evidence in the course of our study that some peers feel overwhelmed by the amount, and in particular the technical detail, of the documents and issues they have to consider. While their Commons equivalents have well-resourced offices and can deploy their researchers to support them in performing their committee duties, there is a distinct lack of resources for members of the Lords' EU committees, who are usually in effect part-timers who share offices and have no staff of their own. (Scrutiny staff are attached to the committees, not to individual peers serving on the committees.)

Even so, the reports produced by the House of Lords EU committees are widely considered to be of high quality and reflect the high level of expertise the House of Lords can deploy. House of Lords reports are valued beyond the UK in the European Commission and other national parliaments. For example, during the Convention on the Future of Europe other national parliaments would use their material and the Lords committee was invited to give evidence to the French Assembly on the new Constitutional Treaty, the House of Lords having been one of the first parliamentary bodies to report on it.

The government also gives importance to these reports. Although the House of Lords does not have the same ability as the House of Commons to cause direct political embarrassment to the government, the government is aware that its EU committees, by way of their expert questioning, have the ability to cause personal embarrassment to a minister. This can be illustrated by a quote arising from our interviews: 'When I was a minister I would prepare many hours for a session with the Lords select committee.' It was clear that the speaker spent much less time in preparation for a session with the House of Commons.

However, we also heard the criticism that the House of Lords devotes too much time and effort to its prestigious reports: their long and in-depth inquiries mean that only a very small number of issues gets scrutinised at all (approximately 10 per cent of all documents), and their reports are often published too late to shape decision-making. To address this problem sub-committee C recently started to produce 'mini-reports' in between or additional to longer inquiries in order to ensure a more timely response to important current issues. In addition great emphasis is now being placed on producing reports on issues which may become relevant in the future.

The difference in working methods between the two Houses ('the House of Commons rush in and out while the House of Lords check the reference books') reflects their different roles. The House of Lords is not the primary legislative chamber to hold the government to account. It is perhaps therefore understandable that it does not wish to consider every European document submitted to it. At the same time its in-depth inquiries may be able to fill a gap which is left in the House of Commons system of EU scrutiny, where there is not enough room for longer inquiries. For this complementarity to function effectively, however, a more formal process of coordination between the two Houses would be desirable. There would undoubtedly be scope for a more structured exchange of information (possibly through the clerks) and for regular meetings between the committees, to discuss priorities in oversight and agree which upcoming EU issues may require particular parliamentary attention.

Reforming parliamentary scrutiny of EU policy

In order to address the problems described above a number of reform proposals for the EU scrutiny system in the UK Parliament have been made. As we note above, the Modernisation Committee in the House of Commons recently published its suggestions on reform.[9] The report broadly follows the government proposals submitted to the inquiry in form of a memorandum[10] by the then Leader of the House – who at the same time held the post of chair of the committee. This close relationship between the committee and the government makes the implementation of something very like the committee's proposals reasonably likely over the course of the new Parliament.

A joint 'grand' committee

The committee's key recommendation is for the creation of a new joint committee of both Houses of Parliament to consider EU matters, a suggestion which was also the preferred reform option of the government. The suggested name for this new committee would be 'Parliamentary European Committee'. It would have two chairs – one from each House – but no core membership (as it will not be voting), with any member of either House being allowed to attend and a quorum of seven (at least two of each House). British MEPs would also be allowed to attend and speak. Meetings are envisaged to take place approximately four times a year, two of which would coincide with the publication by the Foreign Secretary of the government's White Paper on developments in the EU. The other two meetings would be held 'as the need arose', for example on a specific policy area, on a Commission forward planning document or on another EU document.

The two chairs would trigger a decision to hold a meeting in consultation with the government. Procedures in the committee would take a similar form to the pattern set by the previous Standing Committees on the Convention and on the Intergovernmental Conference respectively. This means that a minister, or in the case of the new 'Parliamentary European Committee' possibly a European Commissioner, would make an opening statement at the beginning of the meeting, which would be followed by questions of up to one-and-a-half hours. After this there would be a debate on a specific subject but the committee would not vote on any specific resolution.

The report claims that one of its objectives is to 'mainstream' European business. However, the new joint committee would still treat EU business as a separate issue and meetings are likely to be attended only by members 'according to their interest in the subject under discussion' (as the report rightly states), which essentially means those members who already have an interest in EU affairs. The report suggests that members would attend according to the policy area under discussion (such as agriculture or aviation), although evidence from attendance at meetings of the European standing committees does not support this.

The intention of the Modernisation Committee – and indeed the government – is evidently to increase the profile of EU issues within Parliament (and beyond, in the media) with the creation of this committee, hoping that the appearance of the Foreign Secretary or an EU Commissioner would give a high profile to EU matters both within Parliament and beyond.

There is undoubtedly a need for Parliament to bring EU matters higher up the agenda. But the fundamental problem lies within the lack of interest that the majority of MPs have in the day-to-day oversight of EU matters and this problem will not be solved simply by a high-profile, media-compatible event four times a year. Evidence from the Standing Committee on the Convention, to which this new 'Parliamentary European Committee' is meant to be the successor, shows that the attendance of MPs tended to be very low, with regular difficulties being faced on meeting the necessary quorum. There must also be doubts whether the level of debate on EU matters in Parliament would be improved.

There is inevitable concern that debate in the 'Parliamentary European Committee' would solely turn into political 'grand-standing' between those members holding extreme views on the EU instead of encouraging serious and genuine debate on a particular topic. An example of this danger was provided by the Standing Committee on the European Convention. We heard evidence that at least one witness deliberately used technical and inaccessible vocabulary in speaking to this committee, precisely in order to avoid stirring up fruitless polemic, whether from MPs present at the committee's meetings or journalists reporting afterwards.

From the above it becomes clear that a new joint committee along the lines proposed by the Modernisation Committee and the government will not be an effective tool for overseeing and scrutinising government's day-to-day handling of EU affairs. There may be no harm in creating this committee, and it might indeed assist in raising awareness of the importance of EU affairs (it has been suggested to us that this was the case with the Welsh Grand Committee). But we have been frequently warned during the course of our study about the difficulties posed for an effective grand committee by the underlying differences in political culture between non-elected peers and elected MPs. In theory, such a committee seems to offer the benefit of joining expertise and influence of both Houses. In reality, it runs the risk of perpetuating the problems now endemic to the European standing committees, with little commensurate benefit in terms of expertise or accountability.

Reforming the European standing committees

The Modernisation Committee also suggests ways in which the scrutiny of EU affairs by the European standing committees in the House of Commons might be improved. As outlined above (see page 119), the workings of the European standing committees have repeatedly been the focus of criticism. The Modernisation Committee report makes several suggestions for reform of these committees, designed to increase attendance at their meetings and to improve the level of debate. One is to increase the number of European standing committees from three to five and reduce the core membership of each committee from thirteen to nine. In this way each member would need to attend fewer meetings in total, increasing the likelihood of members attending. At the same time members would then be able to focus more specifically on one policy area and develop specialist expertise, which in turn may improve the quality of debate. In tandem the committees would be renamed, replacing the current designated letters for each committee (European Standing Committee A, B or C) to indicate the policy areas they would cover, with a view to making the work of the committees easier for outside parties to understand.[11]

In response to criticism that the European standing committees are powerless to amend a government motion, the Modernisation Committee proposes that a committee's own motion should be taken to the House for debate in the form of the European Standing Committee's Resolution, and that the government may table an amendment to reverse or modify this resolution. In this way committee members would be able genuinely to influence the motion taken to the House, which in turn may improve interest in (and attendance at) the European standing committees. Interestingly, this proposal is at variance with the governmental view expressed in its memorandum to the committee's inquiry.

The Modernisation Committee's report further suggests that each European standing committee should have a permanent chair, drawn from the Chairman's Panel. This chair would not have the powers of a select committee chairman, but would be a permanent point of contact for the European Scrutiny Committee. The committee also recommends strengthening the links with the European Scrutiny Committee by giving the chairs of the standing committees the power to allow for a brief opening statement from a member of the European Scrutiny Committee, explaining their reasons for referring this specific document to the committee and so making the point of concern clear to its members (see also page 126 below on 'mainstreaming').

A different way of improving the quality of debate in the European standing committees would have been to create a way of selecting MPs for their expertise. The government memorandum, and the European Scrutiny Committee, had suggested an overlap in membership of European standing committees with the respective departmental select committees. The Modernisation Committee report, however, refers to this option only in passing: 'The narrower focus would make it easier for the Committee of Selection to have proper regard to the qualifications of Members nominated to the Committees, perhaps facilitating some overlap with membership of the relevant select committee.'[12]

The reasons for this may lie in the anticipated resistance from the select committees and will be discussed further below.

Mainstreaming European affairs in Parliament

A more radical approach to improving the procedures for oversight of EU matters in the House of Commons would be what is generally described as 'mainstreaming'. This refers to proposals that European legislative proposals should not be dealt with and overseen by a specific 'European' committee, but instead by a committee with expertise in the specific policy area which the legislative proposal would affect.

There are different models under discussion on how this could be achieved. One is that the committee responsible for the specific policy area which an EU legislative proposal will affect would scrutinise such documents. For example European proposals concerning environmental legislation would be scrutinised by the Environment, Food and Rural Affairs Committee. The rationale behind this structure is that EU legislation which may have an impact on domestic legislation should be overseen by the same committee responsible for domestic legislation in the specific policy area.

Another advantage of such a mainstreamed procedure would be that proposals would be considered by a committee of MPs with the relevant expertise to make sense of the often highly technical nature of these documents. In order to cope with the increased workload, committees could be made larger (see page 193); and the larger committees could create sub-committees to deal specifically with EU matters. Already under the current procedures EU matters fall into the theoretical remit of departmental select committees, a remit they are not eager to fulfil.

A different variation of mainstreaming would be to create sub-committees of the European Scrutiny Committee specialising in different policy areas. The European Scrutiny Committee already has the power to create sub-committees, which it has chosen not to pursue. The Standing Orders would need to be changed for these sub-committees to perform the debating role currently undertaken in the European standing committees. There are concerns, however, that this structure would replicate work done by the House of Lords, whose EU Committee follows this structure of sub-committees.

In both cases the European Scrutiny Committee could, under 'mainstreaming', keep its current function of sifting documents.

However, instead of referring those it considers important to a European standing committee it would refer them either to the relevant departmental select committee, or to the appropriate sub-committee of the European Scrutiny Committee.

These mainstreaming options were mentioned in the government's memorandum to the Modernisation Committee, although seemingly as an afterthought after elaborating on the new joint committee. The Modernisation Committee's report only refers to these possibilities in passing. In particular it recommends that the European Scrutiny Committee should forward any early notice from the government on an EU proposal to the relevant select committee as a matter of routine. This procedure, however, seems to be already in operation, as during our study we were assured that EU documents with relevance for a specific departmental select committee are sent as a matter of information to those committees by the European Scrutiny Committee.

Both these models for mainstreaming EU affairs follow the radical approach of abolishing the European standing committees. A third watered-down model has also been discussed in an attempt to combine both approaches. This idea revolves around improving the links between the European standing committees and both the European Scrutiny Committee (to ensure the members of the European Standing Committee are well briefed about the reasons why a specific proposal is deemed important) and the relevant departmental select committee (to ensure their expertise feeds into the deliberation of relevant EU legislative proposals).

A further suggestion in the government's memorandum to the Modernisation Committee, which was, however, not taken up in the committee's report, was to provide members of the European standing committees with better background information on the documents under discussion in order to improve the quality of debate. Evidence heard during our study supported this proposal, but it does have resource implications. Currently the standing committees have no permanent staff attached to them. To provide better information to prepare for debates staff would be required. This could for example be provided by the Scrutiny Unit (see pages 49–50), or additional staff with a specific remit to deal with EU matters could be attached to the departmental select committees and shared with the European standing committees.

It is clear from the Modernisation Committee's proposals that they are aiming towards a more mainstreamed system of European parliamentary scrutiny, while avoiding radical change to present arrangements. However, as long as departmental select committees, or their members, do not get more closely involved in the process any scrutiny system will lack a major component. Although we heard a substantial amount of testimony calling for a thoroughgoing mainstreamed system of EU scrutiny in Parliament, the likelihood of such a system coming about must be low. Models of reform which envisage a fully mainstreamed approach face well-entrenched opposition from departmental select committees fearing an increase of their workload. This opposition is likely to be bolstered by continuing perceptions (to which we have already referred) of the marginal and unappealing nature of work on European scrutiny.

Mandating government ministers in European negotiations

Mainstreaming EU business is the norm in parliaments of many other EU member states. A notable example of this practice is Finland, which was visited by the Modernisation Committee as part of their inquiry.

Two features of the Finnish system stand out: the committee procedures for dealing with EU business and the 'mandating' system. In the Finnish Parliament, EU legislative proposals are first debated in the subject committees responsible for the policy area into which they fall. There is in addition a 'EU Grand Committee' on which all the subject committees are represented. This grand committee discusses with ministers the government's approach on a specific proposal, basing itself on the views of the parliamentary specialist committees.

The EU Grand Committee meets twice each week and discusses with the government the agenda for any forthcoming Council of Ministers meetings taking place the next week. Thus there is a regular and timely dialogue between government and Parliament in advance of EU meetings of all policy formations. Pre-Council scrutiny is in this way a regular and high-priority feature in the Finnish Parliament. The contrast could not be more striking with the UK Parliament, in which sectional Council meetings are in most cases only scrutinised post hoc by a written question by the chair of the European Scrutiny Committee, provoking frequently a bland and uninformative ministerial answer.

'Mandating' is the other remarkable feature of the way the Finnish Parliament oversees EU affairs. It is in the Nordic countries of the EU (Denmark, Finland and Sweden) that this practice of parliamentary oversight of EU affairs is most highly developed. Under this Scandinavian scrutiny system, the Parliament issues a specific mandate for negotiations to a government minister, which this minister is then supposed to pursue at the European level. Supporters see this procedure as an effective way of ensuring the accountability of the government to Parliament. However, there are two concerns regarding this process, one theoretical and one practical. As we point out in the Introduction, we understand oversight as Parliament examining and shaping government policies as they evolve, while at the same time recognising that parliaments do not govern; and elected government has both a proper and actual primacy in policy-making over a legislature (see page 2). Giving a strict mandate to a minister may therefore seem to go beyond a reasonable role for parliamentary oversight.

From a more practical point of view, a system of mandating could cause problems when a proposal being discussed develops and changes during the negotiations. It is part of the nature of membership of multilateral organisations that negotiations are a process in which compromises have to be struck between many differing interests – 25 governments in the case of the EU. 'Tying a minister's hands' with a mandate could make agreement – which is in the interest of all members – substantially more difficult.

There is evidence that some Scandinavian ministers during EU meetings feel themselves obliged to call the chairman of the relevant lead committee in their national Parliament to inform him or her of developments. However, the Finnish example does not necessarily take this strict form of mandating. Instead, it has been described to us as 'more sophisticated than simple mandating'. Based on a continued dialogue between government and Parliament, it gives Parliament the formal and regular opportunity to have its views heard and taken on board by the government. Changes to the negotiating stance are therefore possible during negotiations, but based on continuing discussions with Parliament at the time, and not only reported post hoc.

The example of Finland seems to have had a very positive resonance with some members of the Modernisation Committee, although the committee's report plays down the possibility for strict comparison with the UK Parliament. Of course the Finnish system has to be understood in the context of the Scandinavian political culture and tradition, which is based on coalition government and more consensual politics than is the case in the UK. However, the establishment of a more regular dialogue between Parliament and the government in tandem with the timetable of meetings of the EU Council of Ministers would indeed be possible – and highly desirable – in the UK Parliament. This dialogue could also attract more media and public interest in EU affairs. Greater involvement of departmental select committees – as is the case in Finland – would obviously be vital for this. Unfortunately, this is one area in which the recommendations of the Modernisation Committee's report fall short of the ideal.

Meeting in private

As outlined previously (see page 111) meetings of the European Scrutiny Committee take place in private. The Modernisation Committee suggests for the first time giving the European Scrutiny Committee the possibility on an experimental basis of opening its meetings to the public. As ever, there are concerns about going about its business publicly. For example, the committee could feel obliged to send more documents for debate than actually necessary, in order to create an appearance of appropriate rigour with the public. Scrutiny Committee members expressed to us the concern that the public would receive an unfairly negative impression of the way in which the committee operates – waving through the vast majority of documents on staff recommendation and only discussing a few. They also feared that serious debate in the committee could be compromised during public sessions in favour of 'political point-scoring'. This latter argument is supported by evidence from Finland, where the European Grand Committee meets in private and seems to believe that consensus would be more difficult to find if it changed this rule.

The Modernisation Committee's recommendation is for open meetings of the European Scrutiny Committee. It cannot be denied that this recommendation is in the political spirit of transparent and accountable governance, an issue particularly important when dealing with EU affairs.

Cooperation with the European Parliament and other national parliaments

The fact that there are two parliamentary bodies overseeing EU legislation and policies – the European Parliament and the UK Parliament – has often led to calls for closer cooperation between members of both Parliaments. These calls have given rise to a system of six-monthly meetings between MEPs and MPs and Lords on the EU-related committees in both Houses. These meetings are conducted as a structured discussion around specific issues, such as recently the 'Financial Perspective' for the future finances of the EU. They are generally perceived as worthwhile by participants. Greater contact between the two bodies is certainly to be welcomed. However, these meetings contribute at best indirectly to effective scrutiny procedures.

To achieve greater effectiveness, a more channelled approach would be necessary, bringing together MPs (and possibly peers) and MEPs working on the same individual proposals or issues. This latter proposal has been tried in joint parliamentary meetings between the European Parliament and national parliaments at committee level. Several European Parliament committees have invited members of the corresponding committees of national parliaments to joint meetings. However, the general perception of these initiatives is that there is too much suspicion, in particular from national MPs fearing their counterparts at the European Parliament as competitors or threats, for these initiatives to be effective. At the same time it is difficult for the European Parliament and national parliaments to find a common interest in a subject, as the EP's role as co-legislator gives it a distinctly different role from that of national parliaments.

There have been increasing calls recently for cooperation between the national parliaments of EU member states. This is particularly the case in the relation to the so-called subsidiarity early warning mechanism proposed under the now endangered EU Constitution. There is already an inter-parliamentary body of EU national parliaments, namely COSAC. Evidence suggests however, that the twice-yearly meetings of this body are generally not regarded as worthwhile and in particular not as a potentially effective tool for national parliamentary scrutiny of EU affairs.

The Interparliamentary Exchange System (IPEX), which was created by the Conference of Speakers of National Parliaments, may in the future turn into the tool to coordinate objections by national parliaments to a specific proposal on subsidiarity grounds, an area of responsibility which the proposed European Constitution sought to give to national parliaments. At present, exchanges between national parliaments on European issues tend to be coordinated on an informal basis by the national Parliament representatives in Brussels, although not all national Parliaments have yet decided to follow the route of representation in Brussels.

Producing 'mini-reports' in the House of Lords

Any reform discussion on the system of EU scrutiny tends to focus mainly on the House of Commons. This may not come as a surprise, the House of Commons being the main scrutinising chamber with the remit to hold government to account. At the same time there is (as described above) a broad consensus on the need for reform of the Commons system, while the reports by the House of Lords EU Committee and its sub-committees have an impressive standing.

Nevertheless, our study has identified the need for improvement in some areas. In order to ensure that reports can have an appropriate impact on the policy debate and the government's stance towards a specific issue, they need to be published well in advance of the actual decisions to be taken. However, this is not always the case, as in-depth inquiries can take several months to conclude. The long time spent on in-depth inquiries also means that the committee has to be very selective in the issues it considers.

One suggestion to remedy this weakness is for the House of Lords EU committees to take up producing 'mini-reports' (see also page 121). These would be short inquiries, possibly related to a specific document, which would take place in between or in addition to longer inquiries. These short inquiries would require far fewer evidence sessions than a full report (where twelve sessions would be the norm), and only produce a 'snapshot' of an issue, timed well in advance of the relevant decisions to be taken. This approach is already sometimes practised by Sub-committee C, which has produced four smaller reports, such as on the EU security strategy, in addition to their in-depth inquiry on the EU's strategy document on weapons of mass destruction. It would be useful for other committees to follow this route.

Coordinating Parliament's scrutiny of EU policy

Parliament's scrutiny of EU business could also be improved quite simply by the development of better cooperation between the two Houses in EU affairs. Currently, there is no formal contact between the committees in the two Houses, and even informally contact seems to take place only between the clerks. We were told several times during our study that the House of Lords undertakes the in-depth inquiries the House of Commons has not got enough time to do. But this is not a satisfactory arrangement as long as there is no joint understanding or agreement on what issues are of priority. Regular meetings between the committees, or even only the chairmen, discussing their views on the most pressing EU issues Parliament needs to address, could be a very helpful tool in ensuring that there are no gaps in parliamentary oversight of EU affairs. Currently, however, closer cooperation seems to be inhibited by issues of personality and a certain 'committee pride' to determine their own workload, which formal and regular procedures of exchange may be able to overcome.

The issue of reform of EU scrutiny in Parliament is not likely to be settled at this stage. It is very likely that the issues arising will re-emerge in future inquiries on the topic. Indeed, for the Commons, the Modernisation Committee report refers to the fact that 'the next Parliament also will wish to revisit some of the issues raised in this Report.' Reforms affecting the composition and powers of the Lords will naturally shape its approach to EU affairs. It is clear that there is far from a settled or unanimous opinion on these issues even among members of Parliament convinced of the need for reform. Any conclusions and recommendations must of their nature be contributions to a continuing debate rather than definitive blueprints for a clearly delineated future.

6

Britain's global dealings

British governments take part in decisions made on a global level by a large number of international organisations that reach into every part of domestic life in this country. These organisations determine everything from the rules that govern international telephone calls to the rules that govern global trade. Some of these bodies also have the ability to make international law which binds the UK government and determines UK policy. Given that these organisations do not only determine policies governing relations between states, but can also have a significant impact on the UK's domestic and foreign policy, it is important that Parliament should be able to maintain oversight of the government's participation in their deliberations. This important responsibility is made all the more difficult by the fact that the Foreign and Commonwealth Office does not hold a comprehensive list of international organisations of which the UK is a member.[1]

In this chapter, we consider current parliamentary arrangements for scrutiny of decisions taken at inter-governmental organisations. We do so by considering eight case studies of international organisations in which the UK plays a role, drawing comparisons between them and seeing what lessons may be learned. As we have seen, traditional constitutional doctrine holds that ministers are responsible to Parliament for the decisions they make. Thus the relevant ministers should be held to account by Parliament for decisions taken at international organisations. However, as we shall see, breakdowns and faults in process and practice mean decisions are being taken at international organisations with very little, if any, parliamentary oversight.

The World Bank and International Monetary Fund

The World Bank and International Monetary Fund are closely linked organisations. They were established at the Bretton Woods conference in 1944 to address financial issues at the end of the Second World War. They were originally conceived as mutual assistance organisations, with all members receiving assistance with postwar reconstruction and any balance of payment problems. The internal governance structure of the organisations reflects this original purpose.[2] The two organisations have separate roles and competencies – but their shared history also means that the two institutions have similar governance structures and accountability processes.

However, there are different processes within Parliament for keeping their policies and actions under scrutiny. Different lead agencies within Whitehall deal with them and practices and cultures of the relevant select committees differ. Each organisation will be considered in turn before we move on to the similarities between the accountability structures and the lessons that arise from them.

Governance of the World Bank

The World Bank is not a bank in the traditional sense of the word, nor does it act as a central bank for the world (that role is taken by the Bank for International Settlements – see below). Equally the World Bank is not a single entity; rather it is a group of five different organisations under the 'World Bank umbrella' with a mission to 'fight poverty and improve the living standards of people in the developing world'.

The five organisations under the World Bank umbrella are the International Bank for Reconstruction and Development (IBRD), the International Development Association (IDA), the International Finance Corporation (IFC), the Multilateral Investment Guarantee Agency (MIGA), and the International Centre for the Settlement of Investment Disputes (ICSID).[3] It is not necessary for a country to be a member of all five of these organisations and in fact many are not.

The UK, however, is a member of all five organisations. References to 'the World Bank' normally mean the IBRD and the IDA, the parts of the World Bank Group that provide the grants and low- or zero-interest loans to developing countries. They are the focus of its development activity and, in effect, they act in cooperation to form one institution. The IBRD in particular is often seen as 'the World Bank'.

Formally all powers of the World Bank are vested in the board of governors, the legal embodiment of the World Bank.[4] Each member country of the bank appoints a governor and an 'alternate governor' for terms of five years (though in reality they serve at the pleasure of the government that appoints them).[5] The governors are typically the development or finance minister of a country. As a body the board of governors meets in plenary session annually at 'autumn meetings' and the 'Development Committee', a joint committee of the World Bank and IMF, meets at 'spring meetings'. Other committees of governors meet at both the spring and autumn meetings (the autumn meetings are also known as 'annual meetings'). Votes by the governors are on the basis of 250 votes per country with an additional vote for each share of stock owned by the country. Votes are taken on a simple majority basis, but votes are rarely taken, the aim being a consensus.

The governors make the most politically sensitive decisions, while a board of executive directors runs the World Bank on a day-to-day basis. All the powers of the World Bank are formally vested in the governors, but the practical necessities of running a large international organisation require that many of these powers are delegated to the executive directors. The governors retain only the powers expressly prohibited from delegation under the Articles of Agreement of the bank. Thus the governors exercise the power (among other things) to admit members and determine the conditions of membership; to increase or decrease the authorised capital stock; to suspend members; to make arrangements to cooperate with other international organisations; and to suspend permanently the operations of the bank.[6]

The 24 executive directors responsible for the day-to-day business of the bank each represent either a country or a group of countries. The President of the World Bank chairs its meetings. The executive board meets at least twice a week and must consider both individual projects proposed by the president of the bank as well as organisational policy. The board also functions through five sub-committees.[7]

The allocation of executive directors is a matter of some controversy. Under the Articles of Agreement, five of them represent only one country each – the United States, Japan, Germany, France and the UK, the five largest shareholders in the Bank. They are appointed directly by the governments of those countries. Three other executive directors are elected by a constituency of one country (China, Russia and Saudi Arabia) and are not government appointees, and the remainder are elected by multi-country constituencies varying in size from four to twenty-six countries. Elections take place every two years at the annual meeting.

The share ownership of the countries that each executive director represents determines their voting power, but once again votes are rare. There is always an attempt to reach an agreement by consensus. Directors representing multi-member constituencies must agree the position between all the countries they represent, as they cannot split their votes. This rule limits the extent to which individual countries within a constituency can make their opinions known. The difficulty of one representative for a group of countries is easily seen when one considers that one executive director must represent the interests of both Australia and Cambodia.

The executive directors have a dual remit: they must represent the interests of the country or countries of the constituency that is their responsibility, but they are also collectively, and therefore individually, responsible for the World Bank as an organisation. When questioned about whether this dual function could lead to a conflict of interests the UK executive director, Tom Scholar, a Treasury official, argued that he could not envisage a situation where he would truly believe that something was in the best interests of the World Bank but contrary to UK policy.

The dominance of the major powers reflects the balance of power in the world, but it also means that the poorest countries in the world are vastly under-represented at the board level of the World Bank – the international institution set up to help them. Concern about the unequal balance of power is sharpened by the fact that the remit of the executive directors, who represent the most powerful and richest countries and who have the strongest voices on the board, is to represent the interests of these countries rather than the poorest countries that the bank has a mission to help.

The president is the administrative head of the World Bank. As a result of an informal agreement between Europe and the US, the President of the United States appoints the President of the World Bank, whilst Europe, effectively the European Union, appoints the President of the IMF. The nomination by President Bush of Paul Wolfowitz to head the World Bank has highlighted the illegitimacy of this arrangement. Wolfowitz, previously the US deputy defence secretary, is a prominent neo-liberal advocate of unilateral action by the US in pursuit of American interests. He was one of the moving forces in the drive towards 'regime change' in Iraq. There was naturally concern in the development community and elsewhere that Wolfowitz would shift the bank's policies towards the geopolitical aims of the US administration rather than focusing on poverty reduction (about which he apparently has no expertise).[8] But there is no process for a parliamentary hearing or vote on such a significant appointment in the UK, so no formal forum exists for the expression of these concerns.

The World Bank has recently begun to make an effort to engage directly with parliamentarians. Following the first World Bank conference with parliamentarians held in The Hague in May 2000, the Parliamentary Network on the World Bank was formed. This organisation is administered by the European vice-presidency of the World Bank and established itself as an independent organisation under French law in 2003. The network provides a forum for parliamentarians from around the world to come together and discuss issues relevant to the World Bank. Although it is formally independent, the fact that it is administered through, and funded by, the European vice-presidency of the World Bank, opens it to accusations of capture by the bank. However, it is still a relatively young organisation and there is much potential for a future expansion of its role to allow it to establish a reputation for independent thought and a democratic influence on the World Bank.

The bank has made other moves towards engaging directly with parliamentarians. For example there is a specific questioning facility for parliamentarians which allows both MPs and peers to submit questions directly to the World Bank for answer.

The UK and the World Bank

Responsibility for the World Bank lies with the Department for International Development, within its International Financial Institutions Department (IFID). IFID is based in London and liaises directly with the Office of the UK Executive Director (UKDEL)[9] in Washington on matters to be considered by the executive board. A weekly teleconference is held between the two offices and decisions are made through a process of mutual dialogue. The DFID also consults with the FCO and Treasury when deciding UK policy. The secretary of state, currently Hilary Benn, may be required to make a decision on the more controversial matters; papers are also regularly sent to his office for information. The staff of UKDEL are drawn from the DFID, the Treasury and the Bank of England in about equal proportions, but they have developed a distinct organisational perspective, which is perceived as being close to the World Bank 'house' position. The staff view is that the UK is traditionally seen as a constructive player in the World Bank, promoting progressive change without alienating those on the other side. Non-governmental organisations (NGOs) working in the area do not necessarily agree.

Benn sits on the board of governors and the alternative is the Chancellor of the Exchequer, currently Gordon Brown. Benn's positions at the bank's autumn meetings are determined though IFID in liaison with UKDEL. The international development secretary is formally appointed independently as governor, but his is also an ex officio position. It is therefore unclear to what extent the secretary of state is bound by the ministerial code and relevant UK law such as the International Development Act when sitting on World Bank committees.

As one of the five largest shareholders the UK has the right, under the Articles of Agreement, to appoint its own executive director to the World Bank. The UK executive director, currently Tom

Scholar, also serves as the executive director of the IMF. This 'double-hatting' is not unique, but it is not the normal arrangement. It certainly makes Scholar a most influential figure in development and aid policy.

Parliamentary oversight of the World Bank

The International Development Committee has over the past three years made radical innovations in oversight of UK activities at the World Bank. The committee now holds annual evidence sessions following the autumn meetings of the board of governors, at which the secretary of state gives evidence on the issues discussed at the meetings and answers questions on other World Bank topics. This annual system has proved to be a successful and effective conduit of information from the World Bank to Parliament and gives the committee a regular opportunity to emphasise policy areas that they think are important. It complements the traditional oral statement to Parliament that the secretary of state also makes following ministerial meetings.

However, this is a limited form of oversight because it is, by definition, ex post facto. The committee can exert political influence only by asking questions after the event and has no formal powers to mandate the position of the UK at the World Bank. (This is a common problem for all select committee oversight since the committees are confined to entirely post hoc analysis.)

Tony Baldry, chair of the International Development Committee, told us that 'the process of taking evidence is important in ensuring topics stay on the agenda.' His argument is that the mere existence of the evidence sessions on the World Bank meetings is an essential part of the oversight system as they focus public and political attention on the UK's activities at the World Bank. Thus, though the evidence sessions are after the meetings, ministers and officials must consider the committee's actual and potential position on issues since they know they will have to answer to it afterwards.

We raised the possibility of meeting before and after the autumn meetings with Baldry just before the 2005 election. This would allow for discussion of the issues before decisions are taken and would allow the committee the opportunity to give the minister guidance as to its position. An oral report after the meetings could then consider the various considerations that came to bear on actual decisions and would make possible broader and more informed discussion on UK strategy within the World Bank. Baldry dismissed this as being impractical due to the time constraints on the committee and the limited number of meetings that they then had each year, typically one formal session a week when Parliament was sitting.[10]

Baldry believed that the inquiries that the International Development Committee conducted were important and significantly added to the discussion in certain areas. However, he also noted that committees were better at considering the 'broad sweeps' of policy as they do not have the investigatory machinery for looking at the specifics. As such his, and other committees, are reliant on the Public Accounts Committee and the National Audit Office conducting inquiries, but their inquiries in the international field have been limited in the past. Although the NAO had indicated that it would be carrying out a report into DFID engagement with multilateral development institutions, this will be not a full 'value for money' report to Parliament but a smaller 'good governance' report directly to the DFID.[11]

The lack of institutional transparency at the World Bank also severely limits the degree of oversight that the committee can achieve. Strict anti-disclosure rules make it impossible for the committee to know what happened at meetings of the board of governors or the executive board. The disclosure rules of the World Bank have been relaxed to some extent in recent years, so it is now possible for an executive director to disclose whether he or she supported or opposed an issue discussed at a board meeting. Nonetheless much information still cannot be disclosed, including any formal record of the 'interventions' that are made at the executive board by the individual directors. These interventions are key policy documents that are drafted in advance by the offices of the executive directors on particular projects or internal policy decisions. Because most decisions are made by consensus and there is therefore rarely a formal vote on issues, it is these interventions that represent the formal position of the directors.

Collectively the interventions are the embodiment of decision-making at the World Bank – and are therefore of great importance for its oversight. Without disclosure of these interventions, the potential for effective oversight of this significant world institution is severely limited. It is essential that the UK Parliament and the International Development and other committees – as well as other Parliaments and their publics – have the basic information on the activities of their representatives at the World Bank in order to be able to conduct adequate oversight. Without this information, it is impossible for the International Development Committee independently to corroborate, for example, the effort ministers and officials make to push UK positions on institutional reform at the bank.

The recent Freedom of Information Act does give parliamentarians and NGOs the ability to seek information on the UK's part in bank affairs. But among the Act's many exemptions from disclosure (see Appendix A), Section 27 gives the secretary of state grounds for refusing to release information that might have an adverse effect on UK relations with international organisations. This limits the potential for the Act to provide an effective mechanism for the release of information on UK activities at the World Bank.

At the evidence session in November 2004, Hilary Benn, responding to a written submission to the committee from the Bretton Woods Project and questioning from committee member Hugh Bayley MP, agreed in principle to certain methods of improving transparency and accountability. He referred to his decision to publish an annual report to Parliament on the work of the DFID at the World Bank, and concurred with certain Bretton Woods Project proposals that there should be a debate in Parliament of the annual report, and that UK objectives for the spring and annual meetings of the IMF and the World Bank should be posted at least ten working days in advance of the meetings. The Bretton Woods Project also argued that the UK objectives should be scrutinised in advance of the meetings by the International Development Committee – though that was a matter for the committee itself. Benn said he agreed in principle with the Bretton Woods Project that it should be possible to release transcripts of UK interventions at the World Bank Board, but that he was prevented from doing so by the

World Bank's Articles of Agreement – which are incorporated into UK law. However, his officials were working hard to get the rules changed.[12]

The DFID published the first annual report on its activity at the World Bank in March 2005 (covering the 2003/4 financial year).[13] The importance of a detailed and analytical report to Parliament is recognised in the US. A 'staffer' to the Senate Foreign Relations Committee described the regular report produced by the US Treasury on activities at the World Bank as the 'transmission belt' of information from the World Bank and the US government to both parliamentarians and civil society.[14] An important role of Congress is getting information out to civil society so that people can use it in their campaigning and, in turn, lobby members of Congress on World Bank issues. Thus the report is important both for legislative oversight and the important role of interest groups within a pluralist system such as that in the UK or US.

A recent report on the reporting mechanisms in Canada by the Halifax Initiative, a Canadian NGO, also emphasised the importance of an adequate reporting structure for both Parliament and society as a whole.[15] Canada's situation is different from that of the UK as it is a member of a constituency and does not have its own executive director. However, the principles of reporting remain the same. The Halifax Initiative report called for all issues under consideration in a particular year to be 'characterised, contextualised and analysed' as well as for a 'comparative analysis of year-to-year changes in priorities, concerns and challenges'.

The first DFID report on the UK's activity in the World Bank fulfilled few of these objectives. At only 22 pages in total the report lacks detail and analytical thrust. Rarely does it lay out in clear terms the UK position on a particular issue, specific activities undertaken to achieve it and their results. Furthermore, considering it is a report to Parliament and therefore to non-experts, it presumes knowledge of specialist terms and the background to particular issues and so neglects to 'contextualise'. If the publication of future reports is to provide a basis for parliamentary activity on the World Bank, they will have to be greatly improved. Moreover, Parliament's role extends far beyond its own activities. Its work in the dissemination of information to the media, civil society and the wider public can be as important as conducting inquiries or asking questions for the oversight of the government's activities. Parliament has to gather, spread and recycle information and collaborate in its use with civil society. To do this effectively, parliamentarians must ensure that the government's reports are adequate, and this may include dictating their nature and detail.

The International Development Committee heard evidence from Gordon Brown, as Chancellor of the Exchequer, in its inquiries into the World Bank. We are privately informed that this came about as a result of the close relationship between Brown and Clare Short. However, Brown gave his evidence in November 2003 after the autumn meetings and after Short's resignation as international development secretary, and much of the focus at the session was on the proposed 'International Finance Facility', a personal initiative of Brown's. Whatever the truth of our private information, it is important that the committee should be able to take evidence from Brown. As chair of the Joint IMF–World Bank Development Committee, Brown has a great deal of influence on the bank's international development policy and as such there is a clear link with the remit of the International Development Committee. He did not appear before the committee for the 2004 or 2005 evidence session.

The committee also looks into issues relating to the World Bank and the IMF when it conducts inquiries into specific country developments. For example, during a recent visit to India collecting evidence for an inquiry, the committee heard about the lack of engagement with Parliament in the Poverty Reduction Strategy Paper Process – the mandated process by the World Bank through which a country engages with civil society to determine the specific priorities for poverty reduction.[16] Thus specific policies of the World Bank are considered as well as the autumn reviews of general policy.

The International Development Committee is anxious to raise the profile of development issues and to create a dialogue between government, Parliament and civil society. As noted in Chapter 3, Tony Baldry openly admitted that the committee thus far represented 'a conspiracy in Parliament of those concerned with development'. At the last committee evidence session on the World Bank the committee invited representatives of NGOs to respond directly to the evidence given by Hilary Benn. The committee would also like to go further in Parliament. Its members are concerned that the Commons fails to debate development issues and World Bank policies on the floor of the House. The committee and Benn have stated their intention to raise the World Bank further up the political agenda and push for debates on the floor of the House or in Westminster Hall.[17] Currently, the House has periodically to consent to statutory instruments replenishing funds for the IDA's future grant-making. But this opportunity to discuss World Bank affairs only infrequently involves a debate as most of the orders go through without debate.

Governance of the IMF

The IMF has a broader remit than the World Bank. The IMF was set up to provide short-term lending to counter balance-of-payment crises at the centre of a new international economic system managing fixed but adjustable exchange rates. The system of fixed exchange rates collapsed in the 1970s, but the IMF retained its role in assisting countries with short-term loans. Significantly it also retains a role in the monitoring and reporting on the exchange rate policies of member countries, which amounts to annual 'health checks' on their economies.[18]

The IMF has a board of governors and an executive board, like the World Bank. Departmental responsibility for the IMF lies with the Treasury. The Chancellor of the Exchequer is, therefore, the minister who represents the UK on the board of governors. As we noted above, Brown is also currently the chair of the Development Committee, which meets at the spring meetings of the bank and fund. This committee is the forum through which the World Bank and IMF coordinate development policy. As the chair of this committee, Brown has a great deal of power – yet it is unclear to whom he is accountable.

As with the various parts of the World Bank, voting at the IMF is determined not on the one-country-one-vote basis that is typical of international organisations, but by a quota system representing the participation of a country in the capital of the IMF. The quotas are based on a number of factors, the most significant of which is national income. The UK quota at the IMF on 31 March 2003 was about £9.2 billion, the sum the IMF can be called upon to provide by the government. It is a significant financial commitment.[19] As with the World Bank, its governing structures are open to the criticism that the richer countries exercise too much power at the expense of poor and developing nations.

The IMF's powers over nations

The potential impact of the IMF on Britain's domestic policy was dramatically demonstrated during the sterling crisis of 1976, when the IMF required a dramatic reduction in the public sector borrowing requirement as a condition of their support to the UK economy. More recently, an IMF report during the 2005 general election campaign suggested that there would be a need to address the 'fiscal gap' within the UK's finances. This directly impacted on the debate about taxation policies of all major parties that was of national attention due to the election campaign.

But the IMF's more continuous and significant power is over developing countries through the facility to provide short-term loans in times of financial crisis.[20] The IMF often attaches 'structural adjustment' conditions to these loans, requiring states to adopt neo-liberal economic policies such as privatisation of state-owned industries and liberalising trade – the so-called Washington consensus. This 'conditionality' has been highly controversial and is a feature of loans of the World Bank and the IMF, and is often more severe in the case of the IMF. This policy clearly has a significant impact on the economics and politics of borrowing countries. Such conditionality runs contrary to UK development policy. Therefore, the IMF is important to both UK domestic and international policy.

Current oversight

Just before the 2001 general election the Treasury Committee conducted an inquiry into the accountability of the IMF, focusing on the accountability to the UK Parliament.[21] The committee emphasised the importance of holding UK representatives at the IMF to account for their actions and considered how this might be achieved. Its members put information at the centre of account-ability, arguing:

> For Parliamentary accountability to be properly exercised the Treasury Committee – and our counterparts in other countries – needs to have access to a wide range of information on the activities of the Fund. In addition, it must be clear who has taken decisions about IMF policies and programmes and for what reasons.[22]

The committee had already asked the Treasury to publish reports on the UK and IMF and the Treasury has been doing so for five years. The 2001 report confirmed the importance of reports which detailed the UK positions on issues and particular actions taken by the UK. The Treasury reports on the IMF are far more detailed than the DFID reports on the World Bank. The most recent report concerns the financial year 2002/3,[23] details specific UK policy positions and analyses the broad direction of the IMF. However, there are still problems of coherence and transparency over Treasury objectives at the IMF. In December 2004, the Bretton Woods Project noted in its submission to the International Development Committee that the 'Treasury's work [with the IMF] is not guided by an institutional strategy paper (ISP). Without an ISP, the objectives of Treasury's work with the IMF remains [*sic*] unclear.'[24]

Importantly, the committee recognised the limits on the ability of one committee in the Parliament of one country to improve the accountability of the IMF and encouraged committees in other countries actively to hold their representatives to account.[25] The lines of responsibility mean that each country can only hold their own representatives to account against the priorities of the country. There is no forum for holding the entire organisation to account in a strategic manner.

Although the 2001 Treasury Committee report stated an intention to hold regular hearings with the UK executive director, this has not occurred. Nor does it systematically hear evidence from the

Chancellor of the Exchequer following the autumn meetings, as the International Development Committee does with its own minister. However, it has regularly considered important strategic issues in relation to the IMF – like its recent inquiry in the 2001/2 session on the IMF and globalisation.

The Chancellor of the Exchequer traditionally makes a written or oral statement to Parliament following the autumn meetings, although it may be in response to a question. The brief statements give basic, but limited, information and the Chancellor determines what they contain, in contrast with a formal report to Parliament, where it is more possible for the relevant committee to push for detail and information on specific subjects to be included.

The Commons rarely debates these issues. The most significant recent debate was an adjournment debate in Westminster Hall on the democratic oversight of the World Bank and IMF. This debate was instigated by a backbench MP following a civil society initiative. The debate was more concerned with the internal processes of the fund rather than the policies that it pursues. There has been not broad-ranging debate on the IMF since at least 1992.

Mandating in the United States

The contrast with the legislative oversight of multilateral organisations in the US is striking. There 'legislative mandates' direct the use of 'voice and vote' by US representatives at multilateral development banks (such as the World Bank). These mandates may concern the approval of specific projects. For example, the US executive director of the World Bank is obliged to abstain from any funding of a project in China unless it addresses 'basic human need'. Although decisions made at the board are normally consensual, it is recognised that the US representative must not give support to projects in such cases. The mandates may also address institutional direction and strategy – pushing, for example, for greater institutional transparency. The system of legislative mandates also provides a reporting structure for the US Treasury, as its reports to Congress must set out activities under each head of legislative mandate. Thus the US Treasury cannot simply avoid mentioning a specific issue. However, the heavy reporting burden has created its own problems as the department is simply overwhelmed with the requirements.[26]

Such legislative mandates are the result of a very different institutional structure in the US. The separation of powers and distinct power base of individual members of Congress makes the political parties less powerful and ensures that the policies of Congress and the executive do not always coincide. A powerful committee structure provides an alternative base for the formation of clear policies as well as oversight of the activities of the institutions. However, the US Treasury argues that too many legislative mandates limit its ability to enter into negotiations because of the numerous obligations to vote in a particular way.

The difficulties of parliamentary oversight

The World Bank and the IMF work closely together, but the Treasury and International Development committees pay little attention to their interaction and neglect the possibility of working together. Yet the same civil servant acts as executive director of both organisations and the Chancellor of the Exchequer chairs the important Joint Development Committee at the World Bank and IMF.

The appearance of Gordon Brown at the International Development Committee was a significant sign of the recognition of the inter-connectedness of the Treasury and the DFID in making Britain's international development policy. But the fact that it was probably an ad hoc arrangement that came about through his friendship with Clare Short is a cause for concern. It shows up the limited access and remit of the select committees. Their oversight fails to reflect the reality of the cross-cutting nature of the work of international organisations, as Whitehall and the bureaucratic processes do.

It has been suggested that the International Development Committee is vulnerable to 'capture' by the DFID and may therefore fail to achieve the objective stance that is needed for effective oversight. However, Tony Baldry, the committee chair, rejects this criticism, arguing that the DFID is just a good department and if they were not 'coming up to scratch', the committee would say so.[27]

The two committees have made some progress on the oversight of the World Bank and IMF and are beginning to establish a pattern and structure for thorough scrutiny of international organisations. However, the anti-disclosure rules of the two organisations prevents them gaining the information they need to achieve a proper level of oversight. As for the information that is available domestically, the Treasury Committee fails to take regular evidence and the IDC does not receive adequate departmental reports.

It will always be possible for these international organisations to make decisions that Britain does not agree with. The UK does not hold enough shares to veto a decision and does not provide enough money to enforce change through leverage over resources (as the US does). What is important is that the UK Parliament ensures as far as possible that decisions are made in line with UK law and policy and that British representatives are held to account for their actions at the bank and the fund.

Bank for International Settlements

The Bank for International Settlements (BIS) is an international organisation with 45 members, incorporated as such in 1930 under the Hague Agreements.[28] BIS was originally established for the administration and distribution of the reparations payable by Germany following the end of the First World War. Its members are not states but rather the central banks responsible for financial stability, so it is the Bank of England, not the Treasury, that is the UK member of BIS. Because of the nature of its membership BIS has developed into a forum for cooperation between central banks that promotes discussion and facilitates decision-making processes among central banks and within the financial and supervisory community. The functions of BIS are now two-fold: firstly to provide institutional support for the promotion of greater international monetary and financial stability; and secondly to act as a bank to central banks and other international organisations.[29]

Acting as a central bank for central banks is an important role within the international economic system. However, it is the promotion of international monetary and financial stability that is the source of BIS's influence. BIS carries out this function both through a series of separate bi-monthly meetings that bring together the staff of central banks who are working on particular issues, and through its support of other groupings of financial authorities such as the G10 committees.[30] The G10 forms powerful committees that produce important financial standards and codes which are then propagated under the auspices of BIS.[31] Thus BIS administers 'internal' and 'external' committees that establish international financial standards, and has both a formal and an informal role in establishing the international financial structures upon which the modern economic system is based.

Gordon Brown said of the financial standards and codes emerging from BIS through the G10: '[they are] not incidental to the financial architecture for the new global economy; they are the financial architecture for the new global economy.'[32] As such it is clear that the bank has an important international role that can have a significant impact on the finances of individual countries, both within and without the organisation. In the production of these financial codes and in holding large reserves of international capital BIS influences global financial markets through the use of its large amount of capital and its key role in determining the rules by which this capital is used.

The UK's role in BIS

The UK is one of six countries that has an ex officio director of BIS, the others being Belgium, France, Germany, Italy and the US. There are a further fifteen seats on the board. The ex officio nations are typically represented on the board by the governors of their central banks, with Mervyn King, the Governor of the Bank of England, formally the UK representative. In practice others do the day-to-day work and one or more 'alternates' do the work and represent the Bank of England at meetings of the BIS board of directors. The board of directors has responsibility for the administration of BIS and meets at least six times a year.

Membership of the bank is through a share issue, with the UK holding 5,000 shares, representing a stake in the organisation of almost 9 per cent. The latest annual report from the Bank of England gives the balance sheet investment of £2 million a true value of £256 million, representing almost half of the non-sterling securities that the Bank of England holds.[33] The management decisions made at BIS, therefore, have the potential to have a significant impact on the finances of the UK.

Confusion in responsibility and oversight

It is the Bank of England, an executive non-departmental public body, that is a member of BIS, not the UK as a 'state'. This distinction creates some confusion in the line of accountability to Parliament for work at BIS. Departmental responsibility for BIS falls within the scope of the Treasury, but the Bank of England's independent status has made the position less clear. In March 2003 Ruth Kelly, then Financial Secretary at the Treasury, said in answer to the only parliamentary question[34] on BIS in the last ten years: 'The Treasury has no formal responsibilities with respect to the governance of the Bank for International Settlements. The membership is comprised mainly of Central Banks. The Bank of England is a shareholder and the Governor of the Bank of England is on the Board of the BIS.'[35]

Under the curious logic of the doctrine of ministerial responsibility no Treasury minister will answer a question on matters concerning BIS. There is therefore a block to one of the three traditional methods of oversight in the UK Parliament: debates, the asking of questions and select committees.

For select committee oversight the relationship is more simple, as the remit of the Treasury Committee as defined by the House of Commons is to 'examine the expenditure, administration and policy of HM Treasury, the Board of the Inland Revenue, the Board of HM Customs and Excise, and associated public bodies, including the Bank of England and the Financial Services Authority'.[36] Thus the Treasury Committee clearly has responsibility for the Bank of England and therefore the work of BIS, even if the Treasury does not. Although the responsibility for oversight is clearer, the reality is that the committee has not carried out any inquiries into the work of

BIS, not even when taking evidence on it from the Governor of the Bank of England on the work when he has appeared before the committee to discuss broader questions. Ministerial unwillingness to answer questions in Parliament may also have ramifications for select committee oversight, as the same logic would also apply to ministers giving evidence to a select committee as stops ministers answering parliamentary questions. The committee could call other witnesses, including the Governor of the Bank of England, if it held an inquiry. But who could and should it hold to account if particularly significant issues arose? Would the appropriate minister agree to be answerable?

The Bank's annual reports are tabled in Parliament, but there is very little other parliamentary oversight. There has been only one question in the past ten years relating at all to BIS or its work, and no debates. There have been no questions on the substance of the financial standards coming out of BIS, or interest in its role as a bank with large amounts of reserves upon which it can call. The reports that are received by Parliament are institutional reports, not UK-focused reports on the work of the Bank of England within BIS. Bank of England reports to Parliament give BIS only cursory mention. Occasionally, the Chancellor of the Exchequer may refer to work of the G10 in statements to Parliament following the autumn meetings of the IMF. For example in October 1996, Kenneth Clarke, the then Chancellor, said in response to a written PQ:

> The G10 discussed issues relating to international monetary and financial stability. We welcomed the progress that has been made towards the establishment of the new arrangements to borrow. I emphasised the benefits these arrangements would bring, not only through increasing the resources available to the IMF in the case of a threat to the stability of the international monetary system, but also in involving in the facility a wider range of countries including some of the emerging market economies, recognising their interest in the stability of the international financial system.[37]

Similarly in November 1997 Gordon Brown, as Chancellor, again in response to a written PQ, said:

The G10 meeting welcomed the broad endorsement given to the concerted strategy to promote financial stability in emerging market economies that has been developed in collaboration with representatives of these economies. The finalisation of the Basle core principles of effective banking supervision was welcomed and the importance of their endorsement and implementation by national authorities was stressed.[38]

It is worth noting that these statements refer solely to the work of the G10 and not the other aspects of the work of BIS; they were made only in response to a specific question; and they arose within the context of the IMF autumn meetings rather than being part of parliamentary scrutiny of the Bank and the G10.

The gap in oversight

The lack of clear lines of responsibility in the relationship between the Treasury and the Bank of England has created a gap in the oversight structure. Although it is clear that the Treasury Committee is responsible for the work of the Bank of England, Treasury ministers take the position that they are not as such responsible for the bank's policies or the UK activities within it. Thus though Treasury officials play a significant role in its affairs, no minister will accept responsibility for their work in Parliament and the chain of responsibility between the executive and Parliament is broken. Yet the ability of Parliament to hold a minister to account is the cornerstone of executive–parliamentary relations under the doctrine of ministerial responsibility. This break in accountability and a notable lack of reporting to Parliament is compounded by the lack of interest in the activities of BIS among MPs and peers. Thus there is little pressure from Parliament to ensure that adequate accountability structures are put in place.

This is not an isolated case. British representatives play important roles in numerous international organisations with a remit that can and does have a significant impact around the world and in the UK. However, there is little parliamentary awareness of them or their work and their accountability to Parliament is dubious at best.

Examples include the European Investment Bank, which has a remit to 'contribute towards the integration, balanced development and economic and social cohesion of the Member Countries'; the Codex Alimentarius Commission, which is responsible for the international coordination of international food standards; and the World Intellectual Property Organization, a specialised agency of the United Nations, which promotes the protection of intellectual property rights throughout the world, including medicine patents.

There is a need for Parliament to ensure that there is a comprehensive and systematic structure of scrutiny in Parliament for the oversight of all international organisations of which the UK government or other public body is a member. It could make a start by obliging the FCO to draw up a full list of the international organisations of which the UK is a formal member.

G7 and G8

The G8 has progressed from being an ad hoc and informal meeting to become a highly powerful grouping that sets the global agenda. Tony Blair has signalled its potential by seeking to use the UK presidency of the G8 to relieve poverty in Africa and to reduce global warming. (The influence of this G8 focus in 2005 is clearly demonstrated by the fact that this year's World Economic Forum has also chosen these two subjects as the key themes.[39]) The then French President Valéry Giscard d'Estaing originally brought together the G6 – France, Germany, Italy, Japan, the UK and the US – informally at Rambouillet, France, in November 1975. Canada joined the meeting in 1976 to form the G7 at that year's summit. Russia joined the political summits in 1991 to form the G8 and is to take the presidency in 2006. The EU has been represented at the G8 since 1994 by the president of the European Commission and the leader of the country holding the EU presidency.

The G8 functions through a series of subject-specific meetings throughout the year, with one heads-of-government meeting providing the focus for the year's activities, which it is expected will bring about progress on the key theme chosen by the country that holds the presidency. The subject-specific meetings bring together environment and development ministers, justice and interior ministers, and labour ministers. Each of these meetings is chaired by the relevant minister of the country that holds the presidency.

The G7 is the equivalent group for finance ministers (Russia is still excluded). Their meetings truly set the long-term agenda for the international financial institutions (IFIs) and other international economic policy. The G7 finance ministers meet regularly before the autumn and spring meetings of the World Bank and the IMF. Government ministers refer to these G7 meetings in replies to parliamentary questions concerning the IMF annual meetings.[40] The influence of the G7 within the IFIs is also recognised in the Treasury annual reports on the work of the IMF, which regularly refer to the G7. For example, the 2003 Treasury report described the G7 as a 'valuable forum for the UK, allowing for high-level discussion among leading economies'.[41]

The G7's influence was recently seen when Gordon Brown used the G7 meeting in February 2005 to garner support for the International Finance Facility (which lies within the remit of the IFIs).[42] Similarly, following the Boxing Day tsunami, it was the G7 finance ministers who announced a freeze on the debt repayments from the countries affected ahead of a meeting of the Paris Club of creditor countries. In doing so the G7 demonstrated its power over the financial affairs of other countries and as determinant of global financial policy.[43]

Although the UK government has focused the agenda for 2005 on international development, the focus of the G8 for a particular year is within the discretion of the presidency of the G8. In past years summits have focused on, for example, global non-proliferation and conflict prevention (2004) or the 'global information society' (2000). The themes are inevitably issues that require international action.

As informal gatherings with a rotating presidency, the G8 has no permanent secretariat. Instead 'sherpas' meet roughly every two months to coordinate its activities. The sherpas represent the political leadership in each country and negotiate the agenda in advance of the meetings. Britain, as the current president of the G8, has already made arrangements within the Civil Service to establish a Cabinet

Office group to follow up on the G8 and Africa Commission priorities. Large numbers of staff in the relevant departments are also working on G8 issues.

Parliamentary oversight of the G8

The current parliamentary system of oversight has only limited purchase on the activities of the G8, as its cross-cutting nature, shifting priorities and subject-specific meetings cross over the strict departmental boundaries of the individual select committees. No one select committee has a remit that takes in the G8's manifold activities, though as the FCO takes the lead for the G8 in Whitehall, the Foreign Affairs Committee has the formal parliamentary responsibility for oversight. Within government the Prime Minister's significant interest in the G8 has been reflected in his questioning on the UK G8 priorities by the Liaison Committee.[44] However, because there is no 'Prime Minister's Department' within Whitehall, by extension no select committee exists with the remit to oversee his activities. Moreover, this kind of international interaction is classic prerogative territory in which the Prime Minister and colleagues move beyond parliamentary scrutiny (see page 14).

The UK priorities for the presidency of the G8 were announced to Parliament as part of an oral statement on the Sea Island summit in the USA. With regard to the priority of Africa the Prime Minister said:

> A major part of the agenda for our G8 Summit next year will be the work of the Commission for Africa that we have established. The Commission will report back next spring with a series of agreed recommendations for action. We will then work with the rest of the G8 to take them forward.[45]

With regard to the focus on climate change the Prime minister stated: 'The other major part of the agenda for the UK presidency of the G8 in 2005 will be climate change. We need to make progress with ratification of Kyoto; but we also need to look beyond Kyoto and its 2012 timeframe.'[46]

Tony Blair's statement on the government's G8 priorities was followed by a poorly attended debate in Westminster Hall. There have been a few questions with the usual limitations on the process. Questions on policy discussed at the G8 or G7 were answered in the House of Commons by seven government ministers as well as the Prime Minister in the 2001–2005 parliamentary session.

Analysis

The Prime Minister and government play a major role in this significant inter-governmental forum. The G8 has great influence in global policies, but the royal prerogative and the ad hoc and cross-cutting nature of its activity mean that there is almost zero oversight of the UK role in this forum. The current select committee system in Parliament needs to adjust to the growing reality of such ad hoc groups and events. The G8 is not the only important group of this kind. Other ad hoc groups that have an important influence on the global agenda include the World Trade Organization 'quad' of the EU, the US, Canada and Japan which essentially leads the WTO (as, for example, on the Russian accession talks). There have also been talks about the creation of an informal US–European foreign policy strategy group, involving the US, the UK, France, Germany, Italy and Poland.[47] It is likely that such groups will continue to form within the sphere of international relations; and there are others such as the G77 and the informal 'democracy caucus' within the UN General Assembly that do not include the UK at the moment.

The Liaison Committee questions the Prime Minister on his activities within the G8, but five minutes of questioning at twice-yearly evidence sessions is not the same as a committee that can conduct full inquiries. Bodies such as the G8 are big players in the global policy agenda and it is important that the government is held to account for its activities within them. It is not only a question of parliamentary process, however; the role of the royal prerogative is in urgent need of reform (see page 15).

The United Nations

The United Nations is the major international forum for global affairs and relations. It is a highly hierarchical and complex organisation with a large number of independent specialised agencies. The UN's prime task is the promotion of international peace and security, but these UN agencies also provide forums for international action on a wide variety of issues under the UN mandate to 'achieve international cooperation in solving international problems of an economic, social, cultural or humanitarian character'.[48] The UN was established by an international treaty – the UN Charter – signed in 1945 following an international conference in San Francisco. However, most countries that are now members of the UN were not present at the San Francisco conference and joined after 1945.

The UN functions though six organs which are at the top of the organisational structure: the General Assembly, the Security Council, the Economic and Social Council, the Trusteeship Council, the Secretariat and the International Court of Justice (ICJ) at The Hague (see page 10).[49] The other five organs are based at the UN headquarters in New York. Each of these organs has the ability to create subsidiary organs. Only the ICJ and the Trusteeship Council (which is currently suspended) have no subsidiary organs at all. The Secretariat is responsible for carrying out the work of the UN under directions from the General Assembly. The Secretariat is headed by the Secretary-General of the UN, currently Kofi Annan, a powerful political position which can have significant impact on the shape of the UN as a whole.

All member countries have a seat and equal vote on the General Assembly, which acts as the 'Parliament of States'. The other three councils have a limited membership, but Britain is currently a member of all three. Britain also has one of the five permanent seats on the Security Council, the most important political organ of the UN. Britain is the only permanent member to accept the compulsory jurisdiction of the ICJ. (The impact of this on UK foreign policy is unclear, and the decision was one of policy rather than of law.)

The UN Security Council reflects the geopolitical reality of international relations in 1945 and France, the US, China and Russia are the four other permanent members. The five nations with permanent representation on the Security Council have the right to veto any council resolution that is non-procedural. There are also ten non-permanent members, who are elected for a two-year term by the General Assembly through informal constituencies. As we have seen (page 8), the Security Council has a unique role in international law with regard to intervention in any state. Its remit is to make recommendations 'on the peaceful settlement of disputes' and to take 'enforcement action to deal with threats to the peace, breaches of the peace and acts of aggression'.[50]

Under Article 25 of the UN Charter, all members of the UN agree to 'accept and carry out' the decisions of the Security Council. Thus the Security Council has the power to make binding decisions which create an obligation under international law. However, it is not the rule of law that prevails at the Security Council,[51] rather the 'rule of high politics'. Though the permanent members were all on the winning side of the Second World War, they have rarely all been on the same 'side' since. From the Cold War between west and east, war in Korea and clashes between the US and the communist China to the recent tensions between the US and Britain and France over the war in Iraq, key decisions at the Security Council are often highly divisive.

Oversight of Britain's role in the UN

The FCO is the UK lead department on the UN. Britain is represented at the UN by a permanent mission, similar to missions to individual countries and the EU. The mission is based in New York, but the UK also has a separate mission to the UN bodies that are based in Geneva. The head of the mission has the rank of ambassador and is currently Sir Emyr Jones Parry.

In 2003 the FCO undertook to produce an annual report on Britain's role in the UN. The first of these was published in September 2003,[52] the second in October 2004.[53] These reports represent the first regular formal reporting of activities at the UN to Parliament, but they have not included a great deal of detail or indeed any note of UK policy. For example, the 2003 report covered the General Assembly in two paragraphs:

73. The General Assembly is the main deliberative organ of the United Nations. It is composed of representatives of all 191 member states, each of which has one vote. The work of the United Nations derives largely from the decisions of the General Assembly.

74. The General Assembly's regular session is held from September to December each year. All discussion on economic and social issues take place in the Second (Economic and Financial Committee) and Third Committees (Social, Humanitarian and Cultural Committee).

The 2004 report did discuss the General Assembly in greater detail, but mostly in the context of proposed reforms rather than the activities and positions of the UK at the assembly over the year. There was some improvement on the previous year with a statement of the UK priorities at the General Assembly.

Jack Straw, the Foreign Secretary, has undertaken to ensure that there is an annual debate in Parliament, aimed to coincide with the preparation for the autumn General Assembly meeting. The 2003 and 2004 debates met this target. But it is unclear whether future debates will, as the two-week return of Parliament during September is under review and seems unlikely to continue. Thus there is less chance that Parliament will be able to discuss UK policy at the UN in time for the meeting of the General Assembly. It is not enough that there be a debate. That debate must have a purpose and should provide at least 'soft mandates' for Britain's policy. It would also be better for the debates to take place on the floor of the Commons rather than in Westminster Hall (where the last two debates took place). The demotion of the UN to the secondary chamber of Parliament is symbolically significant.

Prior to these debates on the UN, there were very limited opportunities for discussion of UK strategic policy towards the UN within Parliament. One major debate on the UN happened whilst the House of Commons was waiting for 'messages from the Lords' and therefore was only able to occur as a result of a fluke of parliamentary procedure. Since 1992 there have been only eight debates in the House of Commons on the UN as a whole. Of these debates, five have been in Westminster Hall. But although debates are still limited and determined by the government, it is the case that there are more opportunities for debates on the UN than previously.

There are also debates on specific issues that are relevant to the UN, but these have often been adjournment debates that depend on a backbencher selecting the topic and being drawn out of the hat. These debates have only a very limited time and few MPs are able to speak. The House of Commons held only one debate on the Rwandan genocide while it was taking place and that was an adjournment debate. More recently the genocide in Darfur attracted more parliamentary attention. The government ensured that there were statements to the House on the developing situation and gave MPs and peers opportunities to discuss the issues. However it was the government that determined the different amount dedicated to the two humanitarian crises, through its control of parliamentary business. Thus the oversight of particular government policies at the UN depends on its willingness to allow time for debate.

The FAC has paid little attention to the United Nations, despite its clear, possibly primary, importance for international relations. In fact the last time that the FAC conducted an inquiry into the UN was in the 1992–93 parliamentary session.[54] There has been more focus on specific issues that relate to the UN, with the International Development Committee regularly referring to the work of the UN in various situations – recently looking into the UN response to the situation in Darfur and the possible failings of the UN Security Council in protecting the people of Darfur.[55]

American oversight of the UN

As with the international financial institutions, the US Congress has taken an interventionist position with respect to US policy at the UN, primarily through the use of legislative mandates on the appropriation of the UN assessed contributions. Although these contributions are determined at the international level Congress has, in the past, required the US Treasury to not pay the full amount of contributions and thereby gained significant political leverage over the UN. Some in Congress would characterise this as merely the US 'paying what it ought to pay' and exerting its national right to determine budget expenditure. Although this raised questions of propriety in using the 'power of the purse', and the power rested on the fact that the US is the largest contributor to the UN, it did prove to be an effective method.

There is, however, a second significant way in which Congress can exert legislative oversight of US foreign policy in general as well as at the UN. The President must secure the approval of the Senate for his nominations for ambassadors, including the US ambassador to the UN, under the principle of 'advise and consent'. The effect of this power was recently seen with the controversial nomination of John Bolton by George W. Bush to be the ambassador to the UN. Prior to his nomination Bolton had made a number of disparaging comments about the UN, including the comment that if the UN Tower in New York 'lost ten storeys today, it wouldn't make a bit of difference'.[56]

Normally, for a successful nomination the Senate Foreign Relations Committee must first vote and approve the nomination before it is passed to a plenary session of the Senate. In a number of evidence sessions the committee heard from both Bolton and a number of individuals who made specific accusations against him. The committee was able to consider a wide range of relevant information as to the fitness of the nomination. Numerous delays in the vote on Bolton by the Foreign Relations Committee acted to further raise the profile of the nomination and during the delays the *Los Angeles Times* called for Bolton to step aside from the nomination.[57] This triggered a debate on US policy towards the UN in the media. The Senate Foreign Relations Committee failed to approve the nomination, but contrary to normal procedure it passed to the floor for a vote of the full Senate. After a number of attempts to break the filibuster on the floor of the Senate, President Bush controversially appointed Bolton as ambassador during the Congressional recess, circumventing the normal process.

In exercising their right to oversee and approve the nominations process the Senate Foreign Relations Committee was able to consider the suitability of the proposed candidate for the role, and by extension what characteristics a candidate should have. Because executive appointees exercise much power at multilateral organisations, oversight of the appointments processes allows oversight of the policy. The Foreign Relations Committee also raised the profile of policy-making at the UN and in doing so interacted with the 'softer' forms of oversight that exist through the media and civil society, acting as a conduit for pluralist involvement in the issues. The power of veto that the doctrine 'advise and consent' gives to the US Congress is almost certainly too strong meat for British political traditions, but the ideal of an apolitical diplomatic corps has already been breached, especially by overt political appointments, such as that of Lord Levy as a freewheeling envoy in the Middle East. Some form of parliamentary vetting of appointments across the range of appointees ought to be considered (see page 189).

Oversight of UN a basic duty

The United Nations holds a significant, but contested, global position in the maintenance of peace and world order as well as in major issues such as world health, development and the alleviation of poverty. Britain plays an important and in some respects a central role in its politics as a permanent member of the Security Council, a large contributor to its funding, America's most prominent ally and a member of the EU. Yet there is scarcely any parliamentary oversight of Britain's policies and activities at the United Nations. This is the case even at a time when the future of the UN has been the subject of much international debate and controversy. It is our view that Parliament should cover the basics in its oversight of public policy, and Britain's part on the Security Council and in other UN forums is one of the most fundamental basics in the modern world.

Various government departments deal with different UN organisations. The FCO has, as we have noted, the lead role, but for example the Department for International Development deals with the specialist agency on development – the United Nations Development Programme – whilst DEFRA's concerns embrace UN activities such as the United Nations Environment Programme. These bureaucratic divisions within the UN and national governments can result in a lack of cohesion on international issues, with different priorities being promoted by different government departments and UN agencies. With the agreement on the Millennium Development Goals the UN is going through an international process of promoting 'coherence, coordination, convergence and cooperation' between the agencies. So should the British government and Parliament. Parliament must take a strategic overview of policy priorities and ensure that government departments coordinate their dealings with the UN and its agencies.

NATO

The United Kingdom is a central player in the North Atlantic Treaty Organisation (NATO), both in its own right and as an aspect of the Special Relationship with the US (see Chapter 3). The North Atlantic Treaty of 4 April 1949 was born of mounting concern in the west about the Soviet Union's military and political intentions in Europe, provoked by the recent communist seizure of power in Czechoslovakia and by the Russian blockade of West Berlin. The treaty founded NATO as a military alliance, primarily binding the US into the protection of western Europe, though its signatories committed themselves to a wider strategy (in Article 3) to 'maintain and develop their individual and collective capacity to resist armed attack'.

Following a significant expansion of membership at the end of the Cold War, with former Eastern Bloc countries joining the alliance, there are now 26 members of the alliance.[58] Each member state sends a permanent diplomatic delegation to Brussels which houses the headquarters of NATO. The NATO Council of permanent delegations meets at least once a week and has effective control of NATO policy decisions. The council also meets at higher levels – of either foreign ministers, defence ministers or heads of government – where major decisions are made. All decisions have the same status at whatever level they are made. Decisions are made through unanimity and there is no scope for a majority decision by the alliance's council. The council is chaired by the Secretary General of NATO, currently Jaap de Hoop Scheffer of the Netherlands. It works through a number of sub-committees, the most important of which are chaired by the Secretary General.

Article 5 of the North Atlantic Treaty states:

> The parties agree that an armed attack against one or more of them in Europe or North America shall be considered an attack against them all and consequently they agree that, if such an armed attack occurs, each of them, in exercise of the right of individual or collective self-defence recognised by Article 51 of the Charter of the United Nations, will assist the Party or Parties so attacked by taking forthwith, individually and in concert with the other Parties, such action as it deems necessary, including the use of armed force, to restore and maintain the security of the North Atlantic area.

Though it was the cold war which provided NATO's original *raison d'être*, the 'one for all and all for one' commitment of the NATO allies was not triggered until after the collapse of the Soviet Union. After the Al-Qaeda suicide attacks in the US on 11 September 2001, NATO allies rallied to the US and joined in the US-led invasion of Afghanistan to remove the Taliban regime, which harboured Osama bin Laden and his terrorist structures.

However, this was not the first time that NATO had launched a military operation. The first military action was taken by NATO after the collapse of the Soviet Union with the shooting down of Bosnian Serb aircraft violating the UN no-fly zone in 1994. Later, in 1999, NATO become involved in Kosovo, its first full-scale military conflict. However, it was the attacks on 11 September 2001 that precipitated the first invocation of Article 5.

Britain's part in NATO has been an unquestioned and bipartisan centrepiece of the UK defence strategy since it was founded. Since the US has been the dominant power within the alliance throughout its existence, NATO became yet another aspect of the Special Relationship. The Labour left's drive for unilateral nuclear disarmament, to which the 1960 Labour Party conference briefly committed the party, disturbed the party's commitment to NATO until the mid-1980s, but not that of the party's leaders. They were always resolutely Atlanticist (though in opposition they were often obliged to trim their position, as for example the young Tony Blair did).

Article 5 and other parts of the North Atlantic Treaty cede an important part of national sovereignty to a multinational body. Indeed, the treaty stipulates that parties to it could only leave 'after the Treaty has been in force for twenty years' and then 'one year after its notice of denunciation has been given to the Government of the United States of America', with which all instruments of ratification are deposited.

There is a NATO Parliamentary Assembly, comprising parliamentarians from the member states. Its website describes its primary objective as 'to foster mutual understanding among Alliance parliamentarians of the key security challenges facing the transatlantic partnership'. It does not hold the council formally to account, though the Secretary General responds to its recommendations. One of its lesser aims is 'to provide greater transparency of NATO policies, and thereby a degree of collective accountability'. This vaguely worded statement does not amount to a proclamation of either openness or accountability principles, let alone practice.

Donald (now Lord) Anderson was a member of this assembly as well as being chair of the FAC before he retired as an MP in 2005. He told us that just as the FAC lacked formal power and could only hold the UK government accountable through seeking to influence and encourage, the same applied to the Parliamentary Assembly with respect to NATO. There is no formal procedure for members of the assembly to report back to Parliament on their activities, though Anderson says that it informed their work in a variety of ways.

If the objectives of NATO change, as they have since the Cold War, it is difficult for Parliament to oversee the process. Far-reaching and radical changes of purpose can be agreed between the heads of state, beyond the reach of national Parliaments. The huge change in direction after the ending of the Cold War is a case in point. NATO governments agreed 'The Alliance's Strategic Concept' of April 1999, noting that 'the dangers of the Cold War have given way to more promising, but also challenging prospects, to new opportunities and risks . . . including oppression, ethnic conflict, economic distress, the collapse of political order, and the proliferation of weapons of mass destruction.' They also affirmed that 'the Alliance embodies the transatlantic link by which the security of North America is *permanently tied* to the security of Europe' (emphasis added).

The EU's burgeoning interest in expanding its role in defence and foreign affairs since the end of the Cold War has alarmed the US for they see such interest in a separate EU military force as a threat to NATO and, by extension, to their power base within the alliance. Blair's shuttle diplomacy between the key EU powers and Washington, being at the same time interested in a European military role and anxious not to offend the US, belongs of course firmly in the sphere of the royal prerogative and bilateral negotiation – and so beyond full parliamentary accountability. The Defence, Foreign Affairs and European Scrutiny committees have, however, all taken an interest in the implications of an EU defence policy.[59]

The UK Parliament is in an exceptionally weak position for oversight of NATO since it has no formal role in treaty ratification. Article 10 states: 'The Parties may, by unanimous agreement, invite any other European State . . . to accede to this Treaty.' At the Madrid summit in July 1997, the Czech Republic, Hungary and Poland were invited to join NATO. The agreement, which considerably increased the population and territory of NATO member states, and expanded its borders with non-NATO countries by nearly a third, was subject to each member state ratifying the agreement. Investigating enlargement, the UK Defence Committee remarked in 1999:

> Of the current sixteen NATO member states, only Canada shares with the UK a ratification process which requires no formal involvement from the legislature . . . In many member states parliamentary committees make recommendations to the legislature before the consideration of ratification. In the case of Turkey, the Foreign Affairs and Defence Committees both examine the draft ratification law before it is submitted to the Plenary Assembly. . . . We believe that the current situation, in which the level of involvement of the UK Parliament in treaty-making is decided by the Government's business managers, is unclear and inadequate.[60]

NATO is also highly secretive, not only in itself but also in its influence on the release of official information in member countries. It has resisted attempts to make its security of information requirements public, despite the fact that these impose strict conditions upon the freedom of information regimes of member states.[61]

NATO and the Kosovo conflict

The NATO intervention of 1999 to prevent atrocities against ethnic Albanians in Kosovo raised important issues with regard to the international rule of law and parliamentary oversight. It was carried out without the explicit approval of the UN Security Council (though there were resolutions suggestive of support), was not an act of self-defence, nor was there an 'invitation to intervene'. Thus the NATO allies failed to satisfy the three classic justifications for intervention. The intervention was, as we have seen, justified instead on humanitarian and security grounds (see page 8). But humanitarian intervention requires the approval of the Security Council and the security case was dubious (that instability in the former Yugoslavia endangered European security). The allies intervened regardless, enunciating new rules for humanitarian intervention. But the North Atlantic Treaty refers to 'faith in the purposes and principles of the Charter of the United Nations' and 'the primary responsibility of the Security Council for the maintenance of international peace and security'. For NATO to act without the authority of the Security Council was therefore a breach of the allies' own treaty undertakings as well of international law as it stands.

There is a tension here, with potentially dangerous implications. To its credit, the FAC explored these issues in depth as part of its substantial and prescient Kosovo report of June 2000, making a valuable contribution to an emerging area of debate.[62] The committee took evidence from a variety of international legal experts and 'also sought the opinion of the Attorney General'. However, he declined to give evidence on what he described as a 'matter as sensitive as this', citing the convention of the confidentiality of his legal advice to government. His refusal raises the question of whether Parliament should have its own legal counsel, as indeed does the confusion over his advice to the government on the legality of the invasion of Iraq (see pages 92–5).

As we reported earlier (see Chapter 4), the FAC concluded that 'at the very least, the doctrine of humanitarian intervention has a tenuous basis in current international customary law, and that this renders the NATO action legally questionable.' Nevertheless it argued that 'NATO's action, if of dubious legality in the current state of international law, was justified on moral grounds.' It stated there was a need for

criteria . . . which would establish with as little doubt as possible when humanitarian intervention is justifiable and when it is not, and . . . these criteria must not be so flexible as to legitimise one state's intervention in another's internal affairs simply because of an assertion of humanitarian grounds for doing so.

The FAC also drew attention to possible legal problems with the use of cluster bombs, depleted uranium munitions and attacks on broadcasting stations during the conflict. It supported the use of international criminal tribunals against indicted war criminals.

Anticipating a debate which would be raised by the Iraq war, the committee also noted 'an aspect of constitutional law which is thrown into focus by the Kosovo campaign': that of parliamentary involvement and approval. The committee drew attention to the contrast between the weight of parliamentary interest in the military intervention and Parliament's inability to have a substantial say on the decision to engage the forces.

The committee pointed out that the International Development and Defence committees investigated the Kosovo campaign as well as the FAC itself. From January to June 1999, the Prime Minister made five statements to the House on Kosovo, the Deputy Prime Minister one, the Foreign Secretary five, the defence secretary four and the international development secretary one. The crisis in Kosovo was raised in PQs and backbench adjournment debates. There were four whole-day debates in government time. The Lords also dealt extensively with the subject.

But, the committee went on,

Parliaments in other NATO states had a specific opportunity to approve the decision of their governments to engage in hostilities over

Kosovo. However, the British Government commits our armed forces to any conflict by exercise of the royal prerogative. For that reason, it has become normal for Governments to rely on motions for the adjournment to debate the United Kingdom's involvement in a conflict. These procedural motions are unamendable. This is a traditional means of preventing an alternative proposition to that of the Government being offered to the House.

The FAC concluded: 'The Government should table a substantive motion in the House of Commons at the earliest opportunity after the commitment of troops to armed conflict allowing the House to express its view, and allowing Members to table amendments.'[63]

These serious questions about the government's war-making powers, the legality of war without explicit Security Council approval, and the place of the royal prerogative in a liberal democracy were salient enough at the time. They became questions that aroused Parliament and the public three years later, and remain unresolved to this day. But in 2000 the government was unmoved by the committee's conclusions and they failed to attract any attention in Parliament or the media. Why? Donald Anderson attributed this neglect to the low level of esteem that select committees command in the UK. This is in part down to their essential powerlessness. Anderson also believed that they were simply poor at generating publicity. But the media share in the blame.

World Health Organization

The World Health Organization (WHO) is a UN specialist agency established with the aim of enabling all people to attain the highest possible levels of health. The WHO is established separately from the UN (that is, it is not a subsidiary body) and works with the UN through the 'coordinating machinery' of the UN Economic and Social Council. Its remit is broadly drawn. The WHO pursues activities in a wide range of areas from ensuring international preparedness for a possible worldwide pandemic of avian flu and coordinating a global strategy on obesity, to conducting research on 'burden of diseases statistics'.[64] The WHO was the agency responsible for the eradication of smallpox, and its carries out a wide range of on-the-ground activities such as vaccination programmes.

The World Health Assembly is the supreme governing body of the WHO and is attended by representatives of all member states. Decisions are made at the assembly on the basis of one member, one vote, as at the UN General Assembly. The annual assembly sets the policy for the WHO's activities and is responsible for the biannual budget approval.

The Department of Health is the lead department in the UK for WHO affairs and liaises with the DFID on policy, but shares the process for determining the positions that the UK will take at the assembly – in Whitehall parlance, 'clearing of UK lines' – with the FCO and the Foreign Secretary. Although a UK minister may attend the assembly, this is not necessarily the case. If a minister does attend, it is a minister from the Department of Health. Therefore three UK government departments have a direct input into the policy of the WHO.

On an operational basis the WHO is governed by an executive board of 32 medically qualified professionals, meeting twice a year in September and after the annual assembly. The assembly indirectly determines the make-up of this board by electing the states which will send a delegate to the board for a three-year term. The UK's representative, when on the board, is the Chief Medical Officer.[65] The WHO is headed by a Director General; the executive board interviews and then endorses one of a shortlist of candidates for formal election by the assembly. It is rare for the assembly to act against its recommendation. The Director General is formally accountable to the board and assembly, but as they meet infrequently, he or she has great influence and discretion for the direction of the WHO policy and actions.

The WHO is funded through two distinct financial streams, approved on a biannual basis at the Assembly. The first is the contributions that are assessed on the same basis as those to the UN, by which each country is expected to contribute a certain proportion of the organisation's 'core' budget. The UK's assessed amount is 6.2 per cent (about £16 million in 2003/4) from the health budget. In addition, like other nations, the UK makes voluntary contributions, usually for specific projects. In 2003/4, Britain made voluntary payments totalling £47 million from the DFID and Department of Health budgets.

The WHO has six regional offices. The UK participates not only in the Europe office but also represents the interests of overseas territories in the American and Western Pacific regions. Within the Western Pacific regional organisation, the 47 Pitcairn islanders give the UK government the same voting rights as China with more than one billion people. These regional offices operate on an essentially independent basis dealing with regional health issues. The UK is the only country which has representation in more than one region and so it has influence across a large part of the WHO.

The WHO's influence in the UK

British interest in WHO policy and actions concerns its influence on both UK domestic and external policy. For example, its classification of myalgic encephalomyelitis (ME) as a neurological condition led to questions concerning the NHS classification in Parliament. At an external level, the WHO does not escape international political divisions, such as the issue of whether Taiwan should be allowed to join as a member country. However, its coordinating efforts to combat diseases such as the SARS virus and HIV may be the most important of its activities for the UK. In such work the WHO is the first line of defence against international epidemics that would affect the UK and is, for example, providing an 'early warning system' for the spread of avian flu. This work is of growing importance owing to the dramatic increase in international travel over the past few decades, as the SARS scare of 2003 made clear.

The WHO also has the ability to create international law in two specific ways – creating conventions (treaties) and establishing international health regulations. The first of the WHO conventions on the advertising of tobacco has recently entered into force, but as these conventions are 'opt in' measures, Britain is not necessarily bound by them. But Britain is bound, like all other WHO members (whatever the position of the individual government might be or how they voted), by the international health regulations which are designed to provide maximum security against the global spread of disease.[66] These regulations give the WHO the ability to create binding international law, but they were last updated in 1969. An inter-governmental working group is renegotiating them to take account of the threats from avian flu, SARS and bio-terrorism.

Britain shares responsibilities in dealings with the WHO with the EU. While EU member states have responsibility for health issues in general, the EU has some responsibility for policy on public health and so takes part in negotiations on parts of the international health regulations for all EU member states. It also has a coordinating function for other parts of the regulations where it will attempt to create a consensus between member states.[67] The UK is bound by the EU position with respect to its competencies, but is also, of course, involved in establishing these positions in internal EU discussions.

Lapses in parliamentary oversight of the WHO

As the Department of Health is the lead department for WHO affairs, the Health Committee is responsible for the activities of the government at the WHO. The committee has not conducted an inquiry specifically into the work of the WHO for the past five years, but its reports do make a number of references to its work. For example, the committee's recent inquiry into obesity referred to WHO obesity statistics and the extent to which obesity is a global problem.[68] But while the WHO's work may be used, the committee does not actually scrutinise its policies and activities, or Britain's role in them.

Written questions in Parliament often refer to the WHO's activities across a variety of issues. For example, a recent question to the international development secretary, Hilary Benn, took up the issue of the provision of non-effective anti-malarial drugs in Africa and referred to the work that the WHO was doing in this area.[69] Thus it is not always a health minister who responds to PQs, as they often concern a specific policy area that the WHO happens to be working in rather than its broad institutional strategy and policies.

The decisions and resolutions of the WHO executive board are tabled in Parliament, for information. The FCO annual report on the

UN also reports on the WHO, but only briefly. Just three paragraphs in the 2004 annual report were dedicated to the work of the WHO and they were relatively superficial. No formal reports from the WHO Assembly are tabled in Parliament, although internal departmental reports do exist. Yet as we continually stress, the provision of information is a prerequisite for effective and efficient parliamentary oversight.

These parliamentary references to the WHO and its work do not amount even to piecemeal oversight. The Health Committee pays little attention to the work that is done by the WHO, except that which is directly relevant to domestic health policy, and even then it is limited. Yet the WHO can have a massive impact on the health policies of many countries, including the UK. Although the total mandatory budget contributions are smaller than the budget of a hospital trust, the impact of work being conducted at the WHO is potentially huge, both domestically and internationally, not least in the area of international development, where the UK has clearly stated aims. So the small budget and low level of UK government expenditure is not the only measure of the significance of the WHO. Accountability must be determined not only in financial terms, but with respect for the broader impact an organisation might have.

Once again, Parliament neglects the oversight of government activities in an international organisation that has significant influence on UK domestic and international policy. The Health Committee pays hardly any attention to the regular work or the strategic direction of the WHO. True, much of its work is not directly relevant to British problems, but Parliament should be notified of issues of interest or importance that arise, and not merely domestic issues, and could take a view on whether and how the UK should be involved. The public has a continuing interest in the alleviation of poverty and disease in the world, and the alleviation of poverty in Africa is emerging as a significant government policy. Britain's MPs should reflect this public interest. Departmental policies are often closely entwined with the work of related international organisations, such as the WHO, and to examine the policy and actions of a department without considering what international organisations are doing and what part UK ministers and departments play in their activities limits the scope and value of parliamentary oversight.

World Trade Organization

The World Trade Organization (WTO) is the international organisation with responsibility for negotiating, establishing and enforcing the rules that govern trade between nations. The WTO evolved from the General Agreement on Tariffs and Trade (GATT), the 'interim' international agreement of 1948 that governed international trade. The GATT was administered by an ad hoc secretariat that became the WTO secretariat in 1995. The rules of the WTO are negotiated through a series of 'trade rounds', which have progressively liberalised trade between nations by reducing tariffs and prohibiting other non-tariff barriers to trade (such as state subsidies of specific industries). The rules negotiated at the trade rounds have to be agreed by the unanimous consent of all the parties involved in the negotiations.

The current trade round is the Doha round, which began in November 2001 in Doha, Qatar, at the fourth WTO ministerial meeting. These negotiations are supposed to have a development emphasis and the Doha round is sometimes referred to as the 'development round'.

Britain is a member of the WTO in its own right, but as a member of the EU 'customs union' is not directly responsible for international negotiation at the WTO trade rounds. The EU has taken on this responsibility, with negotiations led by the EU trade commissioner, currently Peter Mandelson. Membership of the WTO and EU also prohibits the UK from entering bilateral trade agreements since the EU is also in charge of any negotiations with countries that are not members of the WTO. However, there is no prohibition on the UK government actively promoting trade with other specific countries; and the government has long sponsored an organisation devoted to promoting trade relations bilaterally. This organisation, now known as UK Trade & Investment, operates in 200 of the FCO overseas posts, to encourage international investment in the UK and assist UK exporters (see also Chapter 4).

The WTO is responsible for the enforcement of the negotiated trade rules through an elaborate dispute settlement mechanism. This mechanism ultimately involves the 'appellate body' of the WTO, which in essence acts as a court determining the rights and wrongs of cases brought before it. The appellate body may permit retaliatory action against a country that has breached WTO rules – for example, this could typically involve allowing the country that has brought the action to introduce punitive tariffs on the import of specific products from the offending country. It only applies to countries that have legal standing before the appellate body, but it is clear that its decisions can have a serious impact on specific industries depending on the outcome of cases.

As the body that sets the international trading rules, the WTO has a huge impact on the economies of all member countries, including the UK. Thus the WTO is a highly controversial organisation which raises political issues which are of importance both domestically and for international development. It has been accused of promoting aggressive economic liberalisation, which benefits developed nations at the expense of developing countries. Developing nations, on this analysis, are barred from protecting essential domestic industries, whilst richer countries continue to be allowed to subsidise agricultural production, limiting market access for developing countries. It has also be suggested that the WTO 'levels down' labour and environmental standards and so weakens the protection of workers' rights and the environment and prevents the creation of international standards.[70] Within the UK, the effect of the WTO in the promotion of free trade has undoubtedly been less, but it has nonetheless resulted in, some would say significant, job losses in those traditional industries, such as textiles, which were uncompetitive in the global market without the protection of tariffs. Regardless of the economic arguments, without the agreements reached at the WTO it is doubtful whether the tariff reforms, and their effect on the movement of jobs overseas, would have been so significant.

Even though the EU is in charge of all trade negotiations, the UK government is involved in the formation of EU policy on international trade and takes an active interest in the WTO negotiations and seeks to influence them, directly as well as through the EU. Thus though Britain cannot be a party to WTO agreements, the UK government, along with all other EU countries, still sends a delegation to the WTO international negotiations. For example, a 35-

strong British delegation, including four government ministers, civil servants from six government departments and one civil society representative, attended the Doha ministerial round in 2001. Ghana, by contrast, had a delegation of six.

Parliamentary inquiry into the role of the WTO

MPs and peers have two formal sources of information regarding the WTO: written statements provided by the government and library research papers. The government provides written statements to the Houses of relevant information, such as framework texts in advance of WTO negotiations. The House of Commons Library has also produced a number of briefing papers on the WTO negotiations, ensuring that there is easily accessed, independent information on the negotiations as well as a briefing that provides a background to the organisation. Together these provide a basis for the oversight of the WTO, ensuring that MPs and peers are informed on its work. Such information is necessary but not sufficient for adequate oversight of the organisation.

Within the House of Commons the responsibility for oversight clearly lies with the Trade and Industry Committee and the Foreign Affairs Committee. They are thus jointly responsible for the oversight of the minister responsible for international trade, Ian Pearson, who is uniquely a Minister of State in both the DTI and the FCO. The Trade and Industry Committee has not recently conducted an inquiry into the WTO. But it took oral evidence on the WTO talks in Cancun in October 2003 when Patricia Hewitt, the then trade and industry secretary, appeared before the committee to answer questions on the breakdown of talks.[71] She had previously made a statement to the House of Commons soon after the collapse of the negotiations. The committee did not produce a full report and, indeed, has not produced a full report on the WTO since it was founded. Given the FAC's known focus on traditional foreign policy, it is not surprising that it has paid limited attention to the WTO, with no evidence sessions or reports in the last eight years.

Other committees have, however, held inquiries into the WTO. The International Development Committee produced a substantial report following the breakdown of the Doha round talks at Cancun in September 2003.[72] In the course of its inquiry, the committee took evidence from the Secretary of State for Trade and Industry, the EU Commissioner Pascal Lamy (who was then responsible for international trade negotiations) and the Secretary of State for International Development. This list of witnesses demonstrates a broad approach to the issue, although it is inevitably development focused. The IDC also produced a report after the Seattle ministerial meeting in 1999;[73] and has established a pattern of closely monitoring the outcome of the Doha negotiations with regular reviews of the ministerial meetings.

Within the House of Lords, Sub-Committee A of the European Union Committee (Economic and Financial Affairs, Trade and International Relations) reports on the work of the EU at the WTO and progress in the various trade rounds. Its most recent report[74] was debated on the floor of the House.[75] The committee also produced a report after the Seattle negotiations[76] which the International Development Committee report used heavily – a happy chance which illustrates the potential for collaboration and cross-fertilisation between the House of Commons and House of Lords.

As well as the committee activity, there have been a number of both written and oral questions on the subject of the WTO since it was founded in 1994. In just over ten years there have been 512 questions with subjects ranging from developments in the negotiations to organisational issues, such as the accession of Vietnam into the WTO and the possible accession of Afghanistan. These questions typically ask the relevant minister to make a statement. There have also been questions on particular policy issues such as cotton subsides and ongoing disputes being adjudicated at the WTO. The very first question on the WTO, asking 'whether the World Trade Organisation will be democratically accountable', was answered on 16 March 1994: 'The proposed World Trade Organisation (WTO) will provide an institutional structure to give effect to the rules and market access commitments agreed between prospective members of the WTO in the Uruguay round. As such it will be fully accountable to its members.'[77]

There have also been a number of debates in both Houses on issues relevant to the WTO. In the 2003/4 session the House of Lords held two debates and the House of Commons three. These debates focused on the failure of the Cancun talks and the need for trade justice through WTO agreements for development. They made reference to the reports on the WTO produced by the committees and show how it is possible for the different forms of oversight to interact.

Thus the UK Parliament takes a very active interest in the work of the WTO, though the WTO falls within the competence of the EU. Other committees have reported on the WTO and trade negotiations, partially making up for the failure of the two lead committees in the Commons to engage with the substance of the WTO process. Many individual MPs are actively involved in the issues, working through the 'good offices' of their position as MPs. Much of this parliamentary interest has been ad hoc as different committees have picked up on WTO activity in relation to their own work. Thus the International Development Committee's interest in the Doha round with its emphasis on development.

However, there are no formal structures within Parliament for coordinating their inquiries. The complementary coverage of the Doha round by the International Development Committee and Sub-Committee A of the House of Lords European Union Committee has come about by fortune rather than design. We have found that where there is overlap between the interests of different select committees in the Commons, British reserve makes committees reluctant to pursue issues where other committees have a potential claim (whereas in the US Congress, committees compete unabashed to cover issues where there is an overlap). Our research has suggested that committee clerks are disinclined to negotiate and coordinate committee initiatives for fear of usurping the rights of the members to decide what they want to investigate. There is also possible cause for concern in terms of the potential for duplication of work by the UK and EU Parliaments, which could result in inefficient use of limited oversight resources.

Our interviews suggest that MPs pay attention to developments at the WTO not only because of the evident impact they can have in their constituencies, but also because of their impact on international development. The accession of specific countries to the WTO is a particular concern. Furthermore the House of Lords has given much attention to the WTO and peers are not moved by the interests of constituents.

Conclusions

There are several common threads of analysis throughout these quite different case studies. Parliamentary oversight is all ex post facto; MPs and peers alike have little scope for continuous oversight of the policies, negotiations and activities of these diverse international bodies and of the British government's role in them. It is notable for instance that the large WTO delegations do not include parliamentarians, other than ministers. Nonetheless it has been suggested that the knowledge of oversight yet to come acts as an influence on government actions.

There is a chronic lack of information to Parliament, even at the most basic level. Ministers rarely give Parliament a clear statement of UK policy on particular issues at these international organisations. In many cases, the government acts as a gatekeeper safeguarding confidentiality. The opaque nature of the international organisations themselves, their rules against disclosure and the restrictive nature of Britain's FOI regime, especially on policy-making and external and security matters, compound the difficulties that parliamentarians face in obtaining the information that they need to carry out effective scrutiny. The government's reluctance to give select committees information that may be used politically is a disgraceful extra obstacle (see also pages 37–8).

The government's use of prerogative powers in making external policies and agreeing treaties, beyond parliamentary oversight, is also a major cause of the inadequate oversight that Parliament gives to external policy, even though such policy has extensive domestic repercussions. We make recommendations for reform in Chapter 7. But these studies also show that Parliament pays too little attention to the significant areas of policy and action in which the UK government is engaged abroad. This is in large part a question of resources, including MPs' time, as Tony Baldry indicated to us (see page 142). But there is also an urgent need for a change in culture that could bring such matters into the parliamentary mainstream.

7

The way forward

In the preceding chapters we have examined the relationship between government and Parliament in the making of external policies and looked in more detail at parliamentary oversight of three main areas of activity – bilateral, or 'traditional', foreign policy; pre-legislative European Union proposals; and the government's role in major international organisations. A number of common themes have emerged. First, the executive has a remarkable and undesirable degree of power over Parliament, and this is especially the case in external policy-making. We began this book by identifying the doctrine of the royal prerogative, which gives ministers (and officials acting in their name) the ability to make and direct policy overseas with only the barest nod towards Parliament. The research underlying this book has amply confirmed our initial impression that these prerogative powers damage democratic oversight of the policies and actions of British governments in and around the world.

As we have shown, decisions taken in international affairs in the globalised world of today affect the everyday lives of the British people more than ever before. This is especially the case with the wide range of EU legislation presented to the UK Parliament, and with the EU's conduct of trade negotiations in which the British government shares. So *parliamentary oversight* of the executive's external policy-making in Europe and the wider world really matters – and by 'oversight', we mean Parliament's ability to keep the executive under scrutiny, to debate and influence policy-making, and to hold government to account for its policies and actions abroad.

Our focus is on parliamentary oversight. We have a general concern about the power that a British Prime Minister and the executive in general can exercise over Parliament and British society, and particularly about its notorious 'informality'. We believe that a more rules-based political system would of itself make government more responsive and responsible, and give Parliament a surer grasp of executive policies and actions. But while the executive's dominance has a profound and determining impact upon Parliament's practical ability to hold ministers to account, our findings suggest that Parliament itself does not have the confidence to fulfil its responsibilities.

We find that this is particularly the case in external policy, where the royal prerogative, consciously or unconsciously, colours the approach of many MPs. We are in no doubt that that a general and underlying cause of the inadequate oversight is the unspoken assumption which still exists among MPs that the government is entitled to exercise a broader unchecked discretion in foreign than in domestic affairs. This assumption has perhaps been diminished, but not entirely banished, by the Prime Minister's almost wholly personal use of this discretion in the run-up to the Iraq war of 2003 and the inadequacy and looseness of the processes that might have secured a more satisfactory outcome. Moreover, the prerogative reinforces the post hoc nature of parliamentary scrutiny of the executive. In a modern democracy, parliamentarians should be involved in advance in the formation of significant policies and the taking of major decisions; they should at least be consulted on the principles underlying such policies and decisions, and should share in them in so far as is possible.

But a number of cultural, administrative and procedural factors contribute to the unsatisfactory way in which Parliament oversees British foreign policy. We of course recognise that the sheer volume and diversity of external policy-making is almost bound to over-whelm MPs and the largely part-time peers, who have a multiplicity of functions to perform. We also recognise that Parliaments around the world, as well as in the UK, are but secondary institutions that are universally inferior to the executives that they seek to call to account. In the United Kingdom, the government rules Parliament through its majority in the House of Commons. The government's command of its MPs means that it is rarely vulnerable to the vote of no confidence that would remove it from power. Thus, as we have seen, from the big set-piece debates over the decision to invade Iraq to the efforts of individual MPs to raise concerns through parliamentary questions, early day motions and other parliamentary devices, the executive can 'play it long' and ride out concerns and dissent. As the veteran MP Austin Mitchell once remarked, MPs are largely reduced to 'heckling the steamroller'.

Select committees are Parliament's major instruments for oversight of the government's foreign, trade and aid policies. We have therefore concentrated on their activities in the course of this study. We have come to the conclusion that they provide unsystematic scrutiny of these policies at best, and often neglect significant areas of activity. There are of course examples of significant select committee inquiries into external policy matters – for example, the Foreign Affairs Committee report in 2000 on Kosovo (see pages 170–2) and the legality of that military intervention. But overall Parliament and its committees are failing the nation and the wider world. For example,

- Parliament has never closely considered the strategic choice of the United States over Europe as the mainstay of foreign and defence policy;
- no parliamentary committees have reassessed the Special Relationship with the US in the light of President Bush's increasingly unilateral foreign policy and commitment to pre-emptive military action;
- there has been no parliamentary inquiry into the policies that took the UK into war against Iraq, in spite of widespread public concern;
- neither the Trade and Industry nor the Foreign Affairs Committee has held an inquiry into the World Trade Organization's policies and the EU role in its affairs, even though the WTO sets binding rules that profoundly affect domestic industrial and commercial prospects;
- at the time of the Rwandan genocide, the Commons held only one debate on the situation, and that was an adjournment debate called by a backbench MP which was confined only to his speech and the minister's reply;
- only half the members of the European Standing Committee attend their meetings to consider draft EU legislation that is

classified as being of political or legal importance;
* the draft EU Working Time Directive was submitted to Parliament in September 2004, but no debate had taken place on it, either on the floor of the House or in committee, when the British government came to discuss the proposal in the Council of Ministers in June 2005.

The committees' weaknesses are in large part attributable to their chronic lack of resources – including MPs' own time and commitment – and the weak powers that they possess in practice to obtain official documents and to interrogate ministers and officials. The retrospective nature of parliamentary oversight severely limits the capacity of select committees to influence events. We discussed these issues with a number of dedicated and able parliamentarians who were anxious to improve Parliament's oversight of foreign policies. But we were struck by the stoic acceptance both of executive dominance and their own powerlessness – which in turn has meant that they are neglected by ministers and the media. Our single most important conclusion is that we need a self-confident Parliament, willing to demand the powers and resources that its committees and members require to hold the executive to account, and able to make use of them.

Taming the royal prerogative

We begin our recommendations with reform of the royal prerogative and the untrammelled powers it confers upon the executive in the field of foreign policy which are denied it in purely domestic affairs. We believe, as a matter of principle, that the royal prerogative has no place in a modern democracy, and that it is actively harmful in seeming to confer otherwise unjustified freedom of action on the British government in its external policies. We therefore recommend that the royal prerogative in the field of foreign policy should be abolished, or at the very least substantially reformed to deprive the British government of the unchecked powers which it currently enjoys.

In the long run, we agree with the PASC that the prerogative should be put on a statutory footing in all its manifestations, but that the executive's powers over military force and treaty-making should be dealt with as a priority. Crucial to this development would be the introduction of an effective War Powers Act, which not merely allowed Parliament to endorse or block the formal declaration of war between the United Kingdom and another nation, but also permitted Parliament to approve or reject any substantial military activity which can reasonably be held as the equivalent of war, as well as the deployment of troops in potentially hostile circumstances – such as for example the intensified bombing in the southern Iraq no-fly zone in the run-up to the invasion (see pages 82–3). Many other democracies have formal provision for the involvement of the legislature in war-making, most notably the US, both through provision in its Constitution and in the 1973 War Powers Act. We can see no reason why Britain should not join their number.

Few decisions taken by the British government have more serious consequences than those involving the deployment in anger of military force. That Parliament should have so little formal involvement in these decisions is a glaring democratic anomaly. A UK equivalent to the US War Powers Act would entail, wherever possible, the government bringing a resolution to the House of Commons in advance of a hostile or potentially hostile military action, setting out its objectives, compatibility with international law, estimated costs, and a timetable for completion. The government would be required to return to the legislature at regular intervals when seeking to renew or alter its mandate for action. Where circumstances do not allow consultation with Parliament in advance of an operation, MPs should be given the opportunity to approve, disavow or halt the action as soon as reasonably possible.

But it is not only in times of crisis that Parliament's role needs to be enhanced. The role of Parliament in the negotiation and ratification of international treaties is marginal at best. Parliament could already do more than it does to participate in and scrutinise the negotiation of treaties (see below). It is, however, in the ratification of international treaties that Parliament's present formal competencies need to be enhanced. When negotiating an international treaty, the British government should have firmly in mind that the treaty's final provisions will be subject to serious scrutiny and in the ultimate case rejection by elected representatives. The task of sifting the 50 or so treaties a year to which the UK becomes party should, we recommend, be taken on by a joint committee of both Houses. The joint committee, perhaps in consultation with relevant select committees, could refer those it considered of the greatest importance to the plenary for a debate and a vote. This debate and vote would be no mere formality, but a genuine opportunity for Parliament to review and if necessary reject the outcome of negotiations which Parliament itself will have been following and shaping.

It is often diplomats and officials rather than ministers who conduct negotiations on international treaties. The contribution that MPs could make to foreign affairs would be significantly improved if Parliament were enabled to scrutinise more effectively than it can now the allocation of important diplomatic posts, especially when these posts are filled by political appointees. This scrutiny should not be confined to British ambassadors formally sent to foreign capitals. It should also extend to informal envoys sent on behalf of the Prime Minister or other ministers to carry out diplomatic tasks in a particular country or region. The proposed Civil Service Act could well provide a tool to enforce Parliament's oversight of these appointments as part of the proposal in the current draft that ministers should report annually to Parliament on their special advisers. However, we also recommend that Parliament should seek to put this measure on the statute book for wider reasons – to reinforce the party-political neutrality of civil servants and to restrain the informality at the centre of government identified in Lord Butler's report.

We believe that such measures, if implemented with imagination and determination, would be both materially and symbolically important. They would confer on the UK Parliament powers of which it should not be deprived; and they would act as a potent signal that the traditional gap in parliamentary accountability between the government's internal and external actions was being bridged. However, members of the legislature must take it upon themselves to make effective use of the instruments at their disposal. The US War

Powers Act has often proved ineffective at securing Congressional influence over informal war-making, owing to a lack of will on the part of Congressmen. We return to the question of will later.

Mainstreaming oversight of foreign affairs

Our second major reform proposal is that Parliament should 'mainstream' its oversight of external policies. As we have pointed out, these policies impact upon the daily lives of most citizens and yet their scrutiny is relegated to the margins of parliamentary business. The first priority would be to remove the artificial barrier which currently exists between the parliamentary specialists in the general field of 'external policy' and their colleagues who specialise in the areas of domestic policy on which external policy increasingly impinges. In a world where, for instance, much of Britain's environmental policy is decisively influenced by European legislation and international treaties, those MPs whose speciality is the environment are best qualified to maintain oversight of what the government is doing in European and international environmental negotiations and to conduct pre-legislative scrutiny of EU legislation. It is rare under our current system for them to be able to do so.

We recommend therefore that departmental select committees in the House of Commons should in future oversee all external policy-making that bears upon their domestic responsibilities. This 'mainstreaming' process would rescue a wide range of significant executive policies and actions overseas from the neglect that they currently suffer. It also makes sense to make the best possible use of the expertise that members of the specialist select committees have amassed, and to bring the government's negotiations with its EU and other international partners more clearly on to the political agenda.

The need for this proposal is most clearly illustrated in the case of the EU. Central to the role of national parliaments in this field is the pre-legislative scrutiny which they carry out of proposed European legislation coming from the European Commission. These proposals are generally highly specific in character, covering a wide range of policy areas for which the EU has shared or exclusive responsibility. If proposals from the EU on agriculture, transport or development aid, for example, are to receive the most effective parliamentary scrutiny, we believe it essential that they should primarily be considered by the appropriate specialist committees, not by the present European standing committees.

These standing committees are a highly unsatisfactory substitute for the specialist select committees, which frequently feel themselves absolved from the need seriously to consider European legislation by the very existence of these other committees. The standing committees, as we have seen (see page 119), play a largely political and inexpert role and are often driven by inappropriate partisan wrangling for and against Britain's participation in the EU. Yet there exists within the Commons select committees a body of relevant knowledge and experience, coupled with access to and familiarity with the specialist media covering their policy areas. It must diminish the effectiveness of the pre-legislative scrutiny to which Parliament subjects proposed European legislation for this knowledge, experience and access to the media not to be fully employed, as it clearly is not now.

Once the first step had been taken of making the oversight of European legislation and international agreements a genuinely core task of specialist parliamentary committees, they would be obliged to reform their working methods in line with their new responsibilities. They would need to adopt a system whereby all important new proposals (particularly proposed European legislation) were reviewed and further work done on those which appeared inadequate or disadvantageous to the UK. The committees would need to keep under constant review the meetings and agendas of the European or international ministerial meetings relevant for their policy areas. They would need regularly to interview the responsible ministers and, where appropriate, heads of UK delegations, timing these interviews to precede and immediately follow important stages in developing negotiations. In short, they would need to ensure that they had access to all the information and analysis necessary to form and present to the government professionally solid judgements on the gamut of international texts which at any stage are in negotiation.

Developing 'soft mandates' in Parliament

One particularly important decision for the committees to take under the new arrangements would be to review the nature of their relationship with the ministers and officials from the government department which they are holding to account. As we have already indicated, the traditional system of ministerial responsibility to Parliament allows for post hoc scrutiny of government policies and actions only. In our view, this system leaves open a damaging accountability gap – for by the time Parliament reviews a policy or action, it is already an accomplished fact.

A number of MPs we interviewed expressed interest in the mandating system which some national Parliaments, such as the Danish and Finnish, impose upon their ministers in European negotiations. Under this system, ministers meet regularly with the appropriate committees in advance of EU meetings and are effectively given negotiating instructions by the committee. No deviation from this mandate is allowed without the permission of the committee or its chairman. We recommend that select committees charged with the pre-legislative scrutiny of European legislation should develop a mandating process for the United Kingdom in advance of negotiations (rather than being informed afterwards what policies had been adopted).

We have in mind a form of 'soft mandating', which would allow ministers room for manoeuvre within parliamentary guidelines for the subsequent negotiations. It would be unlikely that a British version of mandating could be as confining of ministers as that practised in Denmark, where governments with small majorities are particularly wary of upsetting a delicate parliamentary balance by controversy with influential parliamentary committees. We believe that mandating in the British Parliament should aim to create a continuous dialogue between ministers and committees rather than to try and impose formal instructions from committees to ministers.

Our recommendations on mainstreaming and mandating arising from the example of EU legislation apply equally to British policy in other international organisations, such as the World Bank, the United Nations with its subsidiary bodies and NATO. The concept of a form of 'mandating' from select committees to ministers representing the UK at these bodies would represent a major advance in parliamentary oversight. The greater involvement of Parliament in the treaty-making process which we advocate would also reinforce the presence of the legislature in this area.

There is also a case for establishing arrangements for prior parliamentary scrutiny in particular policy areas. One such area, for example, would be advance scrutiny of export licence applications, for which the Quadripartite Committee (see page 97) is already pressing. The committee, which is responsible for oversight of export licensing, has already requested that it should be given advance notification of applications. We endorse this request. Advance oversight would enable parliamentarians to ensure that ethical concerns are not overridden by commercial ones, and that the UK does not become an accomplice in acts of brutality abroad by supplying the equipment which makes them possible.

Giving Parliament better resources

When we discussed proposals for mainstreaming, mandating and other changes with MPs and committee officials, the most frequent response was that the select committees did not have the resources to take on the extra responsibilities we were suggesting. Committee members and officials stressed to us, however, that perhaps the most important missing resource is that too few MPs are involved in committee work; and that those who are involved are too busy to devote adequate time to their committee responsibilities. Thus the committees, in turn, are constrained by the difficulties that their members experience. (We have several times sat in on committees as they sought anxiously to summon up a quorum.)

We regard this as a critical issue. We agree with the Hansard Society Commission on Parliamentary Scrutiny that select committees should be enlarged so that they can perform their duties more effectively and the majority of MPs should be expected to serve on a select committee. (The payroll vote should ideally also be reduced so that more MPs would be freed to take on the responsibilities of oversight on a select committee.) In this sense, the House of Commons would be 'mainstreaming' committee service and raising the profile and status of scrutiny among MPs and the media.

There are various other advantages to this proposal. Larger committees could form sub-committees and break into sub-groups to examine specific issues, as takes place, for instance, in Germany and the US. An added advantage of such an approach would be that the total number of MPs sitting on committees would grow, thereby reducing the relative power of the whips when disbursing committee membership as patronage. We deal below with the enduring problem of the time MPs feel able to devote to oversight of external policies, where we discuss the question of the culture of the House of Commons.

Many of the MPs and officials we interviewed were more sanguine about the resources at their disposal than we are. It is our view – and one that was shared by experienced committee members such as Bruce George – that the resources available to select committees are inadequate to meet their current responsibilities, let alone the large increase in duties that we advocate here. We agree with George that Parliament should have at its disposal highly qualified and know-ledgeable experts rather than (as is mostly the case) able young persons at the beginning of their careers. We therefore firmly recommend that extra resources should be allocated to committees and individual parliamentarians to help them become more effective scrutineers of the government's external actions.

We recommend specifically that two institutions, a **Legal Counsel's Office** for Parliament and a **Parliamentary External Audit Office**, should be established to put Parliament on a more equal footing with the executive. These two new institutions would have a similar function, namely to provide authoritative information and advice on which Parliament could base its con-sidered judgement when reviewing the actions of the executive. The present unbalanced relationship between the UK Parliament and the executive in the conduct of international affairs derives at least partly from the imbalance of information available to both parties. The two new institutions suggested would help to remedy that imbalance.

European and international law is increasingly a central element in controversial government decisions on the international stage; and it is highly undesirable that the executive should be able to draw upon usually confidential legal advice from the Attorney General while

Parliament is deprived its own sources of legal advice. It cannot be possible for Parliament to carry out effective scrutiny on such matters without access to authoritative and impartial legal advice, which a Legal Counsel's Office would provide, primarily to parliamentary committees. (Such an office may also be additionally valuable, for example, in considering the impact of domestic legislation on human rights in the UK.)

Our conception of the External Audit Office is that it would give select committees impartial factual advice about the likely impact in the UK and elsewhere of proposed new European legislation or other international obligations. The EAO could perhaps be attached to the recently established Scrutiny Unit, which services select committees and joint committees carrying out pre-legislative scrutiny. It would in some senses be an external version of the National Audit Office, but with a forward-looking remit that is broader and more policy focused than that of the NAO. It would be for the select committees to form political judgements based on its analysis and advice, but the new External Audit Office would give their members a sound factual basis for those judgements.

In addition to these new bodies, further more traditional resources would also need to be made available to committees and individuals to carry out their increased workloads. Library and research facilities should be enhanced. The number of qualified staff allocated to specialist committees should rise. Money should be made available for international research travel, with the emphasis being placed exclusively on the usefulness of the travel, rather than how much travel to what destinations an individual MP involved had already made that year.

The modest increase in expenditure that these proposals involve might well provoke initial public criticism. Parliamentarians would be well placed to rebut such criticism by pointing out that the only beneficiaries of inadequate funding for their work would be the governments that already escape effective oversight. Moreover, in so far as a more informed and active Parliament was able to make proper use of these additional resources, it is possible that the extra costs would be saved by improved decision-making and the avoidance of the 'policy disasters', such as the recent invasion of Iraq, that cost the

British taxpayer. It is illuminating to compare the expenditure on select committees' scrutiny work with total government expenditures on the policies, actions and services that they are supposed to keep under scrutiny: in 2002/3, the total spend on select committees came to £10.6 million, as against total government spending of £430 billion. We get parliamentary democracy 'on the cheap' – and it shows.

Changing Parliament's culture

Among the reasons why we advocate the abolition of the royal prerogative is its likely psychological effect in reinforcing the role of Parliament as an autonomous political body, in no way inferior to or subordinate to the government, today's beneficiary of the royal prerogative. Even if the prerogative is abolished, however, there will still need to be a further shift of psychology and culture among MPs. For the great majority of MPs, three genuine and understandable pressures are dominant in their personal political ambition: loyalty to the party to which they belong, the desire to make a successful ministerial career for themselves and the need they feel to protect their political base by time-consuming constituency work.

All three of these pressures, in their different ways, are inimical to the ability of Parliament effectively to scrutinise the actions of government and hold it to account. The British executive is traditionally adept at exploiting the preoccupations of backbenchers to ensure that the scrutiny to which it is subjected is as toothless as possible. The problem is particularly acute in the case of scrutiny of external affairs. The prospects for effective scrutiny would improve considerably if fewer MPs regarded their work in the House of Commons as primarily an antechamber to ministerial office, and more was done to give real influence to select committees.

Constituency work gobbles up MPs' time. We recognise that this work does a great deal to maintain a significant and symbolic link between MPs and the public. The constituency link is prized by citizens for its access to political influence and treasured by MPs for the contribution it makes to the incumbency effect. Many MPs use their constituency cases to improve the quality and fairness of public services. On the other hand, many others use their allowances and staff simply to shore up their political position. We regret that few of these MPs have the self-confidence to realise that at least some of their work in their constituencies is of little use either to themselves or their constituents.

We hope to return to the question of how to bring about cultural change in the House of Commons in a later book. One of the causes of Parliament's subordination to the executive is the current electoral system, which generally returns single-party governments with inflated (and unrepresentative) majorities to the House of Commons after general elections. As Donald Anderson said to us, under the German system of proportional representation, which returns an equal mix of constituency and (non-constituency) top-up members to the Bundestag, some 50 per cent of the members are free from constituency pressures and can therefore give more time to scrutiny and other legislative work. Austin Mitchell's executive steamroller would also be brought under more effective control in a representative House elected by proportional representation.

Loyalty is part and parcel of party politics, and as we noted earlier rebellions among government backbenchers almost invariably stop short of giving government 'a bloody nose' or worse (see page 30). But a popular chamber elected under a PR system would be more pluralist in composition and governments could not rely any more on the loyalty of an unearned parliamentary majority.

However, even after the outcry occasioned by the results of the 2005 election, the current government is not likely to give way on electoral reform. Thus we confine ourselves to a number of procedural and administrative changes to the workings of Parliament that are intended to strengthen the self-identity of Parliament as an equal partner in its dealings with the government.

Our goal is a modern 'committee' Parliament in which the oversight duties of select committees take precedence over the set-piece occasions customary in the popular chamber. We expect that our proposals for enlarging committees so that most MPs contribute to their work, mainstreaming external and particularly European affairs and introducing 'soft mandating' of ministers, will lead to a potential virtuous circle, whereby more determined and expert committees will refuse to accept the restrictions on their roles implicit in such conventions as the Osmotherly rules, which limit the access of parliamentary committees to civil servants. The theoretical right of parliamentary committees to send for 'persons and papers' must be made a reality if these committees are to carry out their work of scrutiny properly. There should be a shift in emphasis from old-fashioned post hoc scrutiny to scrutiny and involvement in advance of negotiations, policy and decision-making.

These cultural changes will be difficult but not impossible to bring about. The Commons, urged on by the Liaison Committee, is already slowly evolving into a committee-based body. Some committees are already seeking to establish prior scrutiny and consultation. The recent exchange between the Quadripartite Committee and the then trade and industry secretary, Patricia Hewitt, illustrates both a new parliamentary resolve and the executive's resistance to change. In response to the committee's repeated requests for prior parliamentary scrutiny of export licenses, Hewitt replied in January 2005 that 'it would be unacceptable to blur the line between scrutiny by Parliament of the Government's actions on the one hand, and participation by the Committee in the decision-making process itself on the other.' Any meaningful committee involvement 'in the decision-making process' would inevitably give rise to delay and demand additional resources.

The committee's response was:

> Committees do not simply engage in historical studies of government policy: there is increasingly a real-time engagement with decision-making. However, the confidential nature of arms-export licensing, and the fact that it is justiciable make this situation unusual. Other countries have overcome these difficulties, though, with Sweden, the Netherlands and the USA having some form of advance information provision for, and consultation of, Parliament . . . *We intend to press vigorously for this change to be made in the next Parliament* [our emphasis].[1]

The extra resources we recommend above will certainly need to be devoted to this undertaking. But these resources ought not to become simply a prop for the existing system. They should be used to change the House's underlying culture and to accelerate the change that is already taking place from an old-fashioned debating shop to a modern committee-based legislature. We do not underestimate the difficulties of bringing about this major change in culture, but it is not impossible at least to make further advances.

We expect that involving the great majority of MPs in committee scrutiny and mainstreaming external and European affairs will make scrutiny a more familiar and characteristic experience for MPs that could lead to a potential virtuous circle, whereby more determined and expert committees will refuse to accept the restrictions that the government imposes on their work, such as the Osmotherly rules that limit their access to civil servants, and the obstacles to their theoretical right to send for 'persons and papers'. It is extraordinary that, as Lord Butler no doubt rightly said to the Public Administration Select Committee, the government is reluctant to give information to select committees because their opposition members may take advantage of it. Select committees could and should do more to assert their rights against the executive. It should not be for the scrutinised executive to decide what weapons of scrutiny Parliament will be allowed to deploy.

The governing party's command of parliamentary business is another major obstacle to a more assertive House. Powers over their business that were ceded by earlier, more deferential Parliaments should be retrieved. If most MPs were involved in drawing up committee reports, they would surely begin to rebel against the inadequate responses these reports often elicit from government departments, and the neglect of critical reports or those which contain unwelcome proposals on the floor of the House. We heard from a number of those to whom we spoke that successive governments have been much more willing to discuss in prime parliamentary time committee reports with which they were generally sympathetic, than those with which they were out of sympathy. The government is clearly in a strong position to block any such attempts by committees, but continuous political pressure by an assertive Parliament could overcome this hurdle.

Strengthening Parliament's independent voice

It will be clear that we believe that a strong and confident committee structure in the Houses of Parliament is vital to transforming 'executive democracy' (as Jack Straw styles it) into modern parliamentary democracy. The key to such a change is to hammer away at proposals that strengthen Parliament's political hand in dealing with the British executive.

The Liaison Committee, comprising the chairs of select committees, has already begun to act as their collective voice and has made a series of recommendations designed to strengthen them in their dealings with the executive. We recommend that the powers of the Liaison Committee in the House of Commons be strengthened and that it set up a smaller executive group, as recommended by the Hansard Commission on Parliamentary Scrutiny. The House of Lords, though weakened by its ambiguous status, has a strong reputation for the quality and objectivity of its scrutiny work and more use could be made of its members. We recommend that more joint committees between the House of Lords and the House of Commons be established; and that the House of Lords should consider establishing ad hoc committees to consider major issues of external policy. Both practically and psychologically, greater co-ordination between parliamentary committees between different Houses and covering different policy areas would greatly help to right the traditional imbalance in the UK between government and Parliament, an imbalance particularly observable in foreign affairs.

There is a crucial weakness in arrangements for ensuring that ministers act properly in their dealings with Parliament and the Civil Service. The *Ministerial Code*, the rule-book for ministers, deals in part with their duties towards Parliament. But it is the property of the Prime Minister of the day and has the force only of convention. The Prime Minister has the sole responsibility for enforcing the code and the clash of interest in his or her judgements is self-evident. That the Prime Minister has the sole responsibility of enforcing this code seems to us politically and constitutionally unsustainable. Moreover in significant cases the degree of political support that a minister has on the government back benches is ultimately the determining factor. There have been a number of proposals for reform of this unsatisfactory position. The constitutional committee in the Swedish Parliament may be a model for reform. One of its remits is to consider the conduct of ministers. We suggest that a parliamentary committee, perhaps a joint committee, could be set up to monitor compliance with the code and keep it under review.

We also urge that Parliament should assume the right to recall itself independently of the executive. This would be an important component of a new independent parliamentary identity and would be particularly relevant in the context of foreign policy. We suggest a system whereby a certain number of members of Parliament (perhaps a third), from two or more political parties represented in the House of Commons, could ask the Speaker to recall Parliament. The Speaker would normally accede to that request. In the case of a refusal, he or she would be expected publicly to defend the decision (which would of course be open to subsequent parliamentary debate). We envisage that a set of constitutional conventions would soon emerge for the Speaker's guidance. A number of variations upon this system could obviously be envisaged, but it is a peculiarly flagrant example of executive dominance that Parliament can currently only be recalled at its initiative.

The important organisational and procedural recommendations we make need cost nothing, and would not require Acts of Parliament. For example, the mainstreaming proposal might require changes to the Standing Orders and list of 'core tasks' for select committees. The ability for the House to recall itself could be stipulated in the Standing Orders (as has been suggested by Graham Allen MP). The obligation for ministers to attend a hearing with the relevant select committee before attending international negotiations could be written into the *Ministerial Code* (and the select committee could be required to take evidence as a 'core task').

In general, we believe that the establishment of a self-confident Parliament depends on a radical upgrading of the importance attached to the work of select committees. Their inquiries and reports constitute the core of Parliament's contribution to political discourse in this country. But it is the traditional set-piece debates, stage managed as they so often are, and the negotiations which precede controversial votes, that still seize media attention. The fact that the select committees are largely powerless deprives them of their cutting edge in media attention. But despite recent attempts to improve the presentation of their reports, select committees still limp along in their capacity to publicise their inquiries and reports effectively. The Clerks Department should employ sufficient professional media staff to address this continuing weakness.

Towards an open democracy

Parliament does not exist in a vacuum. It has an important role as a forum for political debate, but this role is nevertheless a part only of the extended political discourse which characterises mature democracies. Parliament benefits from and helps the work of other leading contributors to this discourse, contributors such as the mass media, non-governmental organisations, academics and the judiciary. Access to official information is fundamental to the quality of this interplay of debate in Parliament and society at large. Parliament has an especial interest in promoting the widest possible access to information from which it and those organisations and individuals who share in this political discourse may expect to benefit. We believe that parliamentary scrutiny in external affairs depends crucially upon the free and open flow of relevant information from all government departments. The British official culture of with-holding information for the convenience of the executive is one from which Parliament especially suffers.

From this general principle, a number of consequences naturally follow. To improve its work of scrutiny in foreign affairs, Parliament has every interest in pressing for reform of the Freedom of Information Act's more restrictive exemptions, which bear most heavily upon foreign, defence and trade policies (see Appendix A). Ministerial power over the decisions of the Information Commissioner is an executive safeguard too far. Successive Commons committees have recommended that the Intelligence and Security Committee, formally appointed by and reporting to the Prime Minister, should be reconvened as a committee of the House, thereby establishing its independence from the executive and enabling parliamentary scrutiny of the security and intelligence agencies. So far, the government has refused to yield. The use made by the government before the Iraq war of intelligence material to bolster its political case for the war has fatally undermined any argument that intelligence and security matters have no place in the open political arena. Parliament has traditionally been willing to concede a wide measure of executive latitude on security and intelligence matters. All the events surrounding the build-up to the Iraq war of 2003 have made the concession of such latitude a matter for urgent review and reform.

Conclusion

In reviewing the workings of Parliamentary accountability in the sphere of external relations, we have implicitly accepted that certain elements of our existing political system cannot or will not be changed in the foreseeable future. In particular, we have assumed that the system for elections to Parliament will remain unchanged for now. We believe that the inadequacies we have identified in parliamentary scrutiny of the British executive's external decisions apply more generally to way the political system works.

We should not wish to think that a more assertive Parliament cannot at least achieve some reform and develop a more effective parliamentary arm to our democracy. Our recommendations are designed to assist this process. We believe that they would, if adopted, help Parliament to hold the British government more effectively to account for its actions outside the frontiers of the United Kingdom. This would be a clear net gain not merely for the transparency of the British political process, but also for those many citizens, British and others, who are affected by the external decisions of the British government.

The starting point of our investigation was the ever more obvious blurring, in a globalised society and economy, of traditional lines between external and internal policy. It is not entirely surprising that our conclusions about the way the British Parliament reviews governmental foreign policy have touched also on the general underlying relationship between the executive and Parliament, whether that is manifested in domestic, European or international affairs. It may well be that the recommendations we are making about external policy have wider implications for this underlying relationship at the heart of our unwritten constitution as well.

Appendix A

The secretive state

Official rules on refusing access to information on foreign policy

Exempt information	FOI Act section	Type of exemption
1. Information supplied by, or relating to security agencies, security tribunals, special forces and other specified security bodies.	s. 23	Absolute class exemption
2. Information not exempt under 1 above but otherwise concerned with the safeguarding of national security.	s. 24	Qualified class exemption (a ministerial certificate is required)
3. Information that would, or would be likely to, prejudice the defence of the British Isles or any colony.	s. 26	Prejudice-based exemption
4. Information that would, or would be likely to, prejudice the capability, effectiveness or security of the armed forces.	s. 26	Prejudice-based exemption
5. Information that would, or would be likely to, prejudice relations between the UK and any other state,	s. 27	Prejudice-based exemption

international organisation or international court.		
6. Information that would, or would be likely to, prejudice the interests of the UK abroad or the promotion or protection of those interests.	s. 27	Prejudice-based exemption
7. Confidential information from another state, an international organisation, or international court.	s. 27	Qualified class exemption
8. Information that would, or would be likely to, prejudice the economic interests of the UK.	s. 29	Prejudice-based exemption
9. Information held by a government department . . . relating to: a) the formulation or development of government policy for the UK government . . .; b) ministerial communications; c) the advice of a Law Officer, or a request for such advice; or d) the operation of any ministerial private office. However, statistical information should be disclosed after policy decisions have been taken; and the authorities must consider disclosing background factual information when it comes to the public interest test.	s. 35	Qualified class exemption

10. Any information held by a government department . . . or any other public authority, which is not exempt under 21 above but which in the opinion of a minister or 'qualified' official or office-holder would, or would be likely to, prejudice the maintenance of the convention of the collective responsibility of ministers	s. 36	Qualified class exemption, except for information held by the Commons or Lords, which is subject to an absolute class exemption
11. Any information held by a government department . . . or any other public authority, which is not exempt under 21 above but which in the opinion of a minister or 'qualified' official or office-holder would, or would be likely to, inhibit: a) the free and frank provision of advice to ministers from civil servants; or b) the free and frank exchange of views in policy deliberations.	s. 36	Qualified class exemption, except for information held by the Commons or Lords, which is subject to an absolute class exemption
12. Any information held by a government department . . . or any other public authority, which is not exempt under 21 above but in the opinion of a which minister or 'qualified' official or office-holder would, or would be likely to, prejudice the effective conduct of public affairs.	s. 36	Qualified class exemption, except for information held by the Commons or Lords, which is subject to an absolute class exemption

14. Any environmental information which is to be disclosed under government regulations to implement the 1998 Aarhus Convention on access to environmental information and justice in environmental matters; or which is exempt from disclosure under the same regulations.	s. 39	Qualified class exemption
15. Information obtained in confidence by a public authority from any other person (including another public authority), where disclosure would be a breach of confidence actionable by that or any other person.	s. 41	Absolute class exemption (but the common law duty of confidence does not arise if disclosure would be in the public interest)
16. Information which is a 'trade secret'.	s. 43	Qualified class exemption
17. Information which would, or would be likely to, prejudice the commercial interests of any person or company – including those of the public body holding the information.	s. 43	Prejudice-based exemption
18. Information where disclosure is prohibited by or under any of more than 300 statutory prohibitions.	s. 44	Absolute class exemption
19. All information where disclosure is incompatible with any European Community obligation.	s. 44	Absolute class exemption

Note: This table excludes some exemptions which could prevent or inhibit disclosure of information relevant to external policy. In items 9–12, references to the Welsh Assembly and the Northern Ireland Executive have been removed. Source Analysis in FOI section, www.democraticaudit.com.

Appendix B

The Special Relationship between the United Kingdom and the United States

Extract from Memorandum from the Foreign and Commonwealth Office in evidence to the Foreign Affairs Committee, October 2001[1]

I Introduction

1. The Foreign and Commonwealth Office has prepared this Memorandum for the House of Commons Select Committee enquiry into relations between the United Kingdom and the United States, and the implications of US foreign policy for United Kingdom interests. British Trade International is submitting a separate Memorandum on trade promotion and investment issues.[2] The Committee will be receiving other evidence, written and oral, both before and after their planned visit to the USA.

2. The maintenance of a strong transatlantic relationship has been one of the cornerstones of British foreign policy since the Second World War. Successive British governments have sought to promote the security and prosperity of the UK and advance its global interests by establishing a close European relationship while maintaining a strong link to the United States. The tone and emphasis of this approach has differed over the decades. But the overall aims have remained constant and have continued into the post-Cold War era.

3. The events of 11 September 2001 have highlighted the strength of the British–US relationship. The US – Administration and people alike – are grateful for the solidarity shown by the British. The habit of working closely together, particularly in the security and foreign policy fields, has paid dividends to both parties. Each

partner has a good instinct for the thinking and likely reactions of the other; the personal links are well-established. Well before the terrorist attacks, the Prime Minister had made clear the high priority he attached to the relationship with the new President and his Administration. His visit to Washington in February, followed by President Bush's visit to the UK in July, provided opportunities to work through many of the important issues which have now become central to the coalition against terrorism. With our EU, NATO and other allies, Britain and the US are looking closely at the wider implications of confronting the terrorist challenge to our common values. This challenge has given the kaleidoscope of international relations a vigorous shake, as we consider together the longer-term transformation of relationships with Russia and with China, as well as potential realignments in South Asia and elsewhere.

4. Any British or indeed European government has to recognise the predominant role of the United States in international affairs. It is the world's largest economy. It has the resources, both human and physical, to maintain a technological lead over all other countries for an indefinite period. It also has unrivalled military power and political influence across the globe. It is a key member of the global system of multilateral institutions.

5. Part of the attraction to each other is that the UK and the US share a similar outlook based in part on shared democratic values and principles, as well as a common interest in the maintenance of international peace and order. This is under-pinned by personal, business and social links that go well beyond foreign policy concerns. For example, the US is the largest investor in the UK (as the UK is the largest investor in the US). But in the areas of concern to the Committee, it is fair to say that the UK and US have a close and probably unique relationship over a wide range of subjects. This does not mean however that the UK and the US always agree, or that British governments therefore defer to the US. While US administrations welcome staunch support, they also welcome a frank relationship with a friend and ally.

6. Even with the closer rapport since 11 September, the Government does not and cannot take for granted the long-term health of the

UK–US bilateral relationship or the broader transatlantic one. The United States has a complex political system and foreign policy-making process. This requires not just good high level access but a broad range of contacts across various levels of the Administration. It means taking into account the important role of Congress and the increased overlap between domestic and international affairs. It requires the ability to influence the powerful lobby groups, some of whose interests or outlook may be opposed to those of the UK. It means being able to deal directly with the powerful US media and having a presence at State level not just to promote British commercial links but to influence public opinion and opinion-formers throughout the US. With an eye to the longer-term, it also requires an understanding of the increasingly multicultural nature of US society.

7. In short, the British–US relationship goes far wider than the traditional co-operation over foreign policy and in the political, military and intelligence fields. There are almost no areas of public policy with which UK posts in the US do not deal. They embrace all aspects of the relationship from public health to trade policy, from transport to immigration and civil liberties, from aid policy to financial services and banking, from welfare to education, from drugs control to policing. The response to the events of 11 September 2001 has emphatically underlined the importance of each strand in strengthening the single rope of the overall relationship. But the focus of this Memorandum remains on foreign policy.

II *Current UK Objectives in the United States*

8. Our objectives are:–

   i. To work with the US and others to defeat terrorism world-wide.

   ii. To ensure, in working for a secure United Kingdom within a more stable and peaceful world, that the US is supportive of UK security objectives, including policies towards Northern Ireland, enlargement and modernisation of NATO, the European Security and Defence Policy, Russia, the Balkans, Middle East problems and UN Security Council expansion;

and that Missile Defence is pursued in a way which protects UK interests and minimises divisions within NATO.

iii. To enhance the competitiveness of companies in the UK by sales to, and investment in, the US and by attracting a high level of quality direct investment from the US.

iv. In seeking increased UK prosperity through a strengthened international economic order, to maintain US support for a new, broad-based, liberalising Trade Round; to prevent trade disputes between the EU and the US damaging the wider relationship; to agree more liberal air services arrangements with the US; to minimise the effect of new US legislation affecting UK financial sector interests; to improve co-operation on competition issues; to secure a new Double Taxation Agreement; and to promote UK business in energy, environmental and other technologies, not least through increased cooperation and technology partnerships with the US.

v. In working for a strong international community and hence improved quality of life world-wide, to secure US policies supportive of UK bilateral and multilateral action to promote democracy, good governance, good health, human rights and the rule of law, and to counter the illegal narcotics trade; to work with the US for action on climate change, environmental integrity and sustainable development; and to secure moratoria on the death penalty in US States.

vi. To influence decisions and actions which affect UK interests through use of modern information and communications technology; to facilitate exchanges at all levels (senior Ministers to students); and to provide authoritative and comprehensive information to UK Government Departments, Devolved Administrations and other public and private bodies in the UK on developments in the US relevant to their work and interests by effective reporting, analysis, exchanges and partnerships.

Appendix C

The rules governing arms exports

The Consolidated EU and National Arms Export Licensing Criteria

An export licence will not be issued if the arguments for doing so are outweighed by the need to comply with the UK's international obligations and commitments, by concern that the goods might be used for internal repression or international aggression, by the risks to regional stability or by other considerations as described in these criteria.

Criterion One
Respect for the UK's international commitments, in particular sanctions decreed by the UN Security Council and those decreed by the European Community, agreements on non-proliferation and other subjects, as well as other international obligations.

The Governments will not issue an export licence if approval would be inconsistent with, inter alia:

a) the UK's international obligations and its commitments to enforce UN, OSCE and EU arms embargoes, as well as national embargoes observed by the UK and other commitments regarding the application of the strategic export controls;

b) the UK's international obligations under the Nuclear Non-Proliferation Treaty, the Biological and Toxin Weapons Convention and the Chemical Weapons Convention;

c) The UK's commitments in the frameworks of the Australia Group, the Missile Technology Control Regime, the Nuclear Suppliers Group and the Wassenaar Arrangement;

d) The Guidelines for Conventional Arms Transfers agreed by the

Permanent Five members of the UN Security Council, the OSCE Principles Governing Conventional Arms Transfers and the EU Code of Conduct on Arms Exports;

e) The UK's obligations under the Ottawa Convention and the 1998 Land Mines Act;

f) The UN Convention on Certain Conventional Weapons.

Criterion Two

The respect of human rights and fundamental freedoms in the country of final destination.

Having assessed the recipient country's attitude towards relevant principles established by international human rights instruments, the Government will:

a) not issue an export licence if there is a clear risk that the proposed export might be used for internal repression;

b) exercise special caution and vigilance in issuing licences, on a case-by-case basis and taking account of the nature of the equipment, to countries where serious violations of human rights have been established by the competent bodies of the UN, the Council of Europe or by the EU.

For these purposes, equipment which might be used for internal repression will include, inter alia, equipment where there is evidence of the use of this or similar equipment for internal repression by the proposed end-user, or where there is reason to believe that the equipment will be diverted from its stated end-user and used for internal repression.

The nature of the equipment will be considered carefully, particularly if it is intended for internal security purposes. Internal repression includes, inter alia, torture and other cruel, inhuman and degrading treatment or punishment; summary, arbitrary or extra judicial executions; disappearances; arbitrary detentions; and other major suppression or violation of human rights and fundamental freedoms as set out in relevant international human rights instruments, including the Universal Declaration on Human Rights and the International Covenant on Civil and Political Rights.

The Government considers that in some cases the use of force by a Government within its own borders, for example to preserve law and order against terrorists or other criminals, is legitimate and does not constitute internal repression, as long as force is used in accordance with the international human rights standards as described above.

Criterion Three
The internal situation in the country of final destination, as a function of the existence of tensions or armed conflicts.

The Government will not issue licences for exports which would provoke or prolong armed conflicts or aggravate existing tensions or conflicts in the country of final destination.

Criterion Four
Preservation of regional peace, security and stability.

The Government will not issue an export licence if there is a clear risk that the intended recipient would use the proposed export aggressively against another country or to assert by force a territorial claim. However a purely theoretical possibility that the items concerned might be used in the future against another state will not itself lead to a licence being refused.

When considering these risks, the Government will take into account inter alia:

a) the existence or likelihood of armed conflict between the recipient and another country;

b) a claim against the territory of a neighbouring country which the recipient has in the past tried or threatened to pursue by means of force;

c) whether the equipment would be likely to be used other than for the legitimate national security and defence of the recipient;

d) the need not to affect adversely regional stability in any significant way, taking into account the balance of forces between the states of the region concerned, their relative expenditure on defence, the potential for the equipment significantly to enhance the effectiveness of existing capabilities or to improve force projection, and the need not to introduce into the region new capabilities which would be likely to lead to increased tension.

Criterion Five

The national security of the UK, of territories whose external relations are the UK's responsibility, and of allies, EU Member States and other friendly countries.

The Government will take into account:

a) the potential effect of the proposed export on the UK's defence and security interests or on those of other territories and countries as described above, while recognising that this factor cannot affect consideration of the criteria in respect of human rights and on regional peace, security and stability;
b) the risk of the goods concerned being used against UK forces or on those of other territories and countries as described above;
c) the risk of reverse engineering or unintended technology transfer;
d) the need to protect UK military classified information and capabilities.

Criterion Six

The behaviour of the buyer country with regard to the international community, as regards in particular to [*sic*] its attitude to terrorism, the nature of its alliances and respect for international law.

The Government will take into account inter alia the record of the buyer country with regard to:

a) its support or encouragement of terrorism and international organised crime;
b) its compliance with its international commitments, in particular on the non-use of force, including under international humanitarian law applicable to international and non-international conflicts;
c) its commitment to non-proliferation and other areas of arms control and disarmament, in particular the signature, ratification and implementation of relevant arms control and disarmament conventions referred to in sub-para (b) of Criterion One.

Criterion Seven

The existence of a risk that the equipment will be diverted within the buyer country or re-exported under undesirable conditions.

In assessing the impact of the proposed export on the importing country and the risk that exported goods might be diverted to an undesirable end-user, the following will be considered:

a) the legitimate defence and domestic security interests of the recipient country, including any involvement in UN or peace-keeping activity;

b) the technical capability of the recipient country to use the equipment;

c) the capability of the recipient country to exert effective export controls.

The Government will pay particular attention to the need to avoid diversion of UK exports to terrorist organisations. Proposed exports of anti-terrorist equipment will be given particularly careful consideration in this context.

Criterion Eight

The compatibility of the arms exports with the technical and economic capacity of the recipient country, taking into account the desirability that states should achieve their legitimate needs of security and defence with the least diversion for armaments of human and economic resources.

The Government will take into account, in the light of inform-ation from relevant sources such as United Nations Development Programme, World Bank, IMF and Organisation for Economic Co-operation and Development reports, whether the proposed export would seriously undermine the economy or seriously hamper the sustainable development of the recipient country.

The Government will consider in this context the recipient country's relative levels of military and social expenditure, taking into account also any EU or bilateral aid, and its public finances, balance of payments, external debt, economic and social development and any IMF- or World Bank-sponsored economic reform programme.

Other factors

Operative Provision 10 of the EU Code of Conduct specifies that Member States may where appropriate also take into account the effect of proposed exports on their economic, social, commercial and industrial interests, but that these factors will not affect the application of the criteria in the Code.

The Government will thus continue when considering export licence applications to give full weight to the UK's national interest, including:

a) the potential effect on the UK's economic, financial and com- mercial interests, including our long-term interests in having stable, democratic trading partners;

b) the potential effect on the UK's relations with the recipient country;

c) the potential effect on any collaborative defence production or procurement project with allies or EU partners;

d) the protection of the UK's essential strategic industrial base.

In the application of the above criteria, account will be taken of reliable evidence, including for example, reporting from diplomatic posts, relevant reports by international bodies, intelligence and information from open sources and non-governmental organisations.

Appendix D

The aims and objectives of the Export Credits Guarantee Department

ECGD mission statement

Aim

To benefit the UK economy by helping exporters of UK goods and services win business and UK firms to invest overseas, by providing guarantees, insurance and reinsurance against loss, taking into account the Government's international policies.

Objectives

Consistent with the above Aim:

- To achieve Financial Objectives set by Ministers.
- To operate in accordance with its Business Principles.
- To ensure its activities accord with other Government objectives, including those on sustainable development, human rights, good governance and trade.
- To promote an international framework that allows UK exporters to compete fairly by limiting or eliminating all subsidies and the adoption of consistent practices for assessing projects and countries on a multilateral basis.
- To recover the maximum amount of debt in respect of claims paid by ECGD in a manner consistent with the Government's policy on debt forgiveness.
- To ensure ECGD's facilities are, in broad terms, complementary to those in the private sector.
- To provide an efficient, professional and proactive service for customers which focuses on solutions and innovation.

- To employ good management practice to recruit, develop and retain the people needed to achieve the Department's business goals and objectives.

About the book

This book is the result of a joint venture by Democratic Audit, the Federal Trust and the One World Trust. The research was funded by the Joseph Rowntree Charitable Trust. Our research has involved interviewing a wide range of people from the staff of international organisations to politicians, journalists and civil servants, all of whom have given their time generously. Without them this project would not have been possible. Two research trips were also undertaken to Brussels and Washington and New York for interviews at the European Union and the global organisations that we were researching.

We were fortunate to have the guidance and advice throughout of an expert steering committee of academics, politicians and journalists. This committee consisted of (in alphabetical order) Christine Chinkin, Sam Daws, Paul Hunt, Nicholas Jones, Chris Lord, Andrew Puddephatt, Donald Shell, Andrew Tyrie MP, Lord Wallace of Saltaire, Ngaire Woods, Tony Worthington and Tony Wright MP. Their support, advice, knowledge and searching questions came just at the right time.

About the organisations

The One World Trust was formed in 1951 by the All Party Group for World Government. The trust has built up a considerable knowledge base about the workings and accountability issues of many of the major intergovernmental organisations. The director of the trust is Simon Burall.

Democratic Audit was set up by the Joseph Rowntree Charitable Trust in 1991 to measure democracy in the UK. Attached to the Human Rights Centre at the University of Essex, Democratic Audit draws on a wide range of collaborators, including academics, journalists and lawyers. It has published three major reports on democracy in the UK as well as a number of reports. Its director is Professor Stuart Weir.

The Federal Trust is a think tank founded to promote studies in the principles of international relations, international justice and supranational government. Set up in 1945 on the initiative of Sir William Beveridge, it has always had a particular interest in the European Union and Britain's place within it. The Federal Trust has no allegiance to any political party. Its director is Brendan Donnelly.

About the authors

This book has been a collective enterprise, led by Simon Burall, Brendan Donnelly and Stuart Weir. They and the three research officers – Andrew Blick, Ulrike Rüb and Claire Wren – have shared the tasks of conducting research, interviewing witnesses and preparing and commenting on drafts.

Andrew Blick is research officer at Democratic Audit. He is the author of *People who Live in the Dark* (Politico's, 2004) and *How to Go to War* (Politico's, 2005), which the *Guardian* called a 'mild-mannered Machiavellian tract for the 21st century'. He previously worked as political researcher to Graham Allen MP.

Simon Burall is director of the One World Trust. He is the co-author of the Global Accountability Report and a trustee of VSO.

Brendan Donnelly is director of the Federal Trust for Education and Research. He is a former member of the European Parliament.

Ulrike Rüb is a senior researcher at the Federal Trust for Education and Research. She is editor of *European Governance*.

Stuart Weir is director of Democratic Audit at the University of Essex. He is joint author of several democratic audits of the UK. He is a former editor of the *New Statesman* and founded Charter 88 in 1988.

Claire Wren is the Parliamentary Officer of the One World Trust.

Notes

Introduction

1 Some 25 years ago, the Procedure Committee famously expressed alarm about the imbalance of advantage between Parliament and government, see its First Report, Session 1977–78, HC 588, 1978; and since then countless MPs, scholars and journalists have reiterated their concern about the damage the imbalance does to parliamentary democracy. See for example Weir, S. and Beetham, D., *Political Power and Democratic Control in Britain* (Routledge, London, 1999), and Beetham, D. *et al.*, *Democracy under Blair*, 2nd ed. (Politico's, London, 2002).

Chapter 1

1 See pages 14–15 for further discussion of the royal prerogative.
2 See Beetham, D. *et al.*, *International IDEA Handbook on Democracy Assessment*, (Kluwer Law International, New York, 2001); Beetham, D. *et al.*, *Democracy under Blair*, 2nd ed. (Politico's, London, 2002).
3 The doctrine of judicial supremacy over duly passed legislation is not recognised in the UK; see Beetham *et al.*, *Democracy under Blair*.
4 Report of the Secretary-General's High-level Panel on Threats, Challenges and Change, *A More Secure World: Our Shared Responsibility* (United Nations, New York, 2004).
5 Report of the International Commission on Intervention and State Sovereignty, *The Responsibility to Protect* (International Development Research Centre, Ottawa, 2001).
6 Speech to Royal Institute of International Affairs, 28 January 2000.
7 'Doctrine of International Community', speech to the Economic Club of Chicago, 22 April 1999.
8 Sands, P., *Lawless World* (Allen Lane, London, 2005); *Observer*, 7 March 2004.

Chapter 2

1 Though Britain's treaty obligations with the EU and Council of Europe jointly make 'European law' the final authority. Thus for example the UK Parliament could not reintroduce capital punishment.
2 'The royal prerogative', memorandum from the Treasury Solicitor's Department (MPP09(a)), Public Administration Select Committee, *Taming the Prerogative: Strengthening Ministerial Accountability to Parliament*, 4th Report of Session 2003-2004, HC 422, 2004.
3 Public Administration Select Committee, *Taming the Prerogative*.
4 Royal Commission on the Reform of the House of Lords, *A House for the Future*, Cm 4534 (HMSO, London, 2000).

5 Public Administration Select Committee, *Taming the Prerogative*.
6 Foreign and Commonwealth Office, 'Approval of Treaties', Evidence to the Royal Commission on the Reform of the House of Lords, 1999.
7 Public Administration Select Committee, *Taming the Prerogative*.
8 Foreign and Commonwealth Office, 'Approval of Treaties'.
9 Ibid.
10 House of Commons Defence Committee, *Nato Enlargement: The Draft Visiting Forces and International Headquarters (Application of Law) (Amendment) Order 1998*, 3rd Special Report of Session 1997–1998, HC 903, 1998.
11 Norton-Taylor, R., 'Nuclear weapons treaty may be illegal', *Guardian*, 27 July 2004.
12 Department for Constitutional Affairs, *Government Response to the Public Administration Select Committee's 4th Report of Session 2003–2004*, 2004.
13 Hansard, House of Lords Debates, 18 July 2001, vol. 626, col. 1481.

Chapter 3

1 See, for example, Department for Constitutional Affairs, *Government Response to the Public Administration Select Committee's 4th Report of Session 2003–2004*, 2004.
2 Bagehot, W., *The English Constitution* (Fontana, London, [1867] 1993).
3 See further, Weir, S. and Beetham, D., *Political Power and Democratic Control in Britain* (Routledge, London, Routledge, 1999); Beattie, A., 'Ministerial Responsibility and the Theory of the British State', in Rhodes, R. and Dunleavy, P. (eds), *The Prime Minister, Cabinet and Core Executive* (Macmillan, London, 1995); Woodhouse, D., *Ministers and Parliament: Accountability in Theory and Practice* (Clarendon Press, Oxford, 1994).
4 Interview with George Cubie, 12 November 2004.
5 See reports in the *Independent* and other newspapers of his speech to the Parliamentary Labour Party, 12 May 2005.
6 See for example former minister Clare Short's evidence to the Foreign Affairs Committee, 17 June 2003.
7 Blick, A., *How to Go to War* (Politico's, London, 2005).
8 Interview with Bruce George MP, 10 November 2004.
9 Hansard Society Commission on Parliamentary Scrutiny, *The Challenge for Parliament*, (Vacher Dod Publishing/Hansard Society, London, 2001).
10 Ibid.
11 Interview with Tony Wright MP, 23 March 2005.
12 Wright, T., 'Prospects for Parliamentary Reform', *Parliamentary Affairs*, October 2004, vol. 57, no. 4.
13 Cabinet Office, *Ministerial Code*, 2001.
14 Glover, J., 'Labour MPs clock up record 300 revolts', *Guardian*, 20 December 2004.
15 House of Commons Procedure Committee, *Government Response to the Second Report of the Committee: Parliamentary Scrutiny of Treaties*, 2nd Special Report of Session 1999–2000, HC 990, 2000.
16 Sampson, A., *Who Runs This Place? The Anatomy of Britain in the 21st Century* (John Murray, London, 2004).
17 To rub salt in the wound, he did give evidence to the Hutton inquiry.
18 Cabinet Office, *Departmental Evidence and Response to Select Committees*, 2005.
19 Ibid.
20 House of Commons Liaison Committee, 'Scrutiny of Government: Select

Committees after Hutton', note by the Clerks, 8 January 2004.

21 Foreign Affairs Committee, *Implications for the Work of the House and its Committees of the Government's Lack of Co-operation with the Foreign Affairs Committee's Inquiry into the Decision to Go to War in Iraq*, 1st Special Report of Session 2003–2004, HC 440, 2004.

22 Hansard, House of Commons Debates, 22 October 2003, vol. 411, col. 707.

23 Interview with Bruce George MP, 10 November 2004.

24 Liaison Committee, Oral Evidence, Session 2003–2004, HC 1180-i, 19 October 2004 (uncorrected transcript).

25 Public Administration Select Committee, Oral Evidence, Session 2003–2004, HC 606-vi, 21 October 2004 (uncorrected transcript).

26 Public Administration Select Committee, 'Government by Inquiry: the Use of Investigatory Inquiries by Government: an Issues and Questions Paper', 2004.

27 Hansard Society Commission, *Challenge for Parliament*, ch. 2.

28 Interview with Donald Anderson MP, 22 November 2004.

29 See also the section on choosing an electoral system at www.democratic audit.com.

30 Interview with Mark Hutton, Clerk to Defence Committee, 10 December 2004.

31 Interview with Alistair Doherty, Clerk to International Development Committee, 23 November 2004.

32 A point made by Alistair Doherty.

33 Interview with Bruce George MP, 10 November 2004.

34 House of Lords Liaison Committee, *First Report of Session 2003–2004*, HL 90, 2004.

35 Home Affairs Select Committee, *The Accountability of the Security Services*, 3rd Report of Session 1998–1999, HC 291, 1999.

36 *Report of the Inquiry into the Export of Defence Equipment and Dual-Use Goods to Iraq* (the Scott report), D4.61–2, HC 115, 1996.

37 Public Administration Select Committee, *Ministerial Accountability and Parliamentary Questions*, 3rd Report of Session 2003–2004, HC 355, 2004.

38 'Open government: ministers must back it', editorial, *Guardian*, 31 December 2004.

39 Leigh, D., Hencke, D. and Evans, R., 'Arms firms plan to thwart disclosure law', *Guardian*, 24 December 2004.

Chapter 4

1 Riddell, P., *Hug Them Close* (Politico's, London, 2004). This study of the Special Relationship was the Channel 4 Political Book of the Year.

2 Interview with Roger Beetham, 20 January 2005.

3 Cradock, Sir P., *Know Your Enemy: How the JIC Saw the World* (John Murray, London, 2002).

4 For the full memorandum submitted by the FCO, see Appendix B.

5 Interview with Bruce George MP, 10 November 2004.

6 This has led to the production of six FAC reports since 2002.

7 Foreign Affairs Committee, *Foreign Policy Aspects of the War against Terrorism*, 7th Report of Session 2003–2004, HC 441-I, 2004.

8 Foreign Affairs Committee, *British–US Relations*, 2nd Report of Session 2001–2002, HC 327, 2001.

9 Sands, P., *Lawless World* (Allen Lane, London, 2005).

10 Ibid.

11 Tony Blair, speech to FCO Leadership Conference, 3 January 2003.

12 Defence Committee, *Missile Defence*, 1st Report of Session 2002–2003, HC 290-I, 2003.

13 Norton-Taylor, R., 'Nuclear weapons treaty may be illegal', *Guardian*, 27 July 2004.

14 Liaison Committee, *Evidence Presented by the Rt Hon Tony Blair MP, Prime Minister, on 16 July 2002*, Oral Evidence, Session 2001–2002, HC 1095, 2002.

15 Riddell, *Hug Them Close*.

16 Defence Committee, *Lessons of Kosovo*, 14th Report of Session 1999-2000, HC 347-I, 2000.

17 Braithwaite, Sir R., 'End of the Affair?', *Prospect*, May 2003.

18 Riddell, *Hug Them Close*.

19 Tony Blair, speech at FCO leadership conference, 3 January 2003.

20 Kagan, R., *Paradise and Power: America and Europe in the New World Order* (Atlantic, London, 2003).

21 Stephens, P., 'Married man seeks friendship', *Financial Times*, 16 February 2001, quoted in Riddell, *Hug Them Close*.

22 Kagan, *Paradise and Power*, p. 3.

23 Fisk, R., 'We are all complicit', *Independent*, 18 June 2005.

24 *A & Others* v. *Secretary of State for the Home Department*, EWCA Civ 1123, 11 August 2004.

25 Foreign Affairs Committee, *Foreign Policy Aspects of the War against Terrorism*, Written Evidence, 'International Law and the Use of Force', submitted by Professor Philippe Sands QC, Ev 91, HC 441-II, 2004.

26 *Foreign Policy Aspects of the War against Terrorism*, HC 441-I.

27 See the *Independent*, 23 May 2005.

28 Phythian, M, 'Hutton and Scott: A Tale of Two Inquiries', *Parliamentary Affairs*, 2005, vol. 59, no. 1.

29 Norton-Taylor, R. with Lloyd, M., *Truth is a Difficult Concept: Inside the Scott Inquiry* (Fourth Estate, London, 1995).

30 Intelligence and Security Committee, *Iraqi Weapons of Mass Destruction – Intelligence and Assessments*, Cm 5972, September 2003.

31 For the full text of the Hutton report, along with all the evidence taken, go to www.the-hutton-inquiry.org.uk/.

32 Foreign Affairs Committee, *The Decision to go to War in Iraq*, 9th Report of Session 2002–2003, HC 813-I, 2003.

33 Dickie, J., *The New Mandarins: How British Foreign Policy Works* (I. B. Tauris, London, 2004).

34 Hansard, House of Commons Debates, 27 November 2002, vol. 395, col. 330W.

35 See Blick, A., *How to Go to War* (Politico's, London, 2005).

36 Liaison Committee, 'Scrutiny of Government: Select Committees after Hutton', note by the Clerks, 8 January 2004.

37 Foreign Affairs Committee, *Implications for the Work of the House and its Committees of the Government's Lack of Co-operation with the Foreign Affairs Committee's Inquiry into the Decision to Go to War in Iraq*, 1st Special Report of Session 2003–2004, HC 440, 2004.

38 Committee on Standards in Public Life, *Survey of Public Attitudes towards Conduct in Public Life*, September 2004.

39 House of Commons Liaison Committee, Minutes of Evidence, 21 January 2003.

40 Department for Constitutional Affairs, *Government Response to the Public Administration Select Committee's 4th Report of Session 2003–2004*, 2004.

41 House of Commons Liaison Committee, Uncorrected Transcript of Oral Evidence, 8 February 2005.

42 Kampfner, J., *Blair's Wars*, (Free Press, London, 2003).

43 Foreign Affairs Committee, *Kosovo*, 4th Report of Session 1999–2000, HC 28-I, 2000.

44 Smith, M., 'Blair planned Iraq war from start', *Sunday Times*, 1 May 2005.

45 Smith, M., 'British bombing raids were illegal, says Foreign Office', *Sunday Times*, 19 June 2005.

46 Short, C., *An Honourable Deception?: New Labour, Iraq, and the Misuse of Power* (Free Press, London, 2004).

47 Short, C., 'PM and the case for war', *Independent*, 9 March 2005.

48 Public Administration Select Committee, Oral Evidence, Uncorrected Transcript, 10 March 2005.

49 Sands, *Lawless World*.

50 Foreign Affairs Committee, *Foreign Policy Aspects of the War against Terrorism*, 2nd Report of Session 2002–2003, HC 196, 2002.

51 Committee on Strategic Export Controls, *Strategic Export Controls: Annual Report for 2001, Licensing Policy and Parliamentary Scrutiny*, 2nd Joint Report of Session 2002–2003, HC 474, 2003.

52 Ibid.

53 Committee on Strategic Export Controls, *Strategic Export Controls: Annual Report for 2002, Licensing Policy and Parliamentary Scrutiny*, 1st Joint Report of Session 2003–2004, HC 390, 2004.

54 Committee on Strategic Export Controls, *Strategic Export Controls: Annual Report for 2001, Licensing Policy and Parliamentary Scrutiny*.

55 Committee on Strategic Export Controls, *Strategic Export Controls: HMG's Annual Report for 2003, Licensing Policy and Parliamentary Scrutiny*, 1st Joint Report of Session 2004–2005, HC 145, 2005.

56 International Development Committee, *The Export Credits Guarantee Department: Developmental Issues*, 1st Report of 1999–2000, HC 73, 1999.

57 Foreign Affairs Committee, *Foreign Policy and Human Rights*, 1st Report of Session 1998–1999, HC 100, 1998.

58 Trade and Industry Committee, *Trade and Investment Opportunities with China and Taiwan*, 14th Report of Session 2002–2003, HC 128, 2003.

59 Committee on Strategic Export Controls, *Strategic Export Controls: Annual Report for 2001, Licensing Policy and Parliamentary Scrutiny*.

Chapter 5

1 We do not go on to analyse arrangements within the EU as the focus of this book is on the British Parliament's part in scrutiny of EU legislation and rendering British ministers accountable for their role in EU policy-making.

2 Select Committee on the Modernisation of the House of Commons, *Scrutiny of European Business*, 2nd Report of 2004–2005, HC 465-I, 2005.

3 The range of documents considered by the committee includes any legislative proposals made under the community treaties; documents submitted to the European Council, the Council of Ministers or the European Central Bank; documents relating to the Common Foreign and Security Policy and to Justice and Home Affairs; any other documents published by an EU institution with a view to submitting it to another EU institution as well as any other EU-related document submitted by the government.

4 Generally an explanatory memorandum includes information on the subject matter of the proposal; ministerial responsibility; the legal base of the document; an explanation of the legislative and voting procedures at EU level which apply to the document; the possible impact on UK law; the government's assessment on the document's policy implications; a regulatory impact assessment; the financial implications of the document in the UK and/or the EU; and the likely timetable under which the document will be considered at EU level.

5 Standing Order No. 119. European Standing Committee A – Environment; Food and Rural Affairs; Transport, Local Government and the Regions; Forestry Commission; and analogous responsibilities of Scotland, Wales and Northern Ireland; European Standing Committee B – HM Treasury (including HM Revenue and Customs); Work and Pensions; Foreign and Commonwealth Office; International Development; Home Office; Constitutional Affairs; together with any matters not otherwise allocated; European Standing Committee C – Trade and Industry; Education and Skills; Culture, Media and Sport; Health.

6 Select Committee on the Modernisation of the House of Commons, *The Scrutiny of European Business*, 7th Report of 1997–1998, HC 791, 1998.

7 Sub-committee A (Economic and Financial Affairs, Trade and International Relations); Sub-committee B (Internal Market); Sub-committee C (Foreign Affairs, Defence and Development Policy); Sub-committee D (Environment and Agriculture); Sub-committee E (Law and Institutions); Sub-committee F (Home Affairs); Sub-committee G (Social Policy and Consumer Affairs).

8 House of Commons European Scrutiny Committee, *The Work of the Committee in 2004*, 6th Report of Session 2004–05, HC 38-vi, 2005.

9 See note 2 in this chapter.

10 Select Committee on the Modernisation of the House of Commons, *Scrutiny of European Matters in the House of Commons: Government Memorandum from the Leader of the House of Commons*, Session 2003-2004, HC 508, 2004.

11 The new names would be European Committee for the Environment (dealing with DEFRA and the Food Standards Agency); European Committee for Transport (Department for Transport); European Committee for Trade and Industry (Trade and Industry; Education and Skills, Culture, Media and Sport); European Committee for Home and Foreign Affairs (Home Office, FCO, DFID, Constitutional Affairs, remaining departments); European Committee for Finance (HM Treasury, Department for Work and Pensions).

12 Select Committee on the Modernisation of the House of Commons, *Scrutiny of European Business*, para. 94, sub-section (c).

Chapter 6

1 FCO official, letter to Claire Wren, 18 April 2005. Following freedom of information request.

2 Woods, N., 'Unelected Government: Making the IMF and World Bank More Accountable', *Brookings Review*, Spring 2003.

3 For more information see www.worldbank.org.

4 Article V(2)(a) of the Articles of Agreement of the IBRD.

5 If the member country is also a member of the IFC and IDA the appointed governor for the IBRD and alternate serve ex officio on these boards of governors (Article VI(2)(b) of the Articles of Agreement for the IDA and Article VI(2)(b) of the Articles of Association of the IFC). The organisation of MIGA and the ICSID is based on a different structure.

6 Article V(2)(b).
7 The Audit Committee, Budget Committee, Committee on Development Effectiveness, Personnel Committee, and Committee on Governance and Executive Directors' Administrative Matters.
8 'Dismay at Wolfowitz's nomination', BBC Online, 17 March 2005.
9 Which is also responsible for IMF policy.
10 Interview with Tony Baldry MP, 10 March 2005.
11 National Audit Office official, e-mail to Claire Wren, 14 June 2005.
12 International Development Committee, *Autumn Meetings of the IMF and the World Bank*, Oral Evidence, Session 2003–2004, HC 1251-i, 2004, response to Q. 17.
13 This runs from July 2003 to June 2004 and therefore the report did not cover discussions and decisions at the autumn meetings in October 2004.
14 Interview with Jay Branegan, staff member to the Committee on Foreign Relations, United States Senate, 6 April 2005.
15 Halifax Initiative, *Analysis of the Report on Operations under the Bretton Woods and Related Agreements Act 2004*, 2005.
16 International Development Committee, *Autumn Meetings of the IMF and the World Bank*, Oral Evidence.
17 Ibid.
18 Woods, N., 'The International Monetary Fund and the World Bank', in *The Routledge Encyclopaedia* (Routledge, London, 2002).
19 HM Treasury, *Growth for All: Towards a Stable and Fairer World – The UK and the IMF 2003* (HMSO, London, 2004).
20 This is in contrast to the long-term loans provided by the World Bank, which are for specific development projects.
21 Treasury Committee, *The International Monetary Fund: A Blueprint for Parliamentary Accountability*, 4th Report of Session 2000–2001, HC 162, 2001.
22 Ibid.
23 The report for the financial year 2003/4 has been delayed for undisclosed reasons.
24 International Development Committee, *Autumn Meetings of the IMF and the World Bank*, Oral Evidence, Session 2003–2004, Supplementary Memorandum submitted by the Bretton Woods Project, HC 1251, 2004.
25 Ibid.
26 Interview with Jon Sanford, Congressional Research Service, 7 April 2005.
27 Interview with Tony Baldry MP, 10 March 2005.
28 Constituent Charter of the Bank for International Settlements, Article 1.
29 On 31 March 2004 140 central banks and other institutions held their international reserves with BIS.
30 The G10 is made up of the ten countries that in 1961 agreed to make their resources available to the IMF outside their fund quotas under the General Arrangements to Borrow. They are Belgium, Canada, France, Germany, Italy, Japan, the Netherlands, Sweden, the United Kingdom and the United States.
31 This is not the only work of the G10; it also meets and issues regular communiqués at the autumn and spring meetings of the IMF, exerting a significant influence on the decisions made at these meetings.
32 HM Treasury, 'Text of the speech given by Chancellor of the Exchequer, Gordon Brown, to the Federal Reserve Bank, New York', Press Release 126/01, 16 November 2001.
33 Bank of England, *Annual Report 2005*, (HMSO, London, 2005).
34 By David Kidney: 'To ask Mr Chancellor of the Exchequer, what assessment he

has made of the governance of the Bank of International Settlements, with particular reference to (a) member control and (b) access to information.' Hansard, House of Commons Debates, 3 March 2003, vol. 400, col. 833W.

35 Ibid.

36 Committee, 'About the Treasury Committee', on the website of the Treasury Committee.

37 Hansard, House of Commons Debates, 15 October 1996, vol. 282, col. 838W.

38 Hansard, House of Commons Debates, 4 November 1997, vol. 284, col. 105W.

39 *From Our Own Correspondent*, BBC Radio 4, 29 January 2005.

40 For example, on 15 October 1996 Kenneth Clarke, the then Chancellor of the Exchequer, gave a brief description of the discussion at the G7 finance ministers' meeting (Hansard, House of Commons Debates, vol. 282, col. 838W).

41 HM Treasury, *Growth for All*.

42 'Mandela backs Brown over Africa', BBC Online, 16 January 2005; 'Mandela calls for poverty action', BBC Online, 3 February 2005.

43 'G7 supports tsunami debt freeze', BBC Online, 10 January 2005.

44 It was one of the three themes for the Liaison Committee questioning on the 8 February 2005. Notably this was well after the announcement of the G8 priorities.

45 Hansard, House of Commons Debates, 14 June 2004, vol. 422, col. 520.

46 Ibid.

47 'Cultivating new friends helps old ones flourish, too', *The Economist*, 9 April 2005.

48 Article 1(3) of the UN Charter.

49 For more information see www.un.org.

50 Malanczuk, P., *Akehurst's Modern Introduction to International Law*, 7th ed. (Routledge, London, 1997).

51 Glennon, M., 'Why the Security Council Failed', *Foreign Affairs*, May–June 2003.

52 Foreign and Commonwealth Office, *The United Kingdom in the United Nations*, Cm 5898, (HMSO, London, 2003).

53 Foreign and Commonwealth Office, *The United Kingdom in the United Nations*, Cm 6325, (HMSO, London, 2004).

54 Foreign Affairs Committee, *Expanding Role of the United Nations and Its Implications for UK Policy*, 3rd Report of 1992–1993, HC 235, 1993.

55 International Development Committee, *Darfur, Sudan: The Responsibility to Protect*, 5th Report of Session 2004–2005, HC 67, 2005.

56 'Profile: John Bolton', BBC Online, 12 April 2005.

57 Editorial, *Los Angeles Times*, 20 April 2005.

58 Belgium, Bulgaria, Canada, the Czech Republic, Denmark, Estonia, France, Germany, Greece, Hungary, Iceland, Italy, Latvia, Lithuania, Luxembourg, Netherlands, Norway, Poland, Portugal, Romania, Slovakia, Slovenia, Spain, Turkey, the United Kingdom and the United States.

59 See, for example, Defence Committee, *The Future of NATO*, 7th Report of Session 2001–2002, HC 914, 2002; Defence Committee, *European Security and Defence*, 8th Report of Session 1999–2000, HC 264, 2000; Foreign Affairs Committee, *European Enlargement and Nice Follow-up*, 5th Report of Session 2000–2001, HC 318, 2001.

60 Defence Committee, *NATO Enlargement*, 3rd Report of Session 1997–1998, HC 469, 1998.

61 Roberts, A., 'Entangling Alliances: NATO's Security Policy and the Entrench-ment of State Secrecy', 15 July 2002, draft.

62 Foreign Affairs Committee, *Kosovo*, 4th Report of Session 1999–2000, HC 28, 2000.

63 Ibid.

64 Health statistics concerned with the impact of different diseases on society.

65 The UK served a term on the executive board between 2001 and 2004.

66 Presently cholera, plague and yellow fever are the only internationally notifiable diseases.

67 Department of Health, *European Union (EU), International Health Regulations*, 2004 [online].

68 Health Select Committee, *Obesity*, 3rd Report of Session 2003–2004., HC 23-I, 2004.

69 Hansard, House of Commons Debates, 15 December 2003, vol. 415, col. 721W.

70 House of Commons Library, *Millennium Trade Talks and the "Battle in Seattle"*, Research Paper 99/107, 1999.

71 Trade and Industry Committee, Oral Evidence, HC 1178-I, 2003.

72 International Development Committee, *Trade and Development at the WTO: Learning the Lessons of Cancun to Revive a Genuine Development Round*, 1st Report of Session 2003–2004, HC 92-I, 2003.

73 International Development Committee, *After Seattle – The World Trade Organisation and Developing Countries*, 10th Report of Session 1999–2000, HC 227, 2000.

74 European Union Committee – Economic and Financial Affairs, and International Trade (Sub-Committee A), *The World Trade Organisation: The Role of the EU Post Cancun*, 16th Report of Session 2003–2004, HL 104, 2004.

75 Hansard, House of Lords Debates, 2 December 2004, vol. 667, cols 617–652.

76 European Union Committee – Economic and Financial Affairs, and International Trade (Sub-Committee A), *The World Trade Organisation: The EU Mandate after Seattle*, 10th Report of Session 1999–2000, HL 76, 2000.

77 Hansard, House of Commons Debates, 16 March 1994, vol. 239, col. 741W.

Chapter 7

1 Committees on Strategic Export Controls, *Strategic Export Controls – HMG's Annual Report for 2003, Licensing Policy and Parliamentary Scrutiny*, 1st Joint Report of Session 2004–2005, HC 145, 2005.

Appendix B

1 Foreign Affairs Select Committee, *British–US Relations*, 2nd Report of Session 2001–2002, Minutes of Evidence, 20 November 2001, HC 327, 2001.

2 Foreign Affairs Select Committee, *British–US Relations*, Appendix 12.

Index